Writing Belonging at the Millennium

Writing Belonging at the Millennium

Notes from the Field on Settler-Colonial Place

Emily Potter

Bristol, UK / Chicago, USA

First published in the UK in 2019 by
Intellect, The Mill, Parnall Road, Fishponds, Bristol, BS16 3JG, UK

First published in the USA in 2019 by
Intellect, The University of Chicago Press, 1427 E. 60th Street,
Chicago, IL 60637, USA

A catalogue record for this book is available from the British Library.

Series: Part of the Cultural Studies of Natures, Landscapes and Environments series
Series editors: Rod Giblett and Warwick Mules
Series ISSN: 2043-7757
Electronic ISSN: 2043-7765

Copy editor: MPS
Cover designer: Aleksandra Szumlas
Cover photo: Emily Potter
Production editor: Mareike Wehner
Typesetting: Contentra Technologies

Print ISBN: 978-1-84150-513-8
ePDF ISBN: 978-1-78938-104-7
ePub ISBN: 978-1-78938-103-0

Printed and bound by Severn, UK

To find out about all our publications, please visit
www.intellectbooks.com.
There, you can subscribe to our e-newsletter, browse or download our current catalogue, and buy any titles that are in print.
This is a peer-reviewed publication.

Contents

Acknowledgements

Much thanks are due to many on this book's journey. For their interventions, support and encouragement in the realisation of the manuscript I am particularly grateful to: Clare Bradford, Katya Johanson, Lyn McCredden, Rod Giblett, Alison Huber, Maria Tumarkin, Naomi Tootell, Brigid Magner and Joost Crouwel. I am also indebted to friends and colleagues who read and commented on the book at different stages: Alison Huber, Kirsten Seale, Samuel Meenahan, David Harris, Lisa Slater, Helen Young and especially Robyn Dunlop, who was there both at the beginning and at the end. Thanks to Intellect, and Mareike Wehner in particular, for their attention to detail and open communication. Thank you to my much-loved friends (some of you already named!) and family who keep me going, and with whom I can't wait to – finally – toast this book's completion. As always, it is W, A and T who are closest to my side.

This book is dedicated to a great mentor and friend, Kay Schaffer.

Some of this research has been published in earlier versions which have been revised, altered and built upon for this book:

Potter, Emily (2017), '"No nails new under the sun": Creativity, climate change, and the challenge to literary narrative in Thea Astley's *Drylands*', *TEXT*, 21:1 (April), http://www.textjournal.com.au/speciss/issue40/Potter.pdf.

Potter, Emily (2015), 'Postcolonial atmospheres: recalling our shadow places', in P. Ashton, C. Gibson and R. Gibson (eds), *By-Roads and Hidden Treasures: Mapping Cultural Assets in Regional Australia*, Crawley, WA: UWA Press, pp. 75–86.

Potter, Emily (2012), 'Climate change and non-indigenous belonging in postcolonial Australia', *Continuum*, 27:1, pp. 30–40.

Potter, Emily (2006), 'Andrew McGahan's *The White Earth* and the ecological poetics of memory', *Antipodes: A North American Journal of Australian Literature*, 20:2 (Dec), pp. 177–83.

Potter, Emily (2004), 'Disorienting horizons: Encountering the past in Chloe Hooper's *A Child's Book of True Crime*', *Journal of the Association for the Study of Australian Literature*, 3, pp. 95–102.

Potter, Emily (2001), 'The "empty highway" and the "yelling silence": Moving beyond Nikki Gemmell's landscapes', *Critical Review of New Literatures in English*, pp. 47–52.

Introduction

Grounding stories

It's Adelaide Writers Week in early March 2002, hot as usual under the cover of the signature white plastic tents. To the north of where we are, the Torrens River, that is really an artificial lake, ripples in the breeze but does not flow. To the south of the tents, beyond the gridded city streets, lie the Adelaide Park Lands, unpeopled, dry and exposed to the sun, while cars move in lines around their edges. Back at the tents, British-Australian author Drusilla Modjeska is addressing the crowd. Her topic is the state of Australian fiction at the turn of the millennium. She sees a problem and is not hesitant to put it forward. Australian fiction, she insists, is disengaged from the things that press on the contemporary nation. It is out of touch with 'conditions on the ground' (Modjeska 2002).

Her argument goes like this: the Australian reading public is turning away from home-grown fiction. Non-fiction has soared in popularity. American novelists such as Jonathan Franzen, whose blockbuster *The Corrections* (2001) focused on a modern middle-class American family and the threads of their lives, model the kind of fiction missing from the Australian literary terrain. Instead, Australian authors are fixated with the past, producing historical set pieces that render Australia too abstract to recognize, or too distant to affect. These works have little to say about Australian lives today. Our fiction has become safe, without risk and, correspondingly, the capacity for insight or impact.

The speech is well received by its audience, the usual writers' festival mix of students, retirees and white-collar workers on their lunch break. It is – as with many large-scale arts events in this city – an almost exclusively non-indigenous audience in attendance. In some way, they have heard it all before. Living in this place, with its strange river-lake on one side, and empty civic lands on the other, and in the early years of a new millennium, this narrative is echoic: it bounces back a familiar hum of disquiet to those who are listening. Australian fiction is ungrounded, Modjeska says: and so, goes the implication, are you, too.

Writing Belonging at the Millennium: Notes from the Field on Settler-Colonial Place critically reflects on this disquiet through a particular moment of Australian cultural life – what this book terms 'the millennial years' – loosely defined here as stretching from the mid-1990s to the mid-2000s. In these years, a series of concerns around time, place and ecological pressures coalesced in the heightened reiteration of an anxiety long-held in this colonized country: the status of non-indigenous belonging to land never ceded by Indigenous presence or claim. In response, and in the decade surrounding that Adelaide Writers' Week, a potent articulation of non-indigenous insecurity and alienation found renewed public voice.

The 'notes from the field' of my subtitle refers to my own position as a non-indigenous Australian, inextricable from what I critique here, and to a method of tracking and assembling this period in Australia and the debates that attended it. Rather than a study of non-indigenous belonging as a reality or a possibility, *Writing Belonging* is interested in how the *idea* of non-indigenous belonging – as something desired, asserted, contested and unrealized – was produced and circulated in the millennial years. The 'field' at issue also is the range of practices deployed for this purpose, specifically narrative practices that reiterated and generated different discourses of non-indigenous belonging, across non-fiction and, especially, literary fiction of the time. The book considers these literary practices to be more than representational. While the texts discussed here all engage with questions of non-indigenous belonging thematically and representationally, they also do so performatively, via their poetics, and in the particular focus of this book, through spatialized poetics, or their 'spatial imagination' (Howitt 2001: 242).

Modjeska's concern with the state of Australian literature provides an apt framing to this endeavour. Her frustration with what she perceived as an absence of engagement with the nation's most pressing matters – and its implicit address to a non-indigenous cohort – recalls an expectation that has been attached to Australian literature since British colonization. That is, to undertake work on behalf of the developing nation, to give shape to nascent collective, located identities: identities that were to be 'truly' Australian. What troubled Modjeska about the apparently passive state of Australian literature and informed her appeal to Australian literary authors (from whom she sat consciously askew as a first-generation British migrant) was this imminent expectation to which the national debates of the millennial years posed a challenge.

What was pressing on the nation at this time that Modjeska wanted acknowledged in Australian fiction? September 11 and its geopolitical reactions were still monopolizing attention in the news media, while the recent toughening stance of the Australian government to the issue of border protection and the introduction of off-shore detention was being hotly debated amongst the populace. An anti-globalist sentiment and increasing distrust of institutions, both private and public, was brewing both domestically and internationally. 'When the press is full of government fictions and lies, and corporate fictions and lies', Modjeska quipped, 'it's hard for a novel to compete' (2002).

The 'underside' of global modernity was being explored, both in terms of its human and environmental impacts. And in this, the matter of historical reckoning was key. In postcolonial contexts around the world, the 1990s had seen a move towards official recognition of the damaging pasts of colonial and undemocratic regimes, resulting in the landmark Truth and Reconciliation Commission in South Africa in 1996. Locally, a series of significant legal and cultural events in Australia articulated with this, shaking up the nation's conscience in regards to its colonial legacies and unjust foundations: most prominently (and sequentially), the 1991 National Reports on the Royal Commission into Aboriginal Deaths in Custody; the 1992 Mabo decision that challenged the *terra nullius* doctrine and opened up the possibility of native title claims; and the 1997 *Bringing Them Home* Report on the National Inquiry into the Separation of Aboriginal and Torres Strait Islander Children from their Families. In 1999, the federal referendum held on the question of Australia becoming a republic raised oblique attention to the matter of Indigenous sovereignty ghosting the public debate.

These elicited varying responses amongst non-indigenous Australians, including hostility and refutation, but also calls to make amends for, and reconcile with, the past. In response, a resistant discourse arose, spurred on by the conservative Prime Minister John Howard, that called on non-indigenous Australians to dig in and hold on to their claim to place while also refusing to dwell in a negative, so-called 'black armband' view of the past. 'Australians are not by nature a war-like people', he told a gathering in London, at the height of the History Wars debate that pitted frontier historians against each other over the 'truth' of colonial violence and brought the violent histories of colonization into prominent public discussion.[1] 'There is no tradition of conquest or imperial ambition' (Howard 2003). Modjeska alluded to these tensions in her critique of Australian fiction which, at this time she argued, fixated on the past and a 'non-specific' mythic one at that, which only reinforced long-worn themes of non-indigenous Australian identity – the 'bushie', the squatter, the battler. This generally was a one-sided account of colonization. Such tropes reinforced 'the notion that what we have to offer is exotic, not the stuff of lives lived in this particular experience of global modernity' (Modjeska 2002). They turned away from the hum that was growing apace in contemporary Australia – a hum generated by the realization that the nation, and its account of the past, was far from settled.

These tensions, this book contends, permeated cultural production of all kinds in Australia in the millennial years, and it is not accurate to say that Australian fiction was disengaged from this disquiet. As *Writing Belonging* demonstrates, literary works *were* active and attentive to this time, and in ways not always visible in a thematic account of their interests.[2] To explore this, I look closely at a range of novels by non-indigenous Australian authors writing throughout these years, and bring this into discussion with other cultural texts. These include commentary by public thinkers and scholars who also participated in the discursive ferment that attended questions of non-indigenous belonging at the millennium. I therefore consider literary works as offering narrative modes amongst a range of others that generate or feed imaginaries of non-indigenous belonging. These imaginaries, in turn, give shape to material ways of relating to and inhabiting place and its constituent parts. Narrative, in this view, is productive of reality, not a simple conduit for it.

My focus on spatial tropes and related imaginaries offers a way to understand this. Just how texts deploy and generate poetic relations enables insight into how places are narrated, and in turn, inhabited. This emphasis on spatialized poetics from a literary perspective aligns with scholarly insights from geography that also register the material significance of narrative practice (Howitt 2001; Hones 2008; Anderson 2014). Richie Howitt's suggestion that 'spatial metaphors' produce 'geographies of exclusion' in settler-colonial space is especially resonant, as he implicates the spatial imaginary of colonizing culture in long-term structural realities of racism and inequality in Australia (2001: 233). There is a strong link to be made between the colonizers' narration of stolen lands through self-justifying spatial tropes of the frontier and the continued refusal of Indigenous sovereignty, as well as very alive cultures of fear of and hostility to difference in this country, something that our off-shore detention centres, inflammatory media coverage of the 'Muslim threat', and emboldened extreme right makes clear (Hage 2017). The colonizing project, in these terms, is a poetic process, as much as it manifests in everyday events and structures (Wolfe 1999; Rifkin 2014).

I consider further the production of textual imaginaries through the concept of 'form'. Form is what literary theorist Caroline Levine identifies as the 'ordering, patterning, or shaping' (2015: 3) of elements that constitute a text's poetic ecology. Because of this, form is inherently political. The connections made between things, or the relations refused, within the text have implications outside it. 'Forms matter', Levine writes, 'because they shape what it is possible to think, say, and do in a given context' (2015: 5). In a literary work, forms are usually associated with the form of the text itself: its classificatory type, with particular conventions attached, that indeed shape, style or order, a text's composition (a novel, or a prose poem, for instance). As Levine points out, however, different kinds of forms are active in a text's composition and its ongoing life, in addition to this meta-structural form. These other forms are produced 'within', or by, the narrative composition, and generate relations, and particular spatialities and temporalities, that impel action and discourse in the text.

This expanded sense of form inspires my approach and the connections I advance between renderings of time, space and cross-material relations (relations between humans, and between humans and non-human elements) in the texts I discuss, and the imaginaries that feed and are enabled by these. If form *informs* what conceptual and actual relations are ontologically possible, then imaginaries underscore our ways of thinking about, and acting in, the world. There are differing understandings of 'imaginary', but here I am influenced by philosopher Helen Verran's rendering of the term. She considers imaginaries to be 'conceptual resource[s]' that underpin how we know and how we exist in the world (Verran 1998: 242). These 'are constitutive of, and constituted by, ontic and epistemic commitments' (1998: 239), registering how things have meaning or are made meaningful, and animating practices of living. 'Epistemic norms' are not neutral, but are generated and sustained by practices that are differentially valued and through which authority is conferred (Brattland et al. 2018). Ascendant imaginaries that, in a sense, represent designs on the world (Carter 2009), shaping habit, practice and authority, enable forms that reproduce particular narratives: narratives that can refuse diverse realities and sustain entrenched structures of power.

This book looks in particular to a spatialized imaginary of 'the ground', which discursively figures as both a material surface and a multivalent poetic in Australian colonizing culture. In the texts that I discuss, relations with the ground, and a ground's given qualities of flatness, sharpness, unevenness and instability (in essence, its amenability to domestication) recurrently feed, in Levine's terms, 'what's possible' in prevailing social and cultural imaginaries – and imaginaries for the future. An obsession with the ground is a long-standing feature of settler-colonial Australia, and the manifestation of this in non-indigenous narratives around the millennium activated a well-established imaginary terrain, with its antecedents in a Kantian privileging of stable, planar surfaces (as metaphor and as material site for human endeavour) in Western knowledge and existential traditions. This 'ground fetish', as I term it, must be seen in relation to the colonizers' preoccupations with claiming territory and securing ontological and moral status through surface dominance and the reproduction of what Jane M. Jacobs and Kay Anderson describe as 'the colonial grid', linear, open to unimpeded mobility, and highly exclusionary (1997). It articulates with particular modes of spatiality that are endorsed and desired by the non-indigenous colonizing culture, and that continue to inform how non-indigenous conceptions of place and expressions of ideal belonging are rendered.

Texts and time

Given these through-lines that connect contemporary expressions of non-indigenous anxiety with a never-settled sense of belonging (and legal sovereignty, as the 1992 Mabo decision made clear), the millennial framing of this book requires explanation. The reverberations of the legal and political events outlined above are, of course, central to this. But there were several other factors at play that coalesced in this period, and fed its discourse of non-indigenous belonging. One of these was climate change, which arguably entered and grew in mainstream public awareness during these years. The environment has been an ongoing register of the ambivalent place of the colonizer in Australia, and climate change presented a conceptual site through which belonging anxieties further played out. Relatedly, a proliferating and, for some, alienating techno-media landscape challenged nationalist definitions of the belonging subject. The millennium itself, as an idea and a structural reality, was a factor here too, promising – in the tradition of the *eschaton*, the end of time – a recidivistic rebuff to chronologic progress. As the book argues, the systemic meltdown predicted by the infamous Y2K bug represented this collapse of linear temporality and articulated with an anxious discourse of globalization that contracted time and space, ushering out 'a safer, more secure past' (Collins and Davis 2004: 3).

This was a fear not only of reset technological systems, but also of time itself going into reboot. The forewarned inability of calendar data to cope with the shift from 1999 to 2000 (as twentieth-century software represented the four-digit year with just its last two digits) meant that, in this computational system at least, the twenty-first century would, at a minimum, slide back to the start of the twentieth. This recidivism is exactly what Western constructions of time inculcate against. Its structures are palindromic but cumulative, repetitious while still moving forward. Time is junctural, marked out by pre- and post-temporality. Deborah Bird Rose identifies Western preoccupations with progress as an isolation of present time compressed between two forces of 'ontological significance'. 'Shrunk' into a 'moment of transition', a fleeting station between where we have been and where we are going, the present is devalued in favour of an imaginary of 'future achievement', and a continually generated sense of what is 'almost, already in the past' (Rose 1997a: 100).

As this book argues, while there was specificity to this 'millennium fever', anxious millennial responses are resonant with colonialist imaginaries as well as modern environmental discourses, including those concerned with climate change. Connecting these is the deployment of a certain temporal frame – the normative Western model of time – for the purpose of securing material and psychic claim over place and excluding interests that compete with these. The trope of 'endism', coupled in contradistinction with continuity, involves a particular view of the subject in space where mobility is connected to a specific mode of temporal dwelling, predicated on future-orientation and a stable ground on which to move forward. In the colonial context, where a reset of time was crucial to the imaginary of *terra nullius* in the first place, and the subsequent establishment of 'Australian' history, the possibility of time rewinding spoke to the anxieties underpinning colonial claim.

So, even as *Writing Belonging* considers the events and characteristics of these years as worthy of attention as a distinct period of Australian cultural life, it also recognizes its enmeshment in processes of colonization that have never resolved, and thus as signifying to an Australia that is yet to come. I agree, along with literary critics such as Rita Felski, that 'the box' of context is an inadequate way of understanding the work of the text, when it is confined to a single point of textual origin (2011: 577). With this in mind, *Writing Belonging* does not suggest that the texts it discusses are only meaningful in a specific historical situation, but instead draws attention to certain, significant imaginaries in literary texts and other cultural narratives that are deployed across time and context, in the ongoing enactment of colonial logic and practices. Patrick Wolfe's idea of colonization as a continuing diffuse structure rather than an 'event' is influential here (1999), along with Indigenous American scholar Mark Rifkin's point that colonization is enacted in everyday practice and experience (2014).

So, the text 'travels' (Felski 2011: 580) but it is active in the process, speaking out of, back to and into, a dynamic history of local and global flows. These stabilize, through the narrative practices that I describe, in a period of time at the millennium. Such stabilizations are acts of place-making in the sense that imaginary work has material effects in the ongoing constitution of spaces and communities. To this end, the texts under discussion here are not representative or summative of a time and place in Australian cultural life, rather they contribute to its manifestation in ongoing practices of reading and imagining. The textual examples explored here include Nikki Gemmell's *Shiver* (1997) and *Cleave* (1998), Thea Astley's *Drylands* (1999), Tim Flannery's Australia Day Address, 'The Day, The Land, The People' (2002), Chloe Hooper's *A Child's Book of True Crime* (2002), Janette Turner Hospital's *Due Preparations for the Plague* (2003), Andrew McGahan's *The White Earth* (2004) and Christos Tsiolkas' *Dead Europe* (2005). These texts have been chosen because of their engagement with non-indigenous belonging, either explicitly, or tacitly, via a spatialized register of textual forms that articulates with millennial non-indigenous belonging debates. They all ask what it means to live with uncertain non-indigenous belonging to place, and model different forms for this, as they reproduce, trouble and contest prevailing colonial imaginaries. While contemporary Australian writing during the millennial years reproduced, in near-obsessive ways, forms of belonging with strong provenance in the logic of colonial-capitalist modernity, other imaginaries were mobilized during this time that suggest a counter shift in non-indigenous self-narration, and, consequently destabilize the smooth flow of colonial continuity. From here, and thinking through form in a literary context, social and political possibilities emerge.

Where I deploy the word 'literary', I do so with an awareness that this term is often held in opposition to the 'popular', as a demarcation of value and taste. However, *Writing Belonging* understands 'literary' in a more inclusive sense to reference poetic deployments of language, imagery and concepts in textual forms that include both fiction and non-fiction. All the fictional texts that I discuss are novels: in part, this is because the novel remains the most visible and consumed written fictional form in contemporary Australian culture and the attention received by 'novelists' as voices of the nation is reflective of that. It is also because in a context of modern 'nation-building', the novel has long been given a central, symbolic role as a public barometer and as a generator of new narratives and visions for an emergent nation. It is important to consider, alongside this, that the novel – embedded within its very name – is a literary form of the post-enlightenment world that correspondingly developed as a manifestation of modernity. Its physical structure, most commonly, reproduces chronology, while the narrative's containment by an opening and a conclusion reinforce linear temporality and episodic, containable time. The tensions that manifest in the texts discussed here, and the anxious unsettlements of non-indigenous Australia that they all give voice to, thus intersect with the constraints of textual convention and their connection to cultural imaginaries more broadly. How these novels work from this dissonant place speaks to the colonial milieu from which they arise.

The question of non-indigenous belonging

Arguably, no history is as critical to informing the structural inequities and psychic pathologies of the contemporary Australian nation as the dispossessions and genocidal efforts of colonization. Despite the violence done by the State to other groups, most recently to its asylum seekers and refugees, it is the treatment of Aboriginal and Torres Strait Islander peoples that most profoundly shapes Australia as a material place and imagined community. It is central to the nation's understanding of itself: dispossession, and the 'management' of continued Indigenous presence that challenges the narrative and the power of state legitimacy, was the premise from which the nation unfolded. One result of this is that Indigenous Australians have long been the object of fascination, scrutiny and control by a dominant non-indigenous culture. Moreover, the dysfunctions of the postcolonial state are most commonly acknowledged through a paternalistic focus on Indigenous people. This is true, too, of progressive attempts to make reparations and renew the terms of Indigenous/non-indigenous engagement. The 'reconciliation era' that bridges the years that are the focus of this book, represented a turning point in public awareness of the nation's unjust colonial pasts, and their ongoing consequences for Indigenous lives. As Lisa Slater writes in her study of progressive settler-colonial women, these were 'anxious times' in which 'worrying about Indigenous people [...] [became] a national preoccupation' (2018: 6). Myopia leads to reasserted power relations, however, and a reiteration of Indigenous people as the problem rather than 'the colonial relationship' (Coulthard 2014: 17).

While the privileging of settler-colonial experience in the story of Australia is a danger of a focus such as this book's, the corollary is that non-indigenous Australian culture goes un-interrogated, normalized as the base-line against which aberrance is measured. To break from this outcome, critical focus needs to turn to non-indigenous Australians, who, in the current arrangement and imaginary scope of Australia's polity, are empowered to maintain and reinforce silences and exclusions. Dethroning this power involves exposing its mechanics, and the book's focus on the expression of disconcerted non-indigenous belonging, how it is manifested through narrative and with what effects, is undertaken with this objective – to illuminate and crack open what Damien Riggs refers to as the 'assumptions of privilege that inform non-indigenous belonging' (2004) in a historically situated, but also continuous, context. The favoured markers, forms and discourses of belonging that the book identifies as prominent and active across the millennial years inevitably connect to longer histories of imperial, Western cultures and their enactments of power, hierarchy and privileged ontology. Nunga/Ngarrindjeri scholar Irene Watson's call to 'tell me about you, not about me' (2001), motivates this study and I am not alone in responding to the imperative to interrogate settler-colonial culture, including the fraught question of non-indigenous belonging. Indeed, there was a heightened engagement around and in the wake of the millennium that responded to its resurgent articulation in these years. Some of these studies rehearse anxious belonging, identifying and summarizing non-indigenous pathology only to restate anxiety as an endemic condition of settler-coloniality (Collingwood-Whittick 2007; Trigger 2008). Others much more critically unpack the problematics of the non-indigenous pursuit of belonging, contending that the very proposition of a non-indigenous belonging is a violence in and of itself: a possibility enabled by historic and ongoing dispossession (Probyn 2002; Moreton-Robinson 2003; Kowal 2015; Slater 2018). Some propose ways for an unsettled belonging to be a positive state of inhabitation: the only possible proxy for an impossible rootedness (Howitt 2001; Crouch 2007; Robinson and Tout 2012). Unlike some of these approaches, *Writing Belonging* does not seek to pin down or resolve what non-indigenous belonging is, or what it might be. The book's concern, instead, is the implications of an expressed desire for a particular idea of non-indigenous belonging that has become an informing part of non-indigenous narrative and self-understanding. Its remit is to consider the social and political meaning and consequence of this idea and its persistence in contemporary culture, and the deployment of spatial imaginaries with world-making implications in its pursuit. A note about terminology is necessary here.

While I employ the term 'non-indigenous Australians' in this book rather than 'white Australians', there is overlap between these monikers as they relate to a dynamically constituted group of subjects whose membership is not self-selected nor naturalized by history. It is, instead, practiced through a range of discursive, embodied and structural means that are temporally contingent. I therefore use this word with self-awareness and in a historicized fashion to refer to subjects of particular narrative focus at a specific time in the field of Australian politics. During the millennial years, the words 'non-indigenous' and 'Indigenous' were employed in ways that generated specific but also contingent meanings to refer to two central stakeholders in this political field: those who identify (or are identified) as the First Peoples of Australia, descended from forebears who precede British colonization, and those Australians born or settled here, who do not.

This book is aware of the diverse cultures, experiences and histories that are obscured in collective terms such as these. The terms are made meaningful, however, by use, and in this way, contribute to the active imaginaries of the nation. So, while 'non-indigenous' is potentially all encompassing, in the targeted way it was employed during the millennial years of Australian political and cultural life it came to signify a particular kind of non-indigeneity, one identified with the founding acts of colonization and the legacies of these, especially as they relate to place and belonging. 'Indigenous' conversely described the subjects of these acts, and their descendants, and was a prevalent term deployed at the time. In this way, and unlike the associations of 'white Australians', 'non-indigenous Australia' is not defined by race, although race is a participating marker in its discourses. And it is not a straightforward Other to 'Indigenous'. Both categories are approached in particular, non-totalized ways, as practiced by a range of bodies, relations and stories. This does not deny other meanings of the terms as racial, cultural, political or ontological categories. The book also acknowledges that the preferred nomenclature amongst Australia's First People is not uniform, and that 'Aboriginal and Torres Strait Islander Peoples' is a favoured name for many.

Where I deploy the term 'postcolonial', I am well aware of the contestation that exists around it. The central – and persuasive – critique of the word is that it suggests an end to the colonial process that has yet to arrive, and denies the ongoing, continually enacted nature of colonization in contemporary Australia and elsewhere. *Decolonization* is the focus for many who think and write across these terrains, alongside the assertion that structures of colonialism are deep and persist in multiple ways – discursive, economic, governmental, imaginary (Watson 2002; Veracini 2007; Moreton-Robinson 2013; Liddle and Mason 2016). Emma Kowal describes our current state as a 'postcolony' in a bid to acknowledge the continuance of the colonial in a settler-colonial context, but also the shift from Australian territory as a cluster of colonies of the British Empire to a sovereign nation (2015). I use the term 'postcolonial' in light of these debates: in the millennial years, it was normative nomenclature in critical discussions over the terrain of non-indigenous belonging, and still activates a tacit understanding of its meaning as referring to a state of still-negotiated settler-colonial and colonized relations in the wake of initial invasion.

Diversity amongst Australia's non-indigenous population is of course reflected in its fiction. Most of the novels discussed here, however, address a generalized, arguably Anglo-Celtic dominant constituency, reflecting the terms of public debate around the question of non-indigenous belonging in the millennial years (itself indicative of the dominant political and media voices of the time). Christos Tsiolkas' position as a second-generation Greek Australian raises particular questions of more recent migration that the other novels do not address. Yet all of the texts manifest a keen awareness of unstable belonging claims that are differentially realized and expressed. Tsiolkas' European setting for much of *Dead Europe* – again, distinguishing it from the other Australian-centric settings – allows reflection on relations with the idea of a non-Australian 'home' that all non-indigenous Australians generationally connect to. The international focus of Tsiolkas' text, and the debasing, violent cultures that it exposes, puts Australian experience in a broader context of global modernity that other texts, notably Astley's and Flannery's, also invite. This dynamic between the local and the global is crucial to the processes of colonization that gave rise to Australia and continue to shape it. The specificity of how particular spatialized imaginaries informed and retrospectively justified non-indigenous occupation and the claim of sovereignty is also necessarily attendant to prevailing logics and practices of the Western mind that are in need of challenge in extra-national contexts as well as national ones.

Readers seeking a definition or a determination of non-indigenous belonging will not find it here. Neither is there an attack on, or defence of, the desire to belong. Relatedly, the book does not assume that *Indigenous* belonging is certain and untroubled. Far from it. Belonging for everyone in a settler-colonial country such as Australia is contentious and contested; it divides histories and loyalties. It is collective and individual, geographical, affective, imagined and practiced (Moreton-Robinson 2015; Watson 2002; Coombes et al. 2012; Gorman-Murray 2010). And, of course, the concept signifies different things to different people, and circumstance, as well as subjectivity, plays an informing role in this. What matters, at least to this book, is that we understand the ways in which belonging claims are formed and circulated, and to what effect. For non-indigenous Australians, the ground is definitely not stable. Yet the yearning for this stability continues to structure relations to place as well as relations to history. How we tell stories is informed by the way we think about place and time. Reciprocally, our stories, their words and forms, continue the making of imaginaries that manifest materially in the world. This is where the matter of belonging and the matter of the text intersect – across the field of the future that we are always in the process of making, to both our despair and our hope.

NOTES

1. See Amanda Nettelbeck for a discussion of how the History Wars played out in the context of public remembering in the National Museum of Australia (2007).
2. Ken Gelder and Paul Salzman also refute Modjeska's claim that Australian novels were disengaged during this time, and relatedly discuss a survey of 'historical novels' of the early 2000s that demonstrate 'the way in which colonial history has been enlisted into the political fabric of contemporary, post-settler Australia' (2009: 53).

Chapter 1
Anxious Belonging: Millenial Australia and Andrew McGahan's *The White Earth*

Published towards the tail end of the millennial years, Andrew McGahan's *The White Earth* (2004) looks back in time towards their beginning, book-ending a heightened period of non-indigenous Australian reckoning with colonial history that 'resonated across the continent and roiled the national soul' (Pearson 2012). Its setting is the farming region of the Darling Downs in Southern Queensland, an area known for its conservative, pro-nationalist supporters, and the Mabo decision has just been handed down by the High Court of Australia, rejecting *terra nullius* as the legal principle of Australia's founding, and opening up the (limited) possibility of native title for Indigenous Australians. With this came a discourse of 'coexistence', meaning, as Howitt points out, not a rich conceptualization of coexistent 'Indigenous and non-indigenous interests in particular places', but the specific 'legal interests in property that could exist together' (2006: 51). Property and its ownership subsequently define the relationship of the novel's non-indigenous protagonists' relationship to place – or their stated sense of belonging. As the novel progresses, this is positioned in contrast to Indigenous connections to the land which, against the logics imposed by Mabo, are continuous, a-temporal, relational with the more-than-human world, and irreconcilable with Western concepts of property – like trying 'to fit a sphere on top of a pyramid' (Watson 2002: 257).

The inter-generational non-indigenous farming family that is the focus of *The White Earth*, the McIvors, are pointedly positioned as 'ordinary' Australians – a prominent descriptor deployed in the political language of 1990s Australia that evoked a reactive politics related to nationalist anxieties and a language still prevalent today in defensive pro-white Australian discourse. Despite the heightened events that happen to the family in the course of the novel, they are 'ordinary', and part of this ordinariness, the story reveals, is that the family is bound to haunting and violent, colonial legacies. They are resolutely complicit in history.

While the Mabo decision is contextual to the 'action' of the text, its affective atmosphere as a disturbance of non-indigenous self-perception permeates *The White Earth* and is represented as a touchstone for the collective and personal disaffections expressed by its protagonists and their communities. It reproduces a widely articulated sentiment of the time that the nation's image of itself had been turned on its head, along with the status quo of social and political power. As the text rehearses, defensive and resentful sentiments circulated in response that targeted an Indigenous minority who were perceived as being newly granted special rights and privileges as a 'guilt' reaction against an unfair rereading of history. Opponents of Mabo claimed a reverse racism against 'old Australia' (meaning the Anglo-Celtic majority), who they felt to be marginalized by cultural fashion, government policy and the law. This mood indicated a profound disconcertion over the parameters of non-indigenous belonging, and the reorientations of social capital and privilege that came with this. The narratives that had given legitimacy to the colonial project – that the land was not stolen, and that Indigenous people never had ownership of land, without concepts of property or recognizable 'attachments' to place – were no longer holding.

This chapter considers *The White Earth* in relation to dominant political rhetoric and cultural tensions of the time which the novel reflects in a series of apparently mimetic gestures. As the millennial years came into view as a distinct period of cultural life in postcolonial Australia, the capacity for this time to be 'captured' grew. McGahan's text was generally received in these terms, celebrated as a 'necessary political novel' that 'examines [...] the residual psychic stains of the past on contemporary and future generations' (Starford 2016). The Darling Downs, where McGahan himself was raised, is part of a geographic area associated with the era's figurehead of marginalized non-indigeneity, Pauline Hanson. Her public rise in the mid-1990s from local council member in the small town of Ipswich to Federal Member for Oxley in the national parliament, distilled the concerns of a swathe of post-Mabo, non-indigenous Australians. In keeping with this reflective role, McGahan's text explicitly references the Mabo decision and echoes its fallout, giving voice to Hanson and her supporters through the text's protagonists, most notably the pastoralist John McIvor.

The story follows John's biography, from a youth to an old man, and tells this through his obsession to own Kuran house – a large, once stately, country manor at the heart of the large pastoral run, Kuran Station. John's story is interwoven with his nephew's: William (Will) McIvor, an 8-year-old boy whose father is immolated in a farming accident. Significantly, the novel begins with Will and his family's dispossession from their property following this death, as they take up support from the only family member that offers it, great-uncle John, and move into the downstairs quarters of the dilapidated Kuran House. Throughout the novel, John's obsession with his land, and Will's mother's fixation on obtaining John's inheritance for her son, hang heavily over the boy as he is continually reminded that 'possession was meaningless if it wasn't absolute' (McGahan 2004: 192).

Like Will, John experiences a formative dispossession when he is run off Kuran Station (where he was born to the Station's manager) as a young, and disgraced, employee. This cements his yearning to claim an inviolate sense of place and the social value that he understands is connected to this. Kuran House becomes the potent icon of this goal – the pursuit of irrevocable ownership and belonging. Though dilapidated, rubbished and almost beyond repair when he finally purchases the property, the material state of Kuran House belies its symbolic worth. For John, mythologies of settler struggle and a hard-won claim to place articulate in the very earth of the Kuran Downs. They represent a basis for an authentic non-indigenous ('white') identity, closely bound to the land. In this perspective, a personal sense of belonging – one's own place in the world – is contingent upon both having and knowing a solid and permanent place that one owns or can lay claim to. 'The most important thing', John McIvor realizes, 'was to keep to your own country' (2004: 74).

Will is slowly groomed to adopt this way of seeing. The house that at first appears to Will as a depressing and mouldering wreck, speaking only of the loss that brought him and his mother to it, becomes something to admire and covet, and something that speaks of possibilities. In his eyes, 'It was solid stone, it was permanent and unchanging. It had the sort of strength that he could never possess [...]' (2004: 117). Despite its material fragility, the house's mythical solidity justifies its enduring place in the land, he believes. The conflation of John's autochthonous connection with Kuran Station – born to the land but without the legal claim that can only be acquired – and the house's symbolic value establishes the primacy of ownership as a marker of psychic, as well as material, belonging in the non-indigenous mindset. It enables a reset of time to take the beginnings of legal tenure as a 'first mark' upon the land that then supports a narrative of primal ownership. 'I've walked this property from one end to the other, year after year', John recalls. 'And there are still places where I don't think a foot has ever set down apart from my own' (2004: 60).[1] This is an ultimate colonial fantasy of uninhabited lands, ripe for the taking.

The White Earth – which won Australia's premier literary prize, the Miles Franklin award,[2] in 2005 – seeks to follow this cultural logic and its influence in the reactions to the Mabo decision and their reflexive focus on non-indigenous belonging. John's angry rhetoric exemplifies Pauline Hanson and her One Nation supporters. Hanson's mantra that '[l]ike most Australians, I worked for my land, no one gave it to me' (1996) is echoed repeatedly in the text: 'No one handed me anything [...] I had to fight my whole life to get it' (McGahan 2004: 13). In John's mind his claim to the land is amply justified through 'hard work and self-reliance' (2004: 129), and for those other non-indigenous Australians who have also earned their place, '[e]very square inch of [Australia] is *our* sacred site'. 'The Aborigines are gone', he affirms. 'This is my property now' (2004: 209).

This last point, and its underlying falsity, is key to the anxieties generated by the Mabo decision, and is shown as erroneous in McGahan's text. The fact that Indigenous people had never 'gone', nor relinquished their claim to the land (a claim finally recognized when the Mabo decision came into law as the Native Title Act in 1993), meant that only the wilful suppression or denial of their presence could (re)activate the fantasy. What the text indicates too is that despite a prevalent national silence on matters of colonial violence and dispossession (the 'great Australian silence' famously identified by W. E. H. Stanner [2011]) in the local contexts in which non-indigenous people sought to make their homes, these histories were known and assimilated to a narrative of temporal forward movement, and national development. These stories could be admitted due to the belief that Indigenous people were no longer there. As John tells Will, Indigenous people do not inhabit the Downs because '[they were] shot, or killed by disease, or carted away' (McGahan 2004: 163), '[...] and wouldn't be coming back' (2004: 99–100).

A legacy of unsettlement

The Mabo decision's recognition of prior and ongoing occupation hollowed out the claim of Indigenous 'disappearance' and stoked long-held insecurities amongst the non-indigenous population at large over the legitimacy of its sovereignty – as landowners and as members of an imagined community of Australians, belonging to the land. These insecurities are endemic to the project of colonization, which displaces existing inhabitants as it re-places the newly arrived. They reveal colonization to be a process of unsettlement in the pursuit of a settlement that is never finalized. The loss of prior place for the colonizer and the disorientations of unfamiliar environments – culturally and environmentally – maintained a tension in the project to make Australia home for the original dispossessors and those who followed (Carter 1996; Curthoys 1999). Twinned with the inherent unhomeliness of migration, the colonizer's first-hand knowledge of the immanent possibility of displacement by another, replays itself, as Ann Curthoys describes, in an ongoing 'fear of being cast out, exiled, expelled, made homeless again, [even] after two centuries of securing a new home' (1999: 17).

A result is hostility to those perceived as potentially unseating this claim, abundantly evident in Hanson's rhetoric in the 1990s against the 'threat' of Asian immigration, and in the post-millennium years, through the 2010s against Middle Eastern migrants and Islamic culture more generally (Hage 2017). Ghassan Hage explains contemporary 'Islamaphobia' in Australia as steeped in this discourse of 'reverse colonization' – a 'feeling of being besieged by the very people whom one is colonizing' – which underpins 'the history of colonialism' (2017: 70–71). It is the paradox of the colonizers' mindset. Indigenous Australians are a further, and perhaps more central, threat to the non-indigenous pursuit of secure belonging. The original claimants of home here have endured, and never relinquished their country. *The White Earth*'s explicit title references the 'whiteness' fantasy that has informed Australian politics and culture throughout its 200 plus years and takes the challenge of Mabo to the heart of this imaginary: the fantasy of complete, secured possession by the colonizer, which buttresses against threats from the outside: the migrant and, ironically, the indigene. The admission of continuing Indigenous presence and, moreover, native title, threatens the absolutism of white possession necessary to sustain the fantasy of erasure. It makes Indigenous presence, and claim, intractable.

John McIvor's insistence on Indigenous disappearance is unsettled by the lingering material evidence that Will encounters to the contrary: colonial photographs on a wall in which '[b]lack men [...] [look] on from the shadows' (McGahan 2004: 46); tools and bones scattered across the 'white' earth; spectral forces and creatures that lie in wait (2004: 315). These forms of evidence evoke classic colonial tropes of repression and haunting which McGahan's novel playfully references through the invocation of various narrative genres that articulate the 'horrors' of colonial experience. The fashion for ghost stories in early colonial Australia is referenced here, as the repressed returns in the newly cleared landscapes of 'white' Australia (see Gelder and Jacobs 1996). In these stories, children go missing and fall victim to the lurking horrors of the bush, while ghostly apparitions refuse the forgetting of prior presence, challenging the narrative of a legitimate non-indigenous claim to place.

Exemplifying this is Rosa Praed's 1891 short story 'The Bunyip', which describes a party of bushmen who find the body of a little girl by a billabong and assume her to be victim of the legendary creature. As Gelder and Jacobs point out in their analysis of the story, Praed applies the word 'uncanny' to her narrative description of the bunyip's effects on these men, prefiguring Sigmund Freud's use (1919) to reference a state of unhomeliness, when the familiar becomes strange, and what was assumed to be certain gives way to ontological doubt (Gelder and Jacobs 1996). Children's fiction was another site for securing colonial place against the threat of the 'outside'. Clare Bradford's reading of Ethel Turner's *Seven Little Australians* (1894) suggests that Turner mobilizes similar tropes to Praed but to reverse effect (Bradford 2008). In this Australian children's classic, the unruly Australian landscape causes the death of the wayward non-indigenous child (the character Judy) who is then re-contained in her hilltop grave – both child and land tamed into a little picket-fenced plot in an acceptable, if melancholy, image of national founding.

But Australian literature has also worked against the return of the repressed by promoting narratives of non-indigenous entitlement, commonly involving a hard-fought battle to secure a place on the land. Here, physical labour is a means to 'emotional and spiritual possession' (Huggan and Tiffin 2010: 101), which *The White Earth* clearly evokes. This 'battle' folds into a narrative idealism that has been identified by cultural critics as resonant with the pastoral idyll – an enduring literary mode in the West, associated with spiritually redemptive environmental experiences, and with particular utility in postcolonial contexts where the new ground of nation needs securing (Huggan and Tiffin 2010; Crane 2014). The tradition of the 'pastoral retreat' centralizes human endeavour pursued in 'other' landscapes that can redeem or restore the depleted subject or bring wisdom and bounty to those who suffer trials in its pursuit. In the Australian context, 'battling the land' has frequently been inflected with such pastoral significance and is associated – as John McIvor indicates – with earning the 'right' to possess both land and the moral right to belong.

Julieanne Lamond traces the trope of the Australian 'battler' back to the 1890s and the early twentieth century fiction of 'Steele Rudd' (the pseudonym of A. H. Davis), whose popular characters Dad and Dave, and their wider family, toil amidst poverty and the 'harsh' environment to build lives on the colonial frontier (2007). Lamond points to the echoes of Rudd's battler in *The White Earth*, set in the same location as the Steele Rudd stories, and with its depiction of John McIvor and his cronies rehearsing this battler narrative with its deliberate echoes of Pauline Hanson. Despite the apex of ownership as entitlement, John makes repeated connections between physically working the land and an earned relationship to place: 'No one handed me anything [...] I had to fight my whole life to get it. But you know what? It's better that way. Because things like this station can't just be given to you. You have to earn them, like I did' (McGahan 2004: 136–37).

John earlier praises the first 'settlers' of the Darling Downs to his nephew: 'That's independence for you', he exclaims. 'It means hard work and self-reliance. And that's how Australia began' (McGahan 2004: 129). Precolonial history is overlooked as national origins are located in the epic struggle of (re)making the land. Steele Rudd applauded the 'pioneers' 'who gave our country birth' with 'giant enterprise [and] deeds of fortitude and daring' (in the epigraph to *On Our Selection*; Lamond 2007). Over one hundred years later, this sentiment was echoed by historian Geoffrey Blainey in his 2001 Boyer Lecture (an annual address on the state of the contemporary nation) that valorized the 'work ethic' of rural Australia. Out of this, he claimed a 'slow growth of respect or love for the land' is earned

(2001: 21, 24). Such discourse threaded through Hanson's speeches, too, which frequently made a point of distinguishing between the 'real' Australians – the non-indigenous working class – and the 'elites', generally meaning the professional classes. The battler narrative offers autochthony and lineage as a counter to prior and existing Indigenous presence. It also asserts a hierarchy of belonging amongst the colonizers, from which Indigenous Australians are implicitly excluded. This allows for a strengthening of earned belonging via particular linear relations with the land over time – relations of agricultural labour and utility, moving towards 'productive' goals. As Judith Brett perceives in Hanson's rhetoric, the 'objects of [her] grievance are not [...] the beneficiaries of inherited wealth who have patently worked for their land or money, but people who get government hand-outs, in particular Aborigines and the "fat cats" in the public service who administer them' (Brett 1997: 14). Hanson's, as well as Blainey's, vision of land worked over time, and consequently invested with legal, affective and moral entitlement, relies on a version of belonging premised on private ownership and tenure that admits entry to a common, but still exclusionary, identity. Virtue and legitimacy are conferred by the entrepreneurial utilization of fallow resources – a classic colonial trope. In this logic, entitlement comes with possession (Moreton-Robinson 2015).

This position, given voice in *The White Earth* by John McIvor, attributes the rural non-indigenous landowner/worker with the preeminent attachment to place. Playing into a long-standing association in the Australian imaginary of the non-urban as the location of 'real' Australian identity and its signifiers (an association that Thea Astley's *Drylands* critically leverages), Hanson and Blainey both identify Australian cities – where the majority of the population actually dwell – with 'elite', cosmopolitan interests, implicitly hostile to hardworking rural folk, and thus the true Australia. Blainey reserves particular hostility for the city dweller's fetishization of 'wilderness' that comes with a disdain for agricultural life. He aligns these 'green crusaders' with the Indigenous land rights movement, both complicit in creating and fostering the isolation of rural Australia, whose practices are seen to be exploitative and degrading of land and resources (2001: 17). According to Blainey, these 'national parks, nature reserves, conservation parks and the Aboriginal lands form a straggling but long buffer zone, straddling tropical and central Australia' and essentially breaking up the nation (2001: 30–31). native title claims only promised more of this, from Blainey's point of view. But the perceived ruptures were more than physical, and they reflected back on an historical narrative that became increasingly untenable.

As the Mabo decision and subsequent Native Title Act (1993) debunked the founding myth of Australia's colonization – the myth that no prior claim to the land existed – they broke the illusion of legitimacy in non-indigenous claims to an ultimate, unproblematic and entitled, relationship with place (Atwood 1996;

Collins and Davis 2004). Native title recognized the *possibility* of Indigenous place, even while it problematically put significant limits around this. Indigenous scholars such as Irene Watson have made clear the intractable problems with the Native Title Act, particularly its underlying adherence to Western concepts of property within the law. Watson writes: 'our *ruwi* (country) became enslaved, commodified and entrenched in their rules of property. We never cultivated the land, an idea alien to those who live "in", "on" and not "of" the land' (2002: 257). By refusing to acknowledge or take account of Indigenous understandings of law, place and belonging to country ('law does not exclude in its embrace, it envelops all things, it holds the world together' [2002: 255]), the Native Title Act enabled non-indigenous imaginaries to prevail, and in turn, continue to control Indigenous experience. 'White versions of history and legality' prevail (Rose in Watson 2002: 259). If the law is able to bestow native title, it is also able to deny it, too, with the legal concept of 'extinguishment'. 'There remains a wide discretion and power in the state to continue to do as it chooses in relation to the acquisition of our lands', Watson writes (2002: 264). It's important to acknowledge, then, that for many Indigenous people, this very possibility of native title represented an affront and a perpetuation of colonization.

The ambivalences of Mabo mean that its radical aspects may well lie in its impact on non-indigenous narratives. As the decision initiated the entry of a long-repressed narrative into national life, one that unsettled the noble hero battler, it delegitimized the perception of passive land and the compliant (disappeared) prior inhabitants and spotlighted a history of Indigenous dispossession. In the words of Justices Dean and Gaudron, who handed down the Mabo decision, this experience remains 'the darkest aspect of our history'. Their ruling declared that: 'The nation as a whole must remain diminished unless and until there is an acknowledgement of, and retreat from, those past injustices' (in Brennan 1995: x–xi). Dispossession and injustice publicly became the terms of national founding, and the resulting 'social, political and psychological turmoil' was, according to Indigenous leader, Noel Pearson, something the nation 'always had to have' (in Read 2000: 19). Resonant with this, McGahan's novel depicts a frightened non-indigenous outcry fuelled by misunderstanding of what native title actually means. In the book, a speaker at an Australian Independence League gathering (referencing Hanson's One Nation party) addresses his audience: 'You could be next! The government is lying! Your back yards aren't safe, your beaches and your rivers aren't safe! Native title will steal the lot' (McGahan 2004: 188). These sentiments echo the tenor of public debate in the wake of Mabo, which focused on icons of ordinary Australian-ness – such as the suburban backyard – as (incorrectly) being under threat. This is something that Chloe Hooper's *A Child's Book of True Crime* also explicitly references.

While we might clearly identify the political themes of a millennial Australia, and the anxious responses of non-indigenous Australians to the implications of Mabo, there is a further register of resonance in *The White Earth*. This is one that illuminates the significance of poetic language to the production of normative – or divergent – imaginaries. As I will go onto discuss in the remainder of the chapter, McGahan's text is not just mimetic; it is also performative as it deploys, for the purpose of critical reflection, the particular poetic register of political and cultural debate in these years in Australia. This is a register that looks to spatialized relations as its imaginary frame. Poetic forms are crucial to this process, modelling such relations between things that in turn give shape to the experiential, as well as conceptual, sense of the world. 'If imaginaries are located anywhere', Verran tells us, 'it is in the practices which constitute, say, a pastoral run, or Aboriginal clan lands' (1998: 252).

For Verran, modern theories of knowledge in the West sublimate imaginaries – they refuse to take them into account. Yet, the post-Mabo years gave rise to a new politics of knowledge that put pressure on prevailing imaginaries, a politics, as Verran calls it, of 'what there is and who/what can know it' (1998: 238). This was an outcome of the Mabo decision's acknowledgement of enduring Indigenous occupation as well as precolonial ways of inhabiting and knowing place in its recognition of customary law. Yet, amongst a non-indigenous constituency, Mabo also triggered the reassertion of an imaginary that supported dominant colonial logics and practices of occupation. In the millennial years, political and popular rhetoric responding to the consequences of Mabo and its rejection of *terra nullius* invested strongly in a spatialized and dichotomized poetic register of division and unity, shallowness and depth. Flatness and groundlessness were recurrent motifs harnessed to describe the socially and emotionally flattening capacities of an uprooted or destabilized non-indigenous majority. 'Crisis' was a condition deployed with reference to these different forms, and which recurred in a chorus of responses. High amongst these was the voice of the newly elected conservative Australian Prime Minister, John Howard, who came to the position in 1996 with a popular platform to heal disaffections amongst the non-indigenous majority and 'restore the balance' of power away from 'minority' interests.

It was his intention, Howard famously claimed, to enable non-indigenous Australians to feel 'relaxed and comfortable' about their past (in Rundle 2001: 54). 'Finally', the media echoed, 'we were going to get a government for us' (Glascott 1997: 2): a statement that evoked Howard's reinvestment in 'ordinary' Australians, in contrast to his predecessor Paul Keating's emphasis on Indigenous rights. Howard consistently evoked this idea of redress and restoration of a righteous status quo with a rhetoric of 'balance', 'common sense' (in Manne 2001b: 4) and 'a commitment to fairness' (in Rundle 2001: 55). This was an 'agenda of invisible reunification' (2001: 24), and its vocalization, that worked through spatial imaginaries of unity and coherence to define the virtues of a healthy, normative national body. The valorization of Australians 'travel(ling) a single path' of 'common purpose' highlighted uniformity as a characteristic of belonging, earmarking diversity as something that would disturb 'the pure Australian spirit' (Howard in Rundle 2001: 20, 27). National inequalities were perceived as the result of increased Indigenous rights, inducing the claim that 'the pendulum' of balance had now 'swung too far towards Aborigines' and needed resetting (in Gelder and Jacobs 1998: 136). This appeal to restored equilibrium is one that Howard frequently harnessed. His rhetoric of balance implied a national ground that needed to be settled and stabilized. Discussions over such things as the 'right' 'ethnic mix' for Australia, or the 'equitable' distribution of government assistance and 'special privileges' amongst Australian citizens, complimented debate over the 'balance sheet' of Australian history, which called for the recognition of the nation's successes over its flaws. Whatever the nation's 'failure and its apportion of shame', Howard famously stated, 'in the great balance sheet of history it has been a remarkable success story' (in Burke 2001: 221).

Howard's politics responded strategically to the previous Labour government's support for Indigenous recognition and what entered public debate as 'reconciliation'. Six months after the Mabo decision, then Prime Minister Paul Keating had delivered his famous Redfern speech, in which for the first time any political leader in this country explicitly admitted responsibility for the devastations of colonization on behalf of the non-indigenous Australian community: 'It was we who did the dispossessing. We took the traditional lands and smashed the traditional way of life [...] We took the children from their mothers. We failed to ask – how would I feel if this were done to me?' (Keating 1992b). Keating's speech signalled the need for symbolic, as well as practical, atonement for these wrongs. His focus on un-repressing colonial injustices, coupled with a turn towards the Asia region in preference to the nation's historical Anglo-centric ties, spoke of Keating's desire to transform Australia's self- and international image, in ways 'consistent with the multicultural realities of our society, and the final passing of the vestiges of our colonial past' (Keating 1992a).

Keating is featured in *The White Earth* and, true to his lack of popularity amongst native title opponents and conservative voters resistant to his reformist agenda, is referred to as 'the worst [Prime Minister] yet': 'If he gets in the way', John proclaims to Will, 'rural Australia is finished forever. So yes, I'll fight him and his Native Title' (McGahan 2004: 139). The idea that Keating and his political agenda were divisive and undermining a marginalized majority became a mainstay of Howard's discourse, and provided a logic for his government's determination to limit the Native Title Act, which they did successfully in the 1997 Wik decision. Such a move was vital, Howard argued, as to 'allow a running sore to develop on the national fabric' would be to 'fail Australia' (in Gelder and Jacobs 1998: 138). Conflict resolution through the (as much as legally possible) curtailment of Indigenous land claims was seen to be the only way that national cohesion could be assured.

Howard's antipathy towards 'noisy minority groups' (Rundle 2001: 13) was further evidenced in his refusal to apologize to Indigenous Australians at the Reconciliation Convention in 1997,[3] overtly deviating from the political path set up by his predecessor. For Howard, saying 'sorry' for non-indigenous policies and practices of the past signified a version of positive discrimination that compromised the freedom of all Australians (as it would implicate everyone, regardless of their own history). Inclusive in this liberty, he argued, was the ability of the national subject to exist 'free from anxiety, free from guilt' (Rundle 2001: 18) – in the context of Indigenous reparation, this meant the non-indigenous Australian subject. An apology to a comparative few was thus seen to compromise ontological security, figured as freedom, and as an affront to the national body itself – at its rhetorical extreme, a kind of national treachery.

A threat to the nation, in this discourse, comes to stand for an attack on the rights and belonging of 'the fully realized Australian subject' (Burke 2001: 36). Howard's repeatedly stated belief that '[w]e are special individuals, not special needs' (in Burke 2001: 195) is illustrative of his concept of national harmony as cultural hegemony: individual units moving on the same level playing field without difference or instability. Within national boundaries, and predicated on their continuity, the national subject is thus endowed with the promise of security 'as a guarantee of the future' (Burke 2001: xxxiv). Security was equated with Australian-ness. Informed by similar logic, sociologist Miriam Dixson argued for the importance of a nation that holds, stating that 'the "holding" capacities of a society concern those influences making a social coherence which works at a satisfactory day-to-day level' (1999: 4). Her contention subscribes to the model of nationhood as a maturing structure that in its own cohesive growth provides correlative maturing and nurturing conditions for the subjects it protects. In the absence of this, she insisted, national identity and the multiple identities that come under its umbrella 'risk exploding into psychosis' (1999: 11). If Australians 'are really serious about diversity', she continued, 'we must be equally serious about cohesion' (1999: 7). Dixson gestured towards cultural narratives in which 'common ground, common standards and [a] common frame of reference' (1999: 48) are asserted to achieve the desired emotional ties she outlines. Affective stories of nation and national cultural identity proffering these elements, she argued, would initiate 'solidarity and belongingness' (1999: 163) for those within the nation-space. Reciprocally, a certifying of belonging through identification with these narratives will secure and protect the nation itself.

At this time, expressions such as the 'sorry industry' (Dixson 1999: 67), and the 'black-armband' (1999: 72) approach to Australian history gained popularity and circulated. The 'elite's' (meaning left-leaning cultural elites) 'celebration of guilt' (1999: 72) was denounced by many strongly right-wing voices, with any apology to Indigenous Australians considered as a humiliating regression that would arrest the nation's ability to 'get on with' the future as 'civilized' (Duffy 1997: 11) countries ought. Commentator Paddy McGuiness, for example, accused the 'left-wing intelligentsia' of attempting to change 'the moral balance of power' in Australia over the questions of reconciliation and the Stolen Generations: trying, in a mood of deep 'self-hatred', to 'humiliate' their country [...] by chatter about 'guilt and shame' (Manne 2001a: 72). For historian Keith Windschuttle, these anxious politics prefigured 'the eventual break-up of the Australian nation' (Windschuttle 2000: 8). Howard's refusal to use the word 'treaty' in reference to a document of official reconciliation employed this image of potential break-up for a beleaguered nation. He argued that 'treaty implies two nations within one'. This, he insisted, 'is something I have never accepted and will never accept' (in Burke 2001: 202).

The case for an official apology and historical reparation had been heightened when the 1997 *Bringing Them Home* Report on the Stolen Generations,[4] established by the Keating government in 1995, exposed government driven or sanctioned, decades-long practices of removing Indigenous children from their parents and wider families. These practices were labelled genocidal in intent. At the same time, the work of frontier historians began to circulate to wider audiences, building a picture of dispossession by force and murderous violence. Evidence of frontier massacres entered public debate. While Indigenous activists have sought to bring attention to their circumstances through a similar narrative since colonization,[5] periodically resulting in eruptions of public consciousness (such as the referendum to grant Indigenous people the vote in 1967), at the millennium these events seemed like the crescendo in a decade of significant points of recognition for Indigenous people. Mabo had followed the findings of the Aboriginal Deaths in Custody Royal Commission released in 1991 which highlighted the inequitable rates of Indigenous incarnation and associated deaths in custody in Australia. This, in turn, followed the 1988 bicentenary of the country's 'founding', where Indigenous protests against the official celebration ceremony made an impression in public arenas.

Non-indigenous commentators noted the 'culturally transforming impact' of these legal and policy milestones (Manne 2001a: 5). According to Robert Manne, the *Bringing Them Home* Report, in particular, shifted Indigenous suffering under governmental regimes 'from the margin to the centre of Australian self-understanding and contemporary political debate'. He continued:

> Many Stolen Generations memoirs were now published; films produced; plays staged; songs sung. Hundreds of thousands of citizens signed what were called – in a language borrowed from the Aborigines – Sorry Books. A National Sorry Day was established. It soon seemed to many Australians that no historical question was of greater importance [...] no moral matter of greater significance to the life of the nation than the apology to the Stolen Generations.
>
> (Manne 2001a: 6)

Yet at this time, such 'postcolonial uncertainties' were also seen to be an 'affliction' of non-indigenous Australians (Read 2000: 10). Advocates of Indigenous rights were depicted as cultural wreckers and psychological vandals. Conservative commentator Ross Terrill positioned Australia's 'cultural gatekeepers' (Terrill 2000: 264) as forcing their fellow citizens to feel 'ashamed of our past' (2000: 274), and called on non-indigenous peoples, particularly, to express an 'innocent joy at "being here"' (2000: 308). Dixson also charged leftist elites with fostering a powerful climate of non-indigenous negativity and 'self-dislike' (Dixson 1999: 12). Dixson's argument was at once an admonishment of settlers' resignation to their anxieties in the face of Indigenous and other 'ethnic' challenges to an Australian 'old identity' (1999: 7), and a sympathetic depiction of a nation that, no longer holding together, faces 'pain and loss' and 'terrifying emptiness' (1999: 50).

The idea of an apology to those affected by policies of Indigenous child removal, as identified in the *Bringing Them Home* Report, was opposed by a conservative commentariat who argued that such a 'humiliation' would arrest the nation's ability to 'get on with' its future, as 'civilized' (Duffy 1997: 11) countries ought. The empowerment of Indigenous testimony, voice and legal rights in practical and symbolic terms was read as an assault on national history and as 'psychologically damaging for many people' (Duffy in Manne 2001a: 72). According to Dixson, 'the problems associated with immigration' (1999: 8), a rapidly changing Australian demographic and Indigenous claims to rights and land had diminished the confidence and the sense of belonging of non-indigenous peoples. As Peter Read similarly expressed in the same period, '[s]ome of us took on the burden of guilt so earnestly that we half believed ourselves unworthy even to be here' (Read 2000: 5).

Thus, Dixson insisted, the 'host culture' – as the 'core' – 'is experiencing [...] uprootedness' and 'a powerful grief' (1999: 43) as a result of which the nation was reduced to 'contending factions' (1999: 48). A language of ruin accompanied these predictions for the nation's crumbling social cohesion, replete with 'vandalism, looting and virtual street war' (1999: 28). Non-indigenous Australians, already alienated, shallowly placed on the land and shaken by the effects of (post) colonial uncertainties, were further undermined, in her view, by an intellectual climate imbued by the cultural fashion for postmodernist decentring, favouring the insubstantial and uncertain, and belittling 'ordinary people['s]' (1999: 9) need for 'real' and 'deep' attachments to place. Post-structuralism was aligned with a superficial mode of meaning and existence that in some ways invoked Drusilla Modjeska's cautions against fiction's representations of an untethered and ineffectual subject. In both accounts, 'deeply' grounding narratives were lacking. '[F]latness', for Dixson, resultingly characterized the Australian nation (1999: 28). Little of this discussion considered the reception of Mabo by Indigenous people, nor acknowledged the realities of the decision's extremely limited capacity to practically alter the paradigm of land ownership in Australia.

Rather, repeatedly, poetic motifs of superficiality, surface connections and fracture were deployed to describe the significance of these legal and political shifts to *non-indigenous* identity and belonging. Both those hostile to the cause of recognition and reconciliation, and those in support of it, harnessed these spatial motifs to describe the tenor and the character of contemporary non-indigeneity, and by proxy, of the nation itself. Australia's was 'a culture of forgetting', Manne decried, in which '[n]othing has weight. Nothing has meaning. Nothing matters' (Manne 1996: 137, 191). Defensive responses to the revelations of *Bringing Them Home*, he argued, had only alienated Indigenous Australians further, and signified 'the closing of minds [and] hardening of hearts' amongst non-indigenous Australians (Manne 2001b: 7). A calcification of collective imagination and conscience were seen to go hand in hand. The 'children overboard' scandal of 2001,[6] was further evidence of this for Manne and other commentators. As the series of photographs featuring life-jacketed children both in the water and being hoisted over the sides of a rickety boat were circulated by the conservative government alongside a dehumanizing language of profound abjection – 'people like that' were unassimilable to this country – 'a goodly part of the nation', Manne wrote, become immune 'to the unspeakable cruelties enacted daily' (Manne 2001b: 13) against asylum seekers in Australia.[7]

This was a national landscape expressed, repeatedly, in terms of aridity and division: where 'minds are shut and [...] [once again] hearts have hardened', and disorder and disunity rein (Gaita 2001: 25). 'Our social fabric [has turned to] rags' (Adams 2001: 32), our civil society 'vandalized' and 'besmirched' (Adams 2000: 24). Mungo MacCallum seconded this with his view of a 'damaged' and 'debilitated Australian political landscape' (2002: 72). Images of non-indigenous Australia 'struck dumb by "our" legacy of the past' were seen to reflect a 'shamed nation' (Schaffer 2001: 3), immobilized and disarrayed by its confusion. Echoing this pathologizing of the settler-colonial body, Bob Hodge and Vijay Mishra theorized the non-indigenous Australian subject as condemned to internal division for the refusal to take on the 'unacknowledged secret' (1991: 204) of Indigenous dispossession and its erasure from national texts and narratives.

The non-indigenous majority, they wrote, echoing a common refrain, prefer to forget than to remember, and this forgetting produces a 'schizoid nation', paranoid about hidden messages in social texts and suspicious of difference (1991: xv). As a consequence, the dominant culture of Australia was 'relentlessly superficial' and 'incapable of real relationships', with the non-indigenous majority 'so traumatized by the catastrophe of being here that they cannot think or feel' (1991: 217).

Mabo imaginaries in The White Earth

McGahan's referencing of this time and its discourse, expressing non-indigenous disconcertion over Mabo and its fallout, extends to these poetics in which a non-indigenous constituency is imagined as fractured, insubstantial, but also weighed down by psychic burdens across the 'left' and 'right' political spectrum. While John McIvor and his fellow members of the Australian Independence League make clear their views of Mabo's damaging implications – 'a disaster' for 'people like us' (McGahan 2004: 135) – John's daughter, Ruth, who represents the progressive liberal view in the book, also gives voice to the perception that postcolonial Australia is ravaged by its history of moral failures. A lawyer who is herself working on a Native Title case, Ruth operates as a corrective against John's influence on his nephew, Will, offering a counter narrative to the triumphalist pioneers. She provokes Will to recognize the illegitimacy of settler claims on the land, sustained by a forgotten genocidal history. '[A] stone axe would have been important to its owner', Ruth tells Will. 'And yet they're lying all over the plains as if they were just thrown away like Coke cans. Why do you think that is? [...] Because their owners died, that's why' (2004: 282).

Ruth seeks to make Indigenous presence visible again and in doing so undermine her father's narrative of absence legitimizing claim. Yet, by the novel's conclusion she is dubious of the law's capacity to reconcile past wrongs. More significantly, her final reflection implies the devastation of colonial history as a shared loss or burden that undermines an 'earthed', or firmly grounded, connection to place: 'A memory came. The smell of earth, and of wheat, and the feeling of a familiar hand upon her head, rough with calluses, and so strong. All of it wasted, all of it ruined' (McGahan 2004: 376). Here, the evocation of earth and a primordial, sensorial connection to it aligns with John's own self-affirming rhetoric of belonging. Ruth's challenge to John's possession claims are thus tempered by this suggestion of a potential for affective equivalence between Indigenous and non-indigenous relations to place, an equivalence that John repeatedly argues. As he tells Will, '[t]his country will speak to you too, if you listen. The blacks say it flows into you through your feet, and they're right. But it's not an Aboriginal thing. It's not a white thing either. It's a human thing. Not everyone has it. But I do. And you have it too' (McGahan 2004: 295). Autochthony and endurance are once again the yardsticks of non-indigenous belonging and rightful claim. 'There's only me left', John insists. 'I've been here all along. So *I* claim Native Title' (2004: 294).

The possibility of an equivalent belonging between Indigenous and non-indigenous Australians, resurrected out of the fires of colonial ruin, was a prominent trope of post-Mabo discourse activated on both conservative and liberal sides of non-indigenous debate. The moral right bestowed by birth and long-term place connection was a view repeatedly expressed by non-indigenous people committed to the cause of historical reparation and reconciliation, and this framing of the claim to place became normatively embedded within expressions of anxiety around the possibility of a real or legitimate non-indigenous belonging. As critics observed at the time, 'white Australians are articulating "black hearts" as a way of legitimizing their place in contemporary Australia' (Ellemor 2003: 234). This emphasis on equivalence aligned with the legal language of 'coexistence' that accompanied the Mabo decision (see Howitt 2006) and became a prominent frame for discursively neutralizing the 'threat' of non-indigenous displacement for native title claims. This was indicative of the decision's curtailed symbolic and practical capacity to acknowledge the singular, original relationship between Indigenous people and their country, and to register differently inhabited relations to place. Its interest was not, Howitt writes, 'the coexistence of Indigenous and non-Indigenous interests in particular places, but an abstract conceptualization of legal interests in property that could exist together' (2006: 51). 'Coexistence' hedged bets in terms of historical redress, admitting Indigenous presence (the possibility of 'enduring connection'), but also refusing to allocate particular rights based upon prior occupation and subsequent injustices. It also enabled the claim of equivalence and a way to articulate non-indigenous belonging in 'parallel' (Read 2000: 120).

Historian Peter Read exemplified the popular deployment of 'coexistence' to articulate non-indigenous belonging in his studies of non-indigenous Australians' attachments to specific sites. These he explicitly offered as a counter to the unproductive anxieties festering in the postcolonial collective. Such attachments are attained, Read argued, through meaningful engagements with the land over time, perpetuating this long-standing motif of settler-colonial legitimacy. The specifics of these attachments are not relevant in themselves, but they are anchored in endurance and feeling, and once they are forged, their loss is commensurable, especially when the same sites hold attachments for many. Read's focus on 'place deprivation' for non-indigenous Australians across his key works of this era (*Returning to Nothing* [1996]; *Belonging* [2000]; *The Haunted Earth* [2003]) posits – like McGahan's depiction of his central characters as all unhomed in some way – the loss of place as a universal experience, implicitly reducing the specificity of Indigenous dispossession to this schema.

Such asserted commensurability between belonging claims is not open to all Australians, but to those who have loved their places in identifiable (to Read) modes of affective connection. And while, as Fiona Probyn points out, Read's work problematically takes indigeneity as an idealized subjectivity, his work does not simply assert a desire for the Indigenous other (what Probyn identifies, after Gayatri Spivak, as an 'epistemic violence' [Probyn 2002: 76]); it takes a non-indigenously identified model of place connection, based in the modern Western concept of 'feeling', and applies it in reverse, to assume a knowability, via commensurability, of what belonging means for Indigenous Australians. In this way, a non-indigenously ascribed and derived model of belonging becomes the gauge of indigeneity, even for Indigenous Australians.

Paradoxically, then, it seems, the quest for non-indigenous belonging locates its deepest disconcertion in the negative prefix which attends its identity – the *non*, in non-indigenous – and at the same time limits its imaginary to non-indigenous terms which become normative for all. The 'aboriginalizing' of non-Aboriginal experience and identity (Ellemor 2003: 239) is thus invested with collective as well as individual value. Clearly emergent in the growing discourse of non-indigenous indigeneity is the idea that such aboriginalization is for the good of everyone. Until the non-indigenous majority have their place, the population as a whole is unsettled, 'anxious, restless, unsure of themselves' (Tacey 1995: 73). Attempts to sacralize non-indigenous Australians' relations to place – an extension of 'feeling' as a force of connection – fed this narrative, as writers such as David Tacey called on non-indigenous people to learn from, and draw on, Indigenous spirituality in order to solidify and authenticate settler-colonial belonging, and consequently 'unite us with "our" family, "our" home and "our" concerns' (1995: 152). As a result, non-indigenous culture would attain its own 'aboriginal' identity (with a small 'a') which has its own 'dreaming' (with a small 'd') (in Gelder and Jacobs 1998: 12).

Martin Mulligan similarly found potential in the idea of a 'whitefella dreaming' to allay cultural crisis, and in doing so, located Indigenous people on a continuum of belonging, behind which non-indigenous people follow (2000). There is, he argued, 'richness in what [the latter] have already started to accumulate' in their places: 'Each of us carries our own personal "dreaming of who we are and where we belong"' (2000: 59). There is no monopoly on meaning, Mulligan argues, no 'dreaming' that is more significant than another, and affective experience of whatever kind fertilizes the roots of a true belonging – a deep connection that will transform 'our' so-far 'sterile and ineffective' relation to place (2000: 58). *The White Earth* models this assertion of equivalent belonging and demonstrates the easy shift into a logic of erasure or replacement that the discourse affords. John's own proclamation of proto-indigeneity is significantly made as he shows Will an apparently sacred site, a ring of stones, on Kuran Station, where he intends to hold a rally for the Australian Independence League:

> There are folk out there who believe that the Aborigines are the only ones who understand the land, that only the blacks could have found a place like this and appreciated what it was [...] But that's not true. We can have connections with the land too, our own kind of magic. This land talks to me [...] And I understand what it says, just as well as anyone before me, black or white. I found this ring, didn't I? So I deserve respect too.
>
> (McGahan 2004: 181)

The alignment of *prior* Indigenous significance, foundational non-indigenous claim and nationalist politics challenge the political terms of the 'sacred', and reinstates singular, chronologic, possession as the marker of belonging. 'The truth is', John tells Will, 'the land has to belong to someone to really come alive' (McGahan 2004: 85). It is the turn of white Australians, by implication, to realize this claim. At the same time, Indigenous belonging is rendered not just past, but straightforward, as open to non-indigenous comprehension and, therefore, replication. The positioning of contemporary Indigenous belonging is contrastingly ambiguous – seen as no longer attached to their places in the precolonial mould (disconnected from 'sacred sites', for instance), Indigenous people are more precariously situated than the non-indigenous claimants who now know and love the land. While this rendering of Indigenous belonging sits alongside the anxiety of an inferior non-indigenous relationship to, and thus claim on, place, these seemingly differing positions ultimately cohere in a fundamental way: non-indigenous interest and insecurity set the terms of Indigenous belonging in the dominant public imaginary.

The novel's ruin poetics – most evident, of course, in the dilapidated Kuran House, but also in its real and spectral cast of emaciated, shambolic and abject non-indigenous characters – offer variant readings (some of which will be explored later), but in this schema of non-indigenous anxiety suggest a haunted consciousness that eats away at the fantasy of secure tenure, upending the ground. If, as Dixson asserted, non-indigenous Australians cannot belong unless their 'unwanted ghosts' (1999: 105) of the past are exorcised, then, McGahan's novel insists, they will never belong. These ghosts clamour around us, pushing against the veneer of stability. The novel does not offer the redemption of settlement. There is no home for Will to claim. As his illness intensifies and his proximity to the 'secret' at the heart of the McIvor family grows (the massacre that enabled Daniel McIvor to claim possession of the station), Will is thrown off balance, constantly destabilized in his relation to the ground, as much as to history, and is caught up with dust, blood, odour, pus and the ever-presence of death.

A growing tumour in Will's ear causing literal deafness, and a dark screaming hole that emits no sound in the burning face of John McIvor, evoke a non-indigenous populace in a poetic binary of mute realization and refusal: a 'shamed nation' 'struck dumb by "our" legacy of the past' (Schaffer 2001: 3). While Will parrots his great-uncle and other members of the Independence League – 'The blacks are gone. You just want to rewrite history' (McGahan 2004: 284) – his embodied experience suggests otherwise. Denial is refused in a poetics of resistance. The pain in his ear only intensifies, the promise of release is denied: 'No rain would help, not even a deluge' (2004: 368). His fevered journey through Kuran Station to the heart of its horror – the bones of massacred traditional owners – results in a dry creek bed, empty of its promised waters that, in his yearning to be relieved of the toxic smell and illness he bears, would soothe and heal. Here, a bunyip appears, once more a figure of non-indigenous anxiety. Here, however, unlike Praed's story, the bunyip speaks directly from a place of difference, rather than voicing a non-indigenous unconscious. 'The rivers have run dry. Caves have opened to the sun', it says. 'The dead are ready for you now' (2004: 317).

Will's feverish stumbling, lost in a landscape without the markers of his or his great uncle's single narrative for this place, suggests Irene Watson's point that the 'sovereign state' representing colonial ascendancy 'is unknowingly [...] enveloped inside Aboriginal law' (2002: 266).The past *does* return in McGahan's text, a theme that I explore further in a later chapter, however it is not as a redemptive revelation for a non-indigenous constituency hoping for clear and secured ground. For Will, this stability is never assured; even as he finally finds relief from the pain, his ear pressed to the cooling earth, 'the ground opened beneath him, and he fell into blackness' (McGahan 2004: 370). The stories told to him do not hold. At the text's conclusion, there is no narrative, seeded in the earth, that legitimizes belonging for Will or his family. The next chapter will go onto discuss this investment in stories as a means for non-indigenous belonging at the millennium, with narratives of a certain kind put forward as restorative and vital to a non-indigenous identity unsettled by outside events, and then, with impacts for the nation entire. Notably, these narratives were frequently described in terms of a formal spatial register in which the ground, and ways of relating to it, figured as a referent of belonging. This practice is in keeping, I will argue, with an ongoing colonial obsession with planarity and rootedness, and where a certain and stable surface for inhabitation is considered the hallmark of belonging. The ground can be secured, it has been repeatedly claimed, with the assistance of narratives that affirm a rightful sense of belonging: a claim that continues to ignore the 'embrace' of another reality around it. Australian literature has long been seen as a site for this to unfold.

NOTES

1. Aileen Moreton-Robinson asserts the link between practices and cultures of property ownership and the non-indigenous logic of national possession/sovereignty (2015).
2. The Miles Franklin Award is Australia's most prestigious literary prize, awarded annually to the best published work that depicts 'Australian life in any of its phases' – a definition that has been open to contestation in recent years.
3. The Reconciliation Convention was held in Melbourne in 1997. It was a cross-sector meeting of 1800 Indigenous and other Australians to discuss paths to Reconciliation, and was convened by the Council for Aboriginal Reconciliation, established by Prime Minister Keating in 1991. The *Bringing Them Home* Report on the Stolen Generations was tabled on the first day of the convention. Prime Minister Howard's opening address set a counter tone to the intentions of the delegates, stating that 'in facing the realities of the past [...] we must not join those who would portray Australia's history since 1788 as little more than a disgraceful record of imperialism [...] such an approach will be repudiated by the overwhelming majority of Australians who are proud of what this country has achieved although inevitably acknowledging the blemishes in its past' (Howard 1997b).
4. The *Bringing Them Home* Report was formally tabled as the *Report of the National Inquiry into the Separation of Aboriginal and Torres Strait Islander Children from their Families*. Its commissioners were the President of the Human Rights and Equal Opportunity Commission, Ronald Wilson, and the Aboriginal and Torres Strait Islander Social Justice Commissioner, Mick Dodson, with eleven Indigenous women co-commissioners. Seven hundred and seventy seven submissions were received by the commission, and a 700-page report produced, recommending reparations, agency funding assistance and formal apologies from state and federal governments. The Report concluded that 'When a child was forcibly removed that child's entire community lost, often permanently, its chance to perpetuate itself in that child. The Inquiry has concluded that this was a primary objective of forcible removals and is the reason they amount to genocide' (Human Rights and Equal Opportunity Commission 1997: 190). Prime Minister Howard famously refused to make the recommended apology to the Stolen Generations, and consequently the Parliament of Australia did not formally apologize until 2008, under Prime Minister Kevin Rudd.
5. See, for instance, Shellam (2015).
6. 'Children overboard' related to an incident that occurred during a period of intensification of border control, and correlative hostility towards asylum seekers coming 'illegally' by boat to Australia. In October 2001, Howard government ministers reported that asylum seekers in Australian waters orchestrated the sinking of their boat, during which time the asylum seekers 'threw' their children into the water in order to elicit Australian help and be brought to shore. This was later revealed to be a fabrication.
7. This is an ongoing situation in 2019 where the mandatory, and in most cases, indefinite off-shore detention of 'illegal' asylum seekers is still government policy.

Chapter 2
Literary Expectations: Grounding Belonging

Narrative lack

The millennial years gave rise to a view that inadequate national, or 'shared', narratives were complicit in the making of anxious non-indigenous belonging, and indeed the social disaffections of contemporary Australia more broadly. Nationalist rhetoric mingled with reflections on the moral value of collective stories: Prime Minister Howard, in 1997, expressed his belief in the power of bonding and 'organic' narratives, insisting that for the nation as a whole 'the symbols we hold dear [...] and the attitudes we have [...] are not things generated by [those] who seek to tell us what our identity ought to be. Rather [...] they grow out of the spirit of the people' (Howard 1997a). In a sense, this reiterated a position long-held by the colonizers, that 'Australian' identity lacked cultural narratives generated by autochthony, and that could justify and solidify possession of colonized land. In a context of relatively recent colonization, such long-standing connections for the settler majority were impossible – they had to be summoned up or transposed from elsewhere. Narratives of what one colonist called 'the native born' (in McCann 2006: 49) were required for those who were not Indigenous. Literary texts, as this chapter will discuss, were given a particular role in this project.

Australia's 'youth' is an ambivalent touchstone here, a source of excitement but also self-consciousness in the national image, often extrapolated as a cultural infancy or incompleteness. This cannot be extricated from the intent of the settler-colonial project in general, which is to reconfigure autochthony by restarting history at the colonial frontier. Deborah Bird Rose has powerfully called this the creation of a colonial 'Year Zero' (1997b). A psychic objective of colonization is to render as prehistory what was there before so that new place narratives can be born, narratives of legitimate claim, untroubled connections and deep knowledge of place. These narratives are implicit to the economic and political project of colonization: they enable its operations, support its power and provide a defensible logic to its innate violence. Literary texts, as a circulating source, and site, of these narratives, are participants in this process, charged with the requisite work of making place anew.

It is in this context that expressions of disconcertion over the youth, and consequently the efficacy, of an Australian literature can be seen. Since Charles Darwin famously sneered at the 'very low ebb' of Australian literary culture (McCann 2006) on his visit to the continent in 1836, the need to define and assert 'Australian literature' has underscored how literary texts written in and about this country are positioned and appraised. The expectations of a 'national literature' more broadly are understood as weighted with ideological purpose – the intention to signify beyond the book, and to 'do work' on behalf of the nation – conveying ideas of the ideal national subject and its constitutive places. These ideas are loaded with subjective values regarding race, class, gender and sexuality, shaping discourses about the nation in the public domain related to its 'character', identity and history. To this extent, a national literature is an 'invention' (Turner 1986) because it is identified after the fact of the literature's production – it only signifies retrospectively and is malleable in its signification.

In the postcolonial context, such invention is crucial to the exercise of power. It allows for the production of imaginaries that enable and sustain dominant social structures of inclusion and exclusion. The paradox of a culture that seeks longevity and resolute attachment (a solid history in place), while also needing the blank slate of a Year Zero that implicitly erases the pre-colonial past, is imminent to an Australian literature, however, and continues to inform the expectations brought to it. Australian literary production is accorded the task of bringing cultural weight and solidity to a relatively new and culturally hybrid nation, as well as imagining the nation starting 'from scratch' and projecting it forward. Darwin's snobbishness spoke to the anxious heart of the colonial project. How to forge a literary culture that would secure a story of national founding, and give legitimacy to settler-colonial presence? Indigenous literary cultures, diverse and complex, and incorporating oral and material traditions, could not be included if the fiction of *terra nullius* was to continue to preside.

Early non-indigenous writings were called upon to undertake this work, in concert with the explorers and surveyors who gave new names to places, conjuring up a land without history (Carter 1988). Literary production became yoked to the wider imperative of forging non-indigenous belonging, an ambition that still has sway. This twisted the assumption that a national literature would 'accurately reflect the character of Australia' (Kramer 1981: 9) and instead deployed literary work for the purpose of generating an idealized character. The strong nationalist themes of some of the most successful and remembered nineteenth- and early twentieth-century Australian authors (Henry Lawson and Joseph Furphy, for instance, along with Steele Rudd) evidence a response to this call, developed through a register of autochthonous place and its realization in various markers that recurred in post-Mabo discourse: knowledge of the land, rightful possession gained through hard work and endurance, and masculine fortitude in overcoming environmental hostility (Schaffer 1989). The continuance of these tropes as characteristics of 'true' Australian literature is evident in their over-representation in winners of the Miles Franklin Award, with its criteria for works that depict 'Australian life in any of its phases'. 'Isn't it striking', wrote literary commentator Angela Meyer in 2011, 'that Australian life, according the Miles Franklin judges, is still represented by the past and the outback, and is written in a male voice' (in Case 2011: 42).

Alongside these prominent narratives were those more ambivalent representations of an uncertain and untrustworthy landscape, with lurking spectres and threats, also giving voice to uncertain place in the sense of both familiarity and legitimacy. However, the push for an embryonic national identity developed in literature, free from the complex acknowledgement of history, meant that tropes of erasure and emptiness, of a land to be filled with colonial endeavour, endured. The literary nationalism of Vance and Nettie Palmer across the 1940s and 1950s demonstrates this. As Australia faced a possible threat of invasion from the Japanese to its north in 1942 during World War II, Vance Palmer wondered whether or not the nation's people 'deserve to survive' such an attack. His reasoning adheres to the narrative of lack, and the assumption that autochthonous stories forge belonging:

> We have no monuments to speak of, no dreams in stone, no Guernica, no sacred places. We could vanish and leave singularly few signs that, for some generations, there had lived a people who had made a homeland on this Australian earth [...] How many penetrated the soil with their love and imagination? We have had no peasant population to cling passionately to their few acres, throw down tenacious roots, and weave a natural poetry into their lives by invoking the little gods of creek and mountain.
>
> (Palmer 2012: 69)

For Palmer, 'a natural poetry' signals the realization of a 'tenacious' attachment of non-indigenous Australians to their places (the reference to 'some generations' makes this non-indigenous focus evident), clearly identifying a particular place for literary work in the non-indigenous project of 'making a mark' on Australian ground, physically and metaphorically. More than this, Palmer's assessment of the promise of a 'natural poetry' suggests that poetic texts can actually materialize the conditions of belonging – 'the little gods of creeks and mountains'. Literary work is given the capacity to materially alter the ways in which we live in our places. Invested with a responsibility that is more than representational, literature potentially offers, in this sense, a forging of relations between non-indigenous Australians and their places. This literary native-ism was influential in the establishment of Australian literature as an academic discipline, the formative period of which continued into the 1970s (Dixon 2007). The idea of 'Australian literature', in one sense, needed the idea of the nation, and thus a nationalist literature, as its object of concern. This articulated with the 'new nationalism' in the wider political air of the 1970s, influenced strongly by then Prime Minister Gough Whitlam's call for an independent national identity free from its colonial past and European inheritance (such as the tradition of 'bloody nationalism'), and defined by its 'self-confidence, maturity, originality and independence of mind' (Crowe 2014). The Australian film industry's celebrated revival during this time (signified by the creation of national and state-based government-financed Film Commissions) drew upon adaptations of key literary works by female authors that extended the bounds of the nationalist canon: notably, the films *Picnic at Hanging Rock* (1975) and *My Brilliant Career* (1979), and the TV miniseries *All the Rivers Run* (1983).

By the 1980s, overt nationalism was approached more critically in cultural circles, with the rise of multiculturalism (as both public policy and theoretical frame) and the influence of post-structural theory in the academy. As Graeme Turner has observed, a 'decline of key nationalist mythologies' (Turner 1986: 360) during this era was marked in the embrace of multicultural and feminist narratives across the cultural industries, evidenced by examples such as Rosa Cappiello's satirical account of migrant experience, the novel *Oh Lucky Country* (1984), and the critically acclaimed documentary of hidden female labour in Australia, *For Love or Money* (1983). This was a significant background to the culture wars of the 1990s, which saw popular sentiment swing against these shifts: the fact that the embrace of multiculturalism, and certainly 'post-structural thought' (no matter the hegemonic nature of the term), was seen as an elitist move driven by the academy rather than by 'the people', certainly signified in this context. Nicolas Birns explains, too, that the 1990s also manifested a break in consciousness, amongst Australian literature at least, from the nation's association with other British colonies (identifying as 'Commonwealth' literature, for instance) (Birns 2015: 10). For conservative commentators, the rejection of nationalism and attachments to empire was suspect for its perceived alignment with the elite cultural minority (in terms of 'taste' and cultural influence, not race or cultural background), rather than the majority of Australians – the 'real Australians', championed later by Prime Minister Howard. The fact that literature, too, held an ambiguous place in terms of its status as both an art form of the elite, but also a traditional locus of nationalist work (both representational and performative), meant that it continued to be called upon in debates over non-indigenous belonging and the national project of making the Australian home. Increasing critical assent grew behind the idea that Australian stories of a particular kind were needed to forge the kind of belonging that would finally assuage non-indigenous anxiety, and that, on the whole, these were lacking.

Indicative of this in the millennial years, public intellectual Robert Dessaix admonished non-indigenous Australians for their lack of nativist narratives that would 'cleave' them to their places (1998: 376). 'Our failed attempt to be at home here', he asserts, is evidenced in 'borrowed tales' (1998: 378), abstracted from far off places of settler yearning: '[I]n Australia we don't seem to have a people at all' (1998: 378). Such a rootless culture, ungrounded by narrative, will only produce 'blankness [and] silence' (1998: 380) beyond its superficial noise. Author Marion Halligan agrees. For her, '[l]ucky [cultures] have had myths and legends for a very long time, beyond quite remembering how or why' (Halligan 2001: 3). Non-indigenous Australia is not one of these. Suggesting that common narratives cohere a community and provide the foundation of belonging, Halligan and Dessaix argue for the identity-affirming capacities of narratives that can speak to a national collective, and in doing so maintain a 'fruitful order in the society, the house, we live in' (2001: 12), 'unless our stories are kept we will perish' (2001: 10), Halligan insists. But just what these stories are is the case in point. The implication is that good stories rightly offer settling and cohering effects; they can attach to all, and hold 'us' tight. That is, their assumed effects idealize certain spatial forms. This reiterates a broader millennial refrain that brings the specificity of an anxious postcolonial Australia together with the disenchantments of a globalized world. Australians at the millennium were 'dying for want of story', alienated by 'metaphysical emptiness' and cultural 'lethargy' (Carroll 2001: 6, 9).

The 'new' narratives offered by the Mabo decision, however, were clearly not those intended here. Despite the fact that, as Stephen Muecke optimistically put it, 'Mabo gave Australians the opportunity to say that the country we thought was fully occupied, fully "covered" by a history which has its point of origin and completion in London, is not at all finished' (1997: 228), there was no comforting hearth offered in its stories, no 'Indigenous myths' (with 'Indigenous' meant broadly) that would secure belonging. Instead it opened everything up. It was indeed, as Muecke wrote, the 'next space of creation' (1997: 228) in a national discourse, but a space that yawned as a crisis in national imagining and was met with recalcitrance and resistance rather than untrammelled recognition. Collins and Davis understand this as a defensive response to the perception of Mabo as a 'threat to the nation', an 'assertion of a moral flaw at the heart of national identity' (2004: 6). Mabo initiated narratives – 'shock-waves' (2004: 4) – that challenged the nation-building work of Australian literature.

However, there remained an enduring preoccupation, across a political spectrum, of tasking Australian literature with formative capacities. These capacities were sometimes evoked in sympathetic tandem with declentionist narratives of literature more generally, and the assertion that reading publics were declining throughout the West. In an Australian context, this was interpreted more specifically. Here, readerships of Australian literature were seen to be falling away (according to the discourse) because Australian texts were failing to engage their public and, in turn, rouse their readership to respond with the nation in mind. In a 2003 lecture, public intellectual David Marr made this point, rather brutally framed as a 'new philistinism' (2003) amongst the culture at large, that our literary writers were called on to defy for the destiny of a progressive Australia. The imperative of Marr's address was for literature 'to focus "without flinching" on the current national scene, to observe and engage the "new old Australia" [...] to make a difference' (2003). This was evocative of Modjeska's speech a year earlier, and her appeal for Australian fiction to respond to 'conditions on the ground' in the contemporary nation. The nation-building capacities accorded Australian literature are activated here, even where 'the nation' is seen in a critical light. Australian 'people' are a collective that can be served, or disabled, by its narratives, and its writers are key actors with responsibilities to this process.

This inevitably loops back into assertions of non-indigenous belonging – an authorial claim on the national space, otherwise unscripted or inadequately written – but it also connects to the liberal humanist ideas of the modern Western literary tradition.[1] These situate literature as restorative of a cultivated inner life in the face of industrial alienation and its attendant effects, such as estrangement from the non-human world, the increasing instrumentality of life and its disconnection from the past which is always preferable to the present. 'Literary study', writes Richard Kerridge, 'is an attempt to build a substitute for a premodern culture that has been lost – one in which the arts have public meaning connecting them with ordinary work and leisure' (2012: 15). In this sense, we can see antecedents of Australian literature's assumed capacity to emplace, ground and 'improve' alienated or estranged subjects here. This is essentially a metaphysical vision with political ambitions, including the drive to belong through inviolate claim.

Colonial ground fetish

The significance of 'ground' to the colonial project is embedded in the very logic and motivation of occupation by dispossession, and in the metaphysics and epistemological traditions of the modern liberal subject. Acts of securing ground and firming up one's foundations are profoundly ontological, and in turn, ideological, and they are brought to bear in acts of imagination and discourse as much as in physical and embodied practices. Thus, from the outset of colonization in Australia, the making of 'settled' space was both a literal and figurative process invested with the need to establish non-indigenous possession, and in turn, to extinguish Indigenous sovereignty and erase pre-colonial history. This was the beginning of a long-standing colonial fetish in Australia that approaches the ground in specific, and very controlling, ways.

The 'ground' is a crucial touchstone in Western philosophic traditions as a metaphoric gauge of Enlightenment ideals – reason, clarity, certainty and mastery. Knowledge is aligned with the 'surface of the mind' and, in turn, the surface of the earth, outside and above a 'material worldsphere that has already closed up' (Ingold 2011: 111). This is to be *on* the world, not *of* it. The human within this tradition is considered to be a sovereign, bounded and coherent thinking subject, defined by its capacity for objective reason held against a stable reality that is wholly available to both human mind (knowledge) and body (occupation). 'Reason' demands firm foundations, and an empirical landscape cleared of ambiguity. As a result, spatial theorist Robyn Dripps contends, '[i]t is easy to understand how the earth's rough and bumpy surfaces, its uncertain and shifting fixity and its damp porosity, could be considered qualities that would destabilize physical, political, and even psychological equilibrium' (2005: 59). A goal of modern Western culture has been to overcome this uncertainty by rendering the external environment as passive and open to control: a non-human world without agency, reinforced through spatial practice. In this paradigm, a human mark on a passive ground indicates presence and power – it is an existential and political act. Dominant traditions of place-making in the West have consequently sought to stabilize ground in order to accomplish these ontological ends, and this took particular form in the colonial project.

Libby Porter describes the 'colonies' as offering opportunities for making place that could not be realized elsewhere. Without an 'existing modern pattern of settlement', the colonizer could 'survey a place as new and empty' (2010: 52) (despite its fullness of life) but also, importantly, as flat. This required imagination and projection, as well as techno-material and administrative practices. 'It was in the colonial moment', Porter writes, 'that Europe realized it could determine the arrangement of space on its own abstract terms' (2010: 52): planar, stable and open to the unimpeded movements of progress. This abstraction of space opened up to acquisitional visions – a land for the taking – and much work had to be done to enact this vision in practice. The eradication of native ecology, mostly through land clearance and the movements of domesticated and feral animals, performed an imaginative and ontological function, clearing away any doubt as to the land's submission to colonial rule. This was a theatrical gesture determined to externalize Indigenous environments as a stage for the inauguration of colonial space and time.[2]

The 'colonial stage' thus performed territorial claim: clearing and enclosing, it pushed traces of other presences that contested *terra nullius* into the wings and spotlighted a preeminent colonial body, secured on the ground of a new epoch – a ground cleared of doubt. In this theatrical context, the colonial body was mobile and unencumbered, and a compacted ground facilitated this. A vertical stance was crucial, too, where less erect physical positions on the ground would suggest a regressive subject unable to command its surroundings. Tess Lea et al. (2012) have written about the privileging of white mobile bodies in the colonized space, in distinction to the unsettling qualities of Indigenous bodies, counterposed as either too absent (disappearing on 'walkabout') or too present ('loitering' around). In pathologizing these temporalities, colonial power could (re)enforce behavioural codes that suited the interests of the non-indigenous majority, and gave cause for the spatial regulation of Indigenous bodies (2012). Like self-contained projectiles rolling on this smooth stage, the ideal colonial unit was closed off from discourse with the ground, and symbolically from 'the outside' more broadly (Carter 1996: 13). A paradoxical relationship to stabilized ground thereby emerged in colonial culture. While the ideal ground – cleared and compacted – affords the mobility prized by imperial processes, this mobility brings with it a kind of detachment, or 'groundlessness', which privileges a surface relation to the ground as a sign of cultivation. This is in strong contrast to Indigenous Australian place-making practices that respond to 'ground' as multidimensional, composed in time as well as in space, and via practices that are performed and ongoing (Memmott and Long 2002; Greenop 2006; Potter 2014).

The Western preference to 'skim the surface of the world' (Ingold 2004: 329) meant a resistance to leaving traces of multiple presences that would contest a singular and dominant place-story – multiplicities that the Mabo decision, and the 'opening up' of history it officially initiated, encouraged. The idea of unmarked ground preceding colonial presence (and in turn, Indigenous 'nomadism') was crucial to the lie of *terra nullius*[3]; patterned ground, in contrast, evidenced not just prior cultural occupations, but the ongoing complexity of postcolonial entanglements. In these entanglements, a particular colonial imaginary is challenged, where the colonial body, mobile and commanding, is the site of action and meaning-making. Dispersed agency, between humans and non-humans – all ecological constituents – involves a very different orientation to the ground where the 'unfamiliar' Australian environment is no longer a projection of the interior colonial subject: surroundings that are 'mysterious', 'inscrutable' or 'patient', for instance. As Peter Weir's Irma muses famously at the sight of the monolith in his film version of *Picnic at Hanging Rock*: 'Imagine, waiting a million years, just for us' (1975). In these terms, the environment and its non-human components will only ever reference human interest, as these supranaturally charged theatrics inspire the pursuit of further conquest, to decode the land and bring it into colonial systems of meaning.

Literary clearings and Romantic immersions

Despite the abstraction of space in the colonial imaginary, colonization was always placed. Invasion and occupation unfolded through embodied inhabitation in the enactment of imaginaries with particular coordinates of time and space. Theatrical fantasies could only go so far. A secured ground had to be continually made, and one force for doing so was literary narrative. As an iteration of literary work for nation-building, a dynamic intimacy existed between colonial place-making and the settler-colonial literary imaginary whereby literary works undertook the psychic and physical 'clearing' demanded by colonial logic. This process was not necessarily in the realm of action or description – a story of what happened, where and to whom – rather it also took place at a compositional level, within the very aesthetics and poetic modes that gave shape to the text. Here, spatial forms within the text intersect with textual forms at a more categorical level, reflecting Levine's position that different kinds of forms are always at work in, and across, texts (Levine 2015: 11).

Recent critical work on Australian colonial and postcolonial literature has reiterated textual form – modes of writing and their attendant tropes, techniques and other poetic devices – as a kind of material politics, with a focus on the enduring aspect of textual traditions in a postcolonial context. As scholars such as Andrew McCann, and Graham Huggan and Helen Tiffin point out, certain textual modes endure in the Australian literary landscape because of their material efficacy for the variant aspects of the colonial project, both past and present. McCann, for instance, highlights the almost obsessive employment of Romantic poetics in early settler-colonial literary culture, notably the elegiac and the sublime, that sought to establish certain aesthetized relationships between colonizer and colonized. These relationships asserted a displaced 'prior' sovereignty – the sorrowful lament for the lost race, for example – and consequently affirmed non-indigenous possession in its apparent witness to the 'tide of time' ushered in by modernity.

This 'Romantic strain' (McCann 2006: 49) rehearsed, and gave poetic reason for, the disappearance of Indigenous people from the landscape, providing a logic of inevitability to dispossession and creating an encysted site for the performance of mourning. Essentially, Romantic modes of writing cleared the imaginative ground of the nation. They gave shape to what McCann calls 'the literature of extinction' (2006). Moreover, McCann contends, these are the origins of a national literature tasked with writing indelible presence onto absence, even while it sought to actively erase and displace others in the process. He cites from an 1867 newspaper review that centralizes, in classic Romantic style, the figure of the child as the loci of hope for an embryonic culture: 'The soil must be occupied by a people who have been born to it [...] who love it not only for the hope of transmitting an inheritance to their children, but also for the sweet memories of their own childhood's scenes and attachments' (2006: 49). Such bucolic ideas, of course, rest upon the violent denial of others' belonging, and *their* children's 'attachments'.

The appeal of these themes and techniques was thus a reaction of the colonizers bringing their existing literary frames to bear on the new context in which they wrote, a context considered otherwise bereft. But it was also due to the amenability of these frames for the colonial task at hand, which was to generate a new national literary culture in the ruins of what had now passed. The Romantic 'vision of people bound to the soil' (McCann 2006: 49) that so strongly informs modern nationalism, could be put to work in literary texts that produced and affirmed this, a belonging forged in the presence of absence. 'The void left by a vanished race [...] would [thus] fill the void at the core of the settler's imaginative experience', McCann writes. 'The trope of the doomed race was not bound up only with a fantasy about racial exclusivity and territorial appropriation [...] it was also the condition upon which colonial writers could begin to fashion an intensely affective, Romantic mode of writing fixated on landscape [...] [in] a series of pathos-laden meditations on the fate of Australia's original inhabitants' (2006: 51–52), such as Judith Wright's poem 'At Cooloolah' (1954), which McCann critiques; Eleanor Dark's *The Timeless Land* (1941); or the rendering of an emptied, deathly environment exemplified by Marcus Clarke's melancholic mountain forests (1880).

The call for a national literature to do the double work of generating culture and forging belonging that recurs in discussions of Australian literature must be seen in the context of this colonial history and its literary enactment. While such explicit versions of elegiac Romanticism may be anachronistic in contemporary Australian literary culture, their legacy remains and actively so. Indeed, in McCann's view, Australian literature has yet to escape this literary history in any real way, continuing to reinvest in 'residual if not regressive aesthetic forms' (2006: 54). Huggan and Tiffin's study of the pastoral mode in the literature of postcolonial Australia similarly highlights the enduring appeal of its attendant concerns and devices and connects this to a material politics of belonging throughout settler-colonial history. While the pastoral may be – as Huggan and Tiffin argue, after Lawrence Buell – 'always contingent, always shifting', and without predetermined 'ideological grammar' (Huggan and Tiffin 2010: 85), it is still a non-indigenous mode of imagination and narration that carries with it particular, irrevocable histories of hierarchy and spectral violence, and that is enfolded into romantic literary imaginings.

This is because, as many critics have pointed out, its politics are generally *poetically* obscured. The classic pastoral theme of journeying or yearning for a more 'simple' life than the one currently inhabited belies the 'crisis of ownership' that inevitably attends such a process, especially in the wake of colonization (2010: 85). It is for this reason that Huggan and Tiffin see the pastoral as speaking strongly to the complexity of the postcolonial situation, especially from a non-indigenous point of view, even while its professed concerns may diverge from this. Indeed, not only have these modes endured in Australian literary culture, but their interrelation with cultural discourse more broadly – with publicly expressed ways of seeing and narrating – continues to be strong. Some of the key tropes that attended expressions of millennial non-indigenous anxiety, across and beyond the literary sphere, draw from this tradition. A key one was the expressed desire to retreat or be somehow immersed in the Australian environment as a predicate for a real, or true, experience of belonging.

The experience of 'getting lost' in the landscape is an archetypal colonial trope in art and literature that has been discussed widely by Australian critics.[4] Most particularly, perhaps, it is the trope of the lost settler child – from Rosa Praed's 'The Bunyip', to Fred McCubbin's painting *Lost* (1886) to the most famous disappearance of all, Joan Lindsay's schoolgirls in *Picnic at Hanging Rock* (1967) – that is most apparent; representing for the 'young' colony or nation attempting to find its feet and mature, the lost settler child is a heightened symbol of anxiety around non-indigenous cultural adequacy, and more deeply, of the legitimacy of their claim to colonized land. Lost children stand for the unknown qualities of the Australian landscape, and its assumed threat and potential for violence – in a sense, the ground's lack of stability. But they also stand, as Peter Pierce argues in his study of the trope, 'for the apprehensions of adults about having sought to settle in a place where they might never be at peace' (1999: xii). Another signification can be read in the settler-colonial who leaves an urban (culturally, and erroneously, associated with non-indigeneity) existence to 'go bush' (associated, similarly, with indigeneity) and find, or remake, themselves anew. Here, the 'bush' is loaded with positive meanings that configure it as an affording space for the non-indigenous endeavour to claim their place. To achieve such an outcome means invariably to 'let go' of certain non-indigenous ontological aspects, and to become an Indigenous (non-indigenous) Australian, meaning to be literally settled, no longer occupying insecure ground. Examples include Robyn Davidson's *Tracks* (1980), Tim Winton's *Dirt Music* (2001) and, in an analogic setting, David Malouf's *An Imaginary Life* (1978).

The evident pastoral aspects of this narrative place it firmly within a Western literary tradition, despite its superficial politics of disavowal. The fantasy of rebirth that lies at the heart of the bush retreat not only appeals to the logic of autochthony – identity forged out of the land, a new nativizing – but has antecedents in the colonizing desire for the 'uncivilized' other that underscores the pastoral mode. In this paradigm, getting lost (which seems anathema to the Cartesian logic of modernity) is fine if something is subsequently found or acquired in the process. Conventionally, this is the wisdom and tacit endorsement of the other that enables a restabilization of time and space. Huggan and Tiffin consider the pastoral as highly amenable to the postcolonial context because it allows a disappearance from the present for the purposes of the future: 'Pastoral is usually associated with nostalgic retreat into the past, but its idealism may also have an oppositional character, or [...] an imaginative potential for the assertion of a new, better, world' (2010: 84).

Significantly, however, the pastoral's conventional emphasis on return (its symmetrical 'retreat and return' structure) requires reworking in the postcolonial context, where the colonizer must stay and make their home, even merging with the landscape (Malouf's *An Imaginary Life* is a prime example of this). Here, the urban/outback dynamic takes the place of the colonial origin and the newly colonized land, involving a journey from disaffected civilized life to the wilder reaches of a premodern, and often nostalgically rendered, space. This journey invariably involves the acquisition of knowledge or insight otherwise unattainable in spiritually depleted urban environments, allowing for critiques of modernity and the alienation of modern life to meld with the project of settler-colonial belonging. This is often undertaken on highly individualized and internalized terms, a personal transformation within the parameters of an unshakable social order, which gave Raymond Williams (amongst others) reason for a critique of the form. As Williams famously wrote, 'a rural landscape emptied of rural labour and or labourers [becomes] a sylvan and watery prospect' (1973: 125).

While the fantasy of a wholly uncritical pastoralism may be impossible in the wake of Mabo and its publicity of colonization's violence, the ongoing attraction of the pastoral mode for non-indigenous Australian writers and commentators demonstrates its political flexibility, if not its modal mobility, as McGahan demonstrates in *The White Earth*. Other more recent Australian novels, such as Stephen Amsterdam's *Things We Didn't See Coming* (2009) and Sally Abbott's *Closing Down* (2017) also provide examples of this. Yet, as I go onto explore through the example of Nikki Gemmell's work in Chapter 3, the pastoral, as a literary form for postcolonial Australia, may be fatally flawed, unable to escape non-indigenous and human-centred self-reference. The determined erasures of a compacted ground, a cultivated *terra nullius*, are what the pastoral, and its continuity of colonial spatial imaginaries inevitably returns to, despite any professed politics to the contrary. In terms of a discourse of narrative lack, and a nation suffering and fractured 'for want of a story', stable ground remains a signifier, and a material model, of a long-standing investment in an acquisitive, surface mobility as well as a 'deep' connection to place. These do not contradict but sit together in the colonial imaginary. Activated anew for a post-Mabo sensibility, these tropes of colonial spatial desire and their material forms – moving on and immersion – fold into each other in attempts to reconcile bad pasts with the enduring ambitions of non-indigenous belonging.

NOTES

1. This point is explored more fully in Chapter 5.
2. See Paul Carter's *The Lie of the Land* (1996) for a poetic discussion of the theatricalizing practices of colonization.
3. Bruce Pascoe's *Dark Emu* (2014) demonstrates the settling cultures of Indigenous Australians, including agricultural practices, in contrast to this image.
4. See, for instance, Rosyln Haynes' *Seeking the Centre: The Australian Desert in Literature, Art and Film* (1998) and Peter Pierce's *The Country of Lost Children* (1999).

Chapter 3
Getting Lost with Nikki Gemmell: Reconciliation and Repair

Nikki Gemmell's twin millennial novels *Shiver* (1997) and *Cleave* (1998) exemplify applications of the pastoral mode to a clearly identified problem of non-indigenous Australian alienation and disconnection from place. They each fold specific post-colonial forces – Indigenous dispossession and sovereignty, non-indigenous denial and the pursuit of legitimate belonging – into narratives that set up a classic urban/non-urban binary, with the former signifying a broader Western cultural disaffection with global modernity, and the latter the restorative and redemptive possibilities of 'non-modern' environments. In that folding, restoration and redemption are aligned with the political and moral cause of 'reconciliation', signalling these novels' historical situation at the height of Australia's reconciliation debate.

The discursive context of millennial Australia invested in a particular meaning of 'reconciliation' that was reproduced in a range of cultural and political forums. While the term was in prominent use elsewhere around the globe, notably South Africa and its Truth and Reconciliation Commission (1996–1998), it had strong currency in Australia in the wake of the Mabo decision and the *Bringing Them Home* Report, and the affective unsettlements these generated. In large part, 'reconciliation' came to be associated with the idea of overcoming and leaving behind 'bad' national pasts, meaning the histories of colonization whose recent visibility had challenged celebratory nationalism and were seen to retard what the nation, otherwise, would be. Reconciliation discourse deployed a terminology of redemption and liberty, offering, as Anthony Moran writes of this time, the opportunity to clean up 'a tarnished national image [...] and free the nation of the guilt and shame associated with its foundation' (1998: 101). It was pitched as a mutually beneficial project, in which both 'sides' could seek repair, often rhetorically tied to the project of nationhood. 'Reconciliation', Tony Birch wrote in 1996, 'is not possible in Australia, and nor is the expression of mature identity, unless White Australia is prepared to "reopen the old wounds, so they can heal"' (Birch 1996: 185).

The 'idea' of healing infused progressive reconciliation discourse of the post-Mabo era (Slater 2018), and Gemmell's novels of the time reflect this keenly. Her stories' focus on Australian 'women in tough places' (as *Cleave*'s blurb tell us) clearly reference their contemporary political context, rendering parallel narratives that speak analogously of 'inward' journeys – almost pilgrimages – signifying broader, sociopolitical challenges. Her protagonists' movements towards repair through adventure-filled passages in physically demanding and alienating environments structure the narrative and provide its symbolic core. In this, Gemmell belongs to a Western romantic tradition of testing and transforming oneself spiritually and psychically through environmental ordeal, particularly in 'remote' environments, offering a version of the pastoral idyll that continues to shape the ongoing relationship between Australian land and its non-indigenous inhabitants. What Gemmell demonstrates is the utility of this contextual romantic tradition to the particular political moment of 'reconciliation' in millennial Australia (a tradition that critics at this time, such as Ann Curthoys, discerned as structuring the discourse of reconciliation itself [1999]), and she does this with increasing visibility across the two works.

Shiver and *Cleave* can in this sense be classified as 'Sorry novels', a subset of millennial literature that is a retrospectively defined genre of Australian writing, responding to the reconciliation debate of the 1990s and 2000s, and that straddles the millennial years. The push to say 'sorry' to generations of Indigenous Australians damaged by the forced separation of children from their parents (known as the 'Stolen Generations')[1] gained momentum throughout the 2000s, despite Prime Minister Howard's refusal to entertain the idea. It culminated at the official State level in subsequent Prime Minister Kevin Rudd's Apology to Australia's Indigenous Peoples on behalf of the Federal Parliament on 13 February 2008.[2] 'Sorry novels' can be understood as reactive to this period; they are almost by definition non-indigenously authored and concerned, focused on questions of non-indigenous refusal, denial, guilt and responsibility. Rebecca Weaver-Hightower, for instance, describes the genre as emergent from a 'cultural climate of guilt and ambivalence', and as literary 'apologies that scrutinize the issue of non-indigenous Australian cultural guilt for the dispossession of Indigenous Australians' (2010: 132).

But Sorry novels are also expressions, rather than simply reflections or critiques, of non-indigenous ambivalence. Weaver-Hightower's own study of three such novels – Peter Carey's *Oscar and Lucinda* (1988), Greg Matthews *The Wisdom of Stones* (1994) and Kate Grenville's *The Secret River* (2005) – focuses on the counter-narratives apparent in each that undercut these texts' intentions to problematize and condemn the violence of colonialization and Indigenous dispossession. This countering occurs in notes of defence or disconcertion that can sit alongside critical portrayals, but more prominently it takes place in gestures that assert non-indigenous *indigeneity* as either a reality or a possibility that can grow from the ashes of dispossession. Potentially, Sorry novels rehearse opportunities for non-indigenous Australians to redeem their fraught belonging and reclaim a rightful place, even if this is mediated through violent and discomforting pasts.

Sorry novels assemble with a range of cultural expressions in the post-Mabo years that prioritize the effects of historical recognition and legal redress (and their absence, too) on non-indigenous subjectivity as they simultaneously acknowledge, and keep in public circulation, a reckoning with the same history. Nikki Gemmell's novels are active in this assemblage, working poetically through spatial forms to clear away troubling pasts, and to resettle a disturbed and uncertain personal and national ground – 'getting lost' in order to belong. While my focus here is *Cleave*, *Shiver*'s parallel narrative is worth brief discussion, as it establishes motifs rehearsed and developed in the latter book and offers an interesting symbolic counterpoint to the central Australian setting of *Cleave*. Both novels centre on the journey of young, independent and socially disaffected women into two distinct 'deserts': the Antarctic mainland in *Shiver* and the Tanami desert in central Australia in *Cleave*. Both women are fleeing from personal traumas, and 'healing' is key to their peripatetic drive. More than this, though, both novels position this dialectic of harm and restitution in concert with a critique of the social body at large, specifically the spatial and affective disconnections of global modernity. The ground is an active presence in the text as an arbiter of individual and collective well-being.

The names of the female protagonists – Fin in *Shiver*, Snip in *Cleave* – reflect the women's drive to make clean breaks with their current lives, weighed down by the past; their mobility speaks to this assertion of freedom. Their mobility also affords reflective critique of dominant living practices that Gemmell repeatedly frames in terms of a relationship to the ground. Fin's journey leads her to realize that her Australian urban contemporaries live 'too removed from the earth' (Gemmell 1997: 268); similarly Snip angrily perceives that most non-indigenous Australians 'never celebrate the land' (Gemmell 1998: 82). Each novel begins with the women's location in environmentally and socially degraded urban environments, feeding into the restless alienation that propels them outward. Both novels reproduce ideas of a rootless, or ungrounded, non-indigenous body. Through the various landscapes they depict, each narrative poetically navigates the challenge of belonging through a metaphoric investment in a dialectical poetics of division and reunion. The texts write a postcolonial world full of material and psychic divisions that are contrasted with the 'wholeness' of unbroken vistas and smoothly surfaced environments, rehearsing the pictorial fantasy of Antarctica and the vast Australian 'outback'. Ultimately, however, Antarctica is reproducible as Australia, and vice versa. They come to stand for the same thing: a place where non-indigenous Australians do not belong in any straightforward or unproblematic way. Here, Gemmell picks up on a long-standing connection of the two continents in the modern imaginary (Collis 1999).

Cleave introduces Snip as an always-travelling young woman who heads into the Tanami desert in central Australia, in search of her father, Bud, and the secret that surrounds his disappearance from her life. She is initially characterized through clear metaphors of atomization and mobility and as untethered to place. Never 'long enough in a place for it to seep through her and hold onto her' (Gemmell 1998: 67), she is described as a 'gypsy girl' (1998: 150) 'ferociously addicted to the new' and to a 'life of fragments' (1998: 25). The obvious implication of her surname – 'Freeman' – heralds her commitment to movement, and aligns her with the modern, as well as the colonial, body and what Ross Gibson calls its 'mania for mobility' (2014: 260).

Snip's unattached and self-detaching qualities are emphasized against Dave's, the hitchhiker with whom she sets off from Sydney to Alice Springs at the start of the novel. 'He's got one of those faces that looks like it's never been anywhere' (Gemmell 1998: 156), Snip comments. Though she has shifted between towns and cities her whole life, Snip is identified as 'a country girl', 'a desert girl, sand is her dirt' (1998: 9). Her taciturn nature is contrasted with Dave's naïve optimism, as is each one's relationship to their own personal history. This contrast is manifested in respective spatial modalities. To poetically convey these differences, they are allocated distinct relationships to the ground. While Dave 'chatter[s]' about family and the layers of his own life, Snip's blunt response reflects her need to move on without looking back: 'I don't remember no childhood' (1998: 16). Moreover, Dave is a professional archaeologist, someone place-bound who digs down into the past, 'scrabbling though dirt and peeling off wallpaper and pulling away bricks' to excavate the past (1998: 16) and expose it to light.

Dave's practice associates him with urban contexts that are depicted as superficial and alienating. While the city is tenacious in its grip upon the ground, it is also estranged from any kind of meaningful relationship to the earth on which it weighs. By contrast, the outback is represented as complex and meaning-rich, against the bright fluorescence of urban vacuity. Snip's affinity with the non-urban space suggests her ideal relation to an environment: untethered and always transient. This is the 'place she never graces with the name home' but from 'where she launches her next venture in any direction' (1998: 44). As the narrative unfolds, however, we learn that Snip's response to the ground is tactical, in order to avoid and forget long-secreted pain. It is her childhood home from which she is running – this is the origin of her unsettlement.

Set amongst the bleak mining regions of coastal New South Wales, the surrounds of her youth affirm the text's depiction of 'settled' environments as depthless and blinkered. Her childhood home, we are told, 'didn't let in the sky': 'bunkered against the wind' and 'shut to the world' (1998: 81), it 'never celebrated the land it was on' (1998: 82). This is compounded by the refuse of industry that stains the earth. The litter from the coastal mines, which are soon to close and quietly decay, signifies the violent legacy of colonizing practices, the apparent inability of the settler population to 'cleave' to the land. Snip's resistance to enclosure and her desire for mobility are thus connected to her displacement from a foundational, family home ('a sacred site in modern Australia' [Gelder and Jacobs 1995: 160]), which stands for the dysfunctional national family at large, and post-industrial Western modernity more broadly. Snip's journey in search of her father, and her subsequent forced confrontation with a traumatic past, provides a pedagogical route to necessary repair. The gothic quality of her bunkered family home suggests secrets hidden away, and Snip's childhood memories continually circle this, a secret that also ruptured her father's relationship with his family and sent him running too.

Cleave is cast with a succession of alienated or alienating non-indigenous characters: an exodus of exhausted urban dwellers seeking refuge in the 'outback'. 'It's the place for runners', Snip knows. 'The Territory's full of them, runners from parents and the law and cities and lovers and children and wives' (1998: 213). The non-indigenous population, locked away in houses elevated from the ground, behind 'barbed wire and mesh and bulletproof glass' (1998: 52), is starkly contrasted with the local Indigenous Warlpiri, or Yapa, way of dwelling in the desert: '"Within the walls of a house you cannot see far," says Queenie Nungala Mosquito, a person of this place' (1998: 52). The correlation between an inward gaze and disconnected living, as a trope of non-indigenous experience, is made repeatedly throughout the text. The 'trees planted by Missionaries' (1998: 58) and the 'scattered cattle bones [and] car parts' (1998: 162) are 'wrong in the landscape' (1998: 162). Standing as signs of failed settler belonging, these talismans are juxtaposed with the stories of non-indigenous people and their hollow attempts to claim the outback ground 'as if their rich record somehow justifies being in a place that isn't theirs' (1998: 111). The 'barrenness thousands of cattle hooves have stamped' (1998: 153) into the earth conveys a 'meanness' (1998: 153) in the environment to Snip, a consequence of the way in which 'Europeans have overlain the land, how they've threaded it with bitumen and concrete' in the built-up spaces of 'whitefella world' (1998: 161). She discerns a 'hum of nothing' (1998: 234) that hangs in the desert, as stiffened hides and bleached carcasses shimmer in the sun.

The colonist's desire to repress the lie of the land (Carter 1996) has barely shifted in 200 years. In Gemmell's depiction, social alienation, environmental degradation and human-perpetrated violence are direct outcomes of colonial malpractice and a fundamental failure of non-indigenous culture to connect meaningfully with the ground. An awareness of this, of a failure to belong, informs the two non-indigenous 'types' that recur in the book – the type who denies this and the type who laments it, both evident dispositions in the contemporary public discourse of reconciliation: '[T]hey're in Australia', Snip considers, 'but they've entered a place where the culture and religion are alien and they can't read the paintings and speak the language and they don't have access to the intricacies of the law' (Gemmell 1998: 316). Dave's insistence that '[w]e don't really belong here, Snip' (1998: 310), is echoed in his friend Richard's question: 'Do the Aboriginal people see them as homeless aimless drifters, do they think it's weird these whitefellas being out here, without ties to their own culture and community, away from their family and friends?'. When Richard asks his non-indigenous companions 'what the Aboriginal people think of them [...] No one answers' (1998: 127).

Yet the opportunity to 'get lost' in the desert, in a spatial and subjective sense, offers both Snip and Bud the possibility of long-sought connection. Snip's initial desire to plough through the land slowly dissolves as 'stop like a tonic flood[s] through her' (1998: 59). The corporeal takes on a different temporality as 'changes' are pushed 'over Snip's body': her 'hair copies the colour of dirt' (1998: 78), while a 'hide is thickening on the underside of her feet [...] Her walk is dropping to a slowness [...] It's energy stopping, she's been told... [it's] the Aboriginal way' (1998: 53). Indigenous subjectivity is synchronized with the environment, which reciprocally takes over the body. Bud eventually wears 'a band of red dust [...] ingrained across the extremity of his white shirted stomach' (1998: 72). Father and daughter begin to speak 'Yapa way' in accordance, we are told, with the spare nature of the land, economically '[d]ropping "and" and "the" [...] Saying little one, skinny one, cheeky one' (1998: 74–75). After twenty-one days 'in this place', Snip 'feels like she's lost the art of talk, dinner-party talk [...] as if the wind and dust and sun and stars have blown it cleanly out of her' (1998: 111). Here, a non-indigenous body can arrive and be made over, invested with a connection to country that is indigenously modelled, and for Snip the land is 'rich', 'singing' with what she otherwise lacks, 'spirit and community and family' (1998: 314). 'Nowhere else for her feels like this' (1998: 67). Thus, the Tanami is home for Snip in a way that cities, or her family, are not. More than this, the Warlpiri community signifies what home to Snip *should* be. While Snip has the provenance of space and mobility, Warlpiri people have both space and certain place at once, she believes.

Indigenous kinships and social relations show a different way of being and belonging, juxtaposed with a repressed, disorientated and disordered settler society. Snip is considered 'a woman of value in this place' (1998: 55), accepted as someone who enters and leaves the Yapa lands, and appreciated for her 'bush-bashing car'

(1998: 55) that can take the women out hunting. The nurturing offered to Snip by these women is juxtaposed with her own warring family's stories, while the matriarchal figure of Queenie, in particular, gestures towards Snip's strained contact with both her parents, welcoming her as 'Napaljarri, my daughter' (1998: 56). Snip watches a group of Aboriginal women and children drive past in the night, noting the care with which each child is held, 'tight' (1998: 79) and protected. Folded and tucked into fabric, wrapped up like 'gifts' (1998: 79), these bundled children suggest an alternative way of seeing enclosure: not unbearable and wounding, but warm and sustaining. These are forms of holding that contrast the depth of belonging against an exposed surface of alienation. Her resistance to the threat of being 'pinned down' by another is surrendered in this land, which Snip acknowledges (in the repeated and rather laboured poetic of love and connection in the novel) is 'under my skin' and 'isn't going to let me go' (1998: 311). The ritual of self-recovery that Queenie performs articulates a connection between being with the land and releasing the past. Telling Snip how 'she went back to her people's way by one day going to the riverbed and stripping down and rubbing sand all over her' (1998: 72), Queenie infers the possibilities of self-renewal and 'fixing' (1998: 62) in this landscape, 'beginning a new way' (1998: 60).

Snip notes the 'wind [...] in this place' and its significance to the Warlpiri '[w]hen there's sorry business, when someone has died' (1998: 60), scattering 'all tracks and all traces as it sweeps the spirit to the land' (1998: 60). Such images of restitution are significant in the text, and the 'payback' ceremony she witnesses from behind bulletproof glass further denotes the distinctions between the non-indigenous culture Snip knows and the Indigenous ways of life she observes. 'Payback', held on the local football oval, signifies both communal accountability and responsiveness to an act of wrong. Rather than Bud's self-determined punishment for his violence against Snip's mother Helen, 'payback' is a necessarily public performance, an expression of collective belonging as much as individual and communal hurt. Indigenous elders act on behalf of their community in 'payback', hitting the offenders 'with nulla nullas and sticks' (1998: 76). The men are then speared in the thigh by the family of their victim, as the 'grandmothers and the aunties all beat [...] themselves' (1998: 77). Suffering and healing become constitutive of community, and are equally shared by all in attendance. The scars from 'payback' admit culpability and initiate mourning. They are exposed rather than hidden and included in cultural knowledge rather than excluded from it.

In contrast, the 'scarring' that Bud and Snip inflict upon each other is emblematic of a disabled sociality in which hurt is individualized and privatized. Snip's summation that '[p]eople aren't meant to exist solely for themselves' (Gemmell 1998: 364) is matched by Bud's admission that he has done just that, telling her that 'people in underdeveloped worlds are never as lonely as those in developed worlds'; '[h]e tells her the wisest thing the Warlpiri have taught him is that the family, not the individual, is society's most basic unit and that for him it's too late' (1998: 359). However much Snip seeks to be inside this knowledge, though, she can never access it in full, and despite the changes that occur in her speech and body, and her welcome in the community, she still exists on its ambiguous margins, 'crashing like a bull' into what she will 'never understand' (1998: 56). Kate's insistence that '[t]heir lives and their beliefs are too complex and secret for me' (1998: 56), is re-voiced by Shelly-Anne when she tells Snip 'she's heard the Aboriginal people [...] think whitefellas have no culture, spirituality, and are backward for that' (1998: 75).

Snip's and Bud's final attempt to 'get lost', heading further outback, away from any settled life, is indicative of an inadequate belonging that can never become sufficiently Indigenous. This is a classic narrative of insufficient non-indigenous place on the land as they become marooned and then lost in the unfamiliar environment. While stranded in the desert, Snip and Bud discuss words with two opposing definitions. *Heimlich* is Snip's favourite: something that 'is homely and comfortable and familiar, but also something which is concealed and inaccessible and unknown' (1998: 179), although the latter is *unheimlich* in the Freudian sense. As an obvious symbol of their ambiguous place in the Tanami, this discussion configures Snip and Bud's unsettled belonging in uncanny terms. As much as they feel at home in the land, and are imprinted by their encounters here, they also do not. Thus, when she returns to the Tanami, recovered, but with the 'sun's deep stain' 'branded' on her body (1998: 337), Snip 'knows she has no right to a permanent place in this community' (1998: 315).

The characteristic discourses of this era of non-indigenous anxiety are put to work here, from the settler body's inadequacy and blindness, to the yearning to inhabit Indigenous experience from a position of insufficiency, with their correlate poetics of dysfunction, superficiality, disconnection and closure. 'We hate this country because we cannot allow ourselves to love it', Germaine Greer wrote in 2003. 'We know in our hearts that it is not ours' (Greer 2003: 7). In this vein, Gemmell's text ambiguously shifts between an acceptance of a non-indigenous belonging that can never be like that of Indigenous Australians, and its negative representation as indicative of cultural and individual ignorance and – importantly – the inability to attach to the ground. This failure is directly linked to colonial practices and legacies. The 'land she grew up in feels like corrupted land to her', we are told, 'because it's been swept clear of the people who told stories about it over thousands of years, it's been swept of the people who sang for it' (Gemmell 1998: 314).

Gemmell's non-indigenous protagonists are products of a destructive history, and their alienation is compounded by the 'real' belonging modelled by Indigenous people, deeply connected to the ground. Yet Gemmell also suggests a way forward for a disconnected community, and a fractured, unreconciled nation. Here, the pastoral comes to use again in the 'healing' qualities of the romanticized premodern. Almost dead in the desert, delirious, badly burnt and severely dehydrated, Snip is finally rescued by an Indigenous tracker – saved by the knowledge of one who 'truly' knows this country. The metaphors at work here leap off the page: it is an explicit image of reconciliation, of the colonized resetting the future for non-indigenous belonging.[3] The pastoral journey is completed as Snip returns to 'modern' life when she fully wakes up in the closed, controlled environment of an Alice Springs hospital. 'Welcome to the real world, Miss Freeman', she hears, as 'the white man takes over' in a 'place seared by white' and overhung with 'the smell of bureaucracies' (1998: 276).

This journey is not just a physical one, of course, it is a psychic one, too, and the text makes Snip's story a clear analogue for the necessary journey of the postcolonial nation itself. Snip's personal reconciliation with her past is played out in a symbolic register of settled spatialities. It is therefore in the course of Snip 'scrubbing her life clean' (1998: 67) that a wider sense of redemption is proposed. Here, Emma Kowal's concept of the 'white anti-racist' is useful, a subjectivity that she locates in the reconciliation period and is characterized by a desire for 'self-effacement' amongst 'progressive Whites' (2011: 315). This is informed by the inversion of white social status as a self-acknowledgement of the exploitative violence of colonialism and imperialism that attaches itself to contemporary non-indigeneity. This is a form of 'White stigma' taken on by 'White' people themselves: the 'stained' environments and personal histories that *Cleave* so evidently presents. Problematically, according to Kowal, this leads to strategies of 'stigma management' that paradoxically involve self-scrutiny (Snip's critical assessments of her dysfunctions as part of a failed non-indigenous family/community) and the pursuit of redemption: the idea that, ultimately, this intractable position can be transcended.

The latter, Kowal identifies, is commonly attempted via the subordination of non-indigenous status to Indigenous authority, with a particular mobilization of child/parent relations. Colonialism is riven with paternalistic/maternalistic patronage and violence over Indigenous subjects, and by inverting this power dynamic, the non-indigenous (or 'White') subject can look to the authority and expertise of Indigenous people on matters of culture, community and the land. 'As a child', Kowal writes, 'the White anti-racist cannot exploit Indigenous people' (2011: 325). Moreover, this inversion entails a new dynamic of care, in which the White adult-child is taken under the wing of Indigenous elders in an opportunity to be restored and remade, and in the process, 'cleansed of stigma' (2011: 326). The hope of redemption is thus opened up. This trope is evident throughout *Cleave*, in the points of contrast continually made between Indigenous and non-indigenous ways of living, being and relating, and Snip's process of 'giving herself up' to the land. Belonging does not mean simply inhabiting an Indigenous subject position, however, and the text is clear on this point: 'She's made up her mind. She has to find her own country' (Gemmell 1998: 316). What it does make clear is that in the pursuit of one's own country, a journey of maturation takes place from stigmatized, disabled non-indigenous subject, to a renewed, regrounded member of a postcolonial community, with the tacit endorsement of Indigenous Australians.

Clearing a space for non-indigenous belonging

The distinct spatial practices accorded to Snip and Dave come to stand for the differing ways that each relate to the past: Snip the runner and Dave the excavator. The text resolves with these two polarities brought into a harmonious coexistence, prefigured by the redemptive desert scene, where the rift between a desire to forget and the impulse to claim is overcome. As Snip learns through her experiences and reflections on the insufficiencies of her past behaviour, her eventual alliance with Dave signals the potential for reconciliation between their spatialized differences and the politics of inhabitation embodied in each. This, Elizabeth Graver suggests in her review of the novel,[4] represents an attainment of 'balance [...] [in] a fractured and difficult world' (1999: 2). Snip must learn, Graver continues, 'accommodation' amongst her 'defiance' (1999: 2), and certainly the more she realizes her affinity with Bud, both of them running, hurt from a past they consider irredeemable, the more she concedes the necessity of changing her ways. The restorative nature of the desert is compounded by the revelation of what has prevented the settling of Snip and Bud, brought to the surface from its psychic depths. Here, their years of running conclude as, physically worn down and stripped of clothes in the heat-filled space, they experience a simultaneous evacuation of repressed pasts.

Dave's techniques of mining through the ground to a time and a place are echoed by Snip as she and Bud dig down to their disremembered 'bad things', cutting into the 'foundations and brickwork' (Gemmell 1998: 161) of a causative moment. The importance of uncovering the past, and bringing it to light, is asserted in this narrative. Bud's insistence that 'you can never have any idea what's in another person's mind. All the deep-down secret stuff [...] no-one else can ever dig [...] out' (1998: 255–56) is met with his daughter's recognition that 'there are some things she has to know or they'll rattle in her head and give her no peace until she dies' (1998: 241). To finally overcome not belonging, it is suggested, remembering is vital. Thus, Bud's revelation means a release for Snip, a common history opened to revelation and recovery. '[H]e's letting her in', she narrates. 'And it could be a way out' (1998: 250–51). The potential for healing and transcendence is activated: the end of one thing, and the beginning of the new. The sky above the desert in which they uncover hidden pasts 'is stained an eery, apocalyptic pink and the desert holds its breath before the dust storm smacks into it' (1998: 195), evoking reckoning and rebirth. There is a 'fermenting dread of something coming to an end' (1998: 253) in the non-indigenous tradition of outback mythology, a space, as Paul Longley Arthur writes, 'where experience is [considered] extreme or ultimate', 'in some way the end or the beginning of the world' (1999: 138).

While Gemmell's non-indigenous characters are called on to face the past, they are propelled to ultimately 'let it go', and once again with Indigenous endorsement (1998: 66). Snip comes to realize that whatever she learns of the past, it will tell her 'everything and nothing' (1998: 300). Waking to find her father gone once more, after their final confrontation, suggests to Snip that however close to the truth she gets, there will never be a final revelation that remakes the world. It is at the point of *this* realization that Snip is finally rescued from her desert ordeal, precariously close to death and emerging anew 'as if layers have been scrubbed from her' (1998: 290). Snip's acceptance of what she cannot know shapes a philosophy of the past in *Cleave*. Her recognition that 'there are too many gaps' (1998: 362) in her father's story lets Snip consider her need to unbury forgotten things outside absolute terms. 'In an archaeological dig', Snip realizes, not all parts of the object will be retrieved. The traces that are found, or the pieces that survive, can be encountered and restored, 'nurture[d] [...] back into life' (1998: 344). Dave's hands on her body, as if he is sifting through a ruin 'to save it, to peel back its layers and dig out its history' (1998: 344), repair in just this manner. With him, Snip knows, 'she wants to settle'; '[s]he wants to begin a new way' (1998: 295). Reconciliation is therefore modelled by the text as the location of 'neutral territory'. '[T]hat's what we need', says Dave, '[a] place new to both of us' (1998: 343), and Gemmell locates the possibility of a non-indigenous settled belonging in the attainment of such a 'new place', a place predicated on the 'letting go' of the past. It is as if the acknowledgement of what evades total knowledge or comprehension defuses its effects. Homeliness opens up to Snip as her acceptance of the past and all its gaps solidifies her place on the ground.

Reconciliation is represented as a central concern of and for non-indigenous Australians. Its demands require work on non-indigenous subjectivity alone, as a singular product of colonial pasts. The 'new home' (1998: 343) where Snip and Dave eventually settle is poetically significant in this regard – a landscape of neither city boundaries nor propulsive horizons, but the water-heavy, 'deep earth' (1998: 347) of Tasmania which is a pointed focus for the text's climax of ontological and national renewal. This is a land 'soaked in blood', according to Snip, 'a ghost-land – beware' (1998: 342–43), and once again she comments on the absence she feels in this environment: '[S]mug' (1998: 344) English-style towns and names cover over a history of Indigenous decimation. However, it is in this landscape that Snip finally finds the ability to stop, to rest, to be in place, and here her ontological strategy is transposed onto the state of the nation itself. In our 'worst place', national redemption must be found. '[S]he has to leave Bud behind', Snip emphatically decides, 'to move on. She has to move on' (1998: 336).

This is the key to Bud's own restoration, too. As their unsettlements are interconnected, they both require the experience of transcendence and healing. Consequently, when Bud joins his daughter in Tasmania he 'touches the earth lightly' (1998: 350), a sign now not of displacement but of belonging. He has acquired the capacity to start 'a new way' (1998: 60). As the Warlpiri spirit is swept to the land, with tracks cleared and things renewed, Bud's swim out to sea at the novel's conclusion represents this renewal and the instigation of beginnings. It also confirms his disavowal of the alienated (dis)order of Western modernity. Baptismal imagery asserts Bud's remaking. For many years a preacher in the Tanami, he tells Snip that he has 'given up on churches [...] [he] tells her God is in his heart and in the land but not, for him, in the walls of a building' (1998: 357). With his daughter watching from the shore, Bud 'dives his bulk at a small wave, as if his body is falling into it' (1998: 363), surrendering a contained and ego-centric self to an unlimited and overwhelming space. '[J]ust a speck now in the vastness of the ocean [...] a swell rises above him and he's gone for a moment and bobs back' (1998: 364), his firm edges dissolved in the fluidity of motion as the 'remnants of waves rush over [Snip's] toes' (1998: 368). Bud's swim out to sea, presumably to his death, mirrors his physical evacuation: emptied out to be refilled. Snip notes, on this arrival in Tasmania, 'the scars of his journey. Sharp cliffs in his cheekbones. A scalp fragile and pink [...] And something missing' (1998: 348). They are implicated in this rebirth together, and as 'the bay sings with Bud's spirit', Snip 'feels free and scrubbed, as if a great weight has been lifted from her' (1998: 368).

Fin, *Shiver*'s protagonist, expresses a similar sentiment as she returns to Australia from her Antarctic journey, feeling as 'though life itself has been bellowed out of me; I feel ready to begin all over again, clean' (Gemmell 1997: 226). Fin's parallel pursuit of immersion, forgetting and renewal in an ultimate place of oblivion and pastoral escape in the Western imaginary (the great 'white land') offers a performative reflection on the non-indigenous fantasy that underlies Snip's revelation. Antarctica is Australia's uncanny mirror: a desired expanse of 'nothingness' to be claimed and written over by imperial endeavour. Its smooth frozen surface epitomizes the affordances of a passive, colonized space. The idea of 'immersion' as a form of claim evokes the classic Western ground: to be immersed is to assert an indelible relationship to place. Even in an unsettled continent such as Antarctica, this is a stable and inviolate one.

Back in *Cleave*, colonial spatial practice is reiterated as the pre-eminent mode for non-indigenous belonging. At the text's conclusion, Bud's fluid movements through water and Snip's metamorphosis expressed in her work – with 'light in the colours and serenity in the strokes' (Gemmell 1998: 373) – depicts the subject free from constraints and able to merge into land. 'Removed, floating, all-seeing' (1998: 364) as she turns her back on Bud in the swell, Snip articulates a sense of immersion that is simultaneously restorative, free from the urge 'to scratch at the scab of her wounds' (1998: 367). 'Let's go home', Dave tells her (1998: 370). The purgatorial journey of Snip and Bud, incurring suffering, loss and self-confrontation in the desert, finds its pastoral reward in the watery space of foundational narrative. Her prize-winning picture that 'seem[s] to float from the canvas' (1998: 373) is fitting for the novel's final image; unloaded, untied, unburdened now, Snip's 'own country' – her belonging – is gained through a reunion of divided parts, and a redemptive return to beginnings that are the origin and end of unsettlement.

The novel's title participates in this, and as Bud and Snip further discuss words with two meanings 'cleave' comes to mind, meaning 'a splitting apart or a binding together' (1998: 178). A 'strong biblical word' (1998: 178) (thus enhancing the baptismal quality of this resolution), 'cleave' encapsulates the key assertion of the text: that relations of unity or division confer a firm or disconnected place for the non-indigenous subject. Unsettlement must be undone to enable belonging, and in the smooth passage from splitting to merging the stability of the ground is restored. The possibility of recuperated beginnings lies only on a clear and secure ground. *Cleave* ultimately embraces the same colonial clearance tactics that it ostensibly condemns, reinvesting in the spatial practices that continue to endorse a secure narrative of non-indigenous place. Though Gemmell resists a straightforward appropriation of Indigenous subjectivity, the remaking of imbalanced belongings in Australia through the correction of a disordered non-indigenous self allows a gathering together of singular pasts and their effects in an image of a future prospect for all Australians. The repetition of 'cleanness' in the text as an ideal ecological and ontological state, and its opposition to the 'mess' by which Snip's past is described, posits the healed national subject as conclusively purified, evacuated and refilled through the transcendence of damaging pasts. There is no account taken of the past as an ongoing presence. Whereas 'mess' stands for hard, sharp and balled up relations in the text, a clean subjectivity is imagined without tensions or irregularities.

Further, the centrality of personal experience in Gemmell's narrative, coupled with Snip's condemnation of Bud's singular life, without accountability to the community/family, suggests that shared damage can be resolved through individual acts of redemption. Timothy Murray argues for the productive capacity of this strategy in which 'the pathos of the personal is intermixed with the trauma of the social' (2000: 105). Here, 'critical energy' (2000: 106) can be generated in a collusion between the two. However, the images of a reconciliation that Gemmell's text offer diffuse the energy of ongoing negotiations in favour of a newly imagined coherent national body – with sovereignty issues resolved. Gemmell's emphasis on common responsibility and sharing disconcertingly flattens difference and dissent as she assumes that belonging *for all* is the goal of healing bad pasts.

What the text ultimately advocates is an idealized non-indigenous belonging that advantages the non-indigenous subject above all, 'cleansing the stigma' of colonial complicity as the primary defacement of the contemporary nation, rather than the complex and violent legacies, and continued activation, of colonization in Australia. Gemmell draws on a spatialized register of postcolonial relations, enacted through formal tropes that elevate surface over depth, and holding together over separation, in its advocacy of this ideal. The reconciliatory imagery and poetics of the text connect morality (Bud's 'wrongness', for example) to legitimacy, thereby invoking the notion of a 'right' Australia that has made up for its past. While Gemmell insists upon differences between non-indigenous and Indigenous historical experience, in her final image of recovery and the attainment of home, complexity is obscured under the sign of national healing, a transcendence instigated by the no longer guilt-locked and repressed settler subject. As the desire for a clean, unmarked body in a context of 'bad' and 'dark' national pasts implies, suffering and ruin are linear predicates for the promise of ontological rebirth. Narratives of settler struggle and survival, once again, feed a legitimizing discourse of non-indigenous claim to the land, and although Snip professes to distance herself from these self-justifying stories, Gemmell's text can be seen as re-employing this tradition. Curthoys points to the currency of pilgrimage narratives in millennial Australia, taken symbolically for a nation in the pursuit of reconciliation. Given its epic proportions of battle, survival and atonement, official reconciliation at this time was frequently endowed with the properties of redemption and healing for the national body (Curthoys 1999: 3). Yet, while Snip attains the promise of the future, her redemption is wholly self-contained, devoid of networked consciousness.

The troubling nature of Snip's isolation of the 'origin' of her personal, and through this, national trauma lies in her enactment of these modalities, despite professed intentions to condemn and escape colonial pasts. Her construction of a foundational narrative in which the originary point of damage is identified, invokes a particular meaning of historical connections that perform the clearing-space of imperial time. In both *Shiver* and *Cleave,* while the subject can return to uncover its past as an experience of 'crisis', the effects of this past are forbidden a similar capacity for activation and contemporaneity. The danger here, as I explore further in this book, is that such a discourse performs erasure, just as the isolation of ruins involves a closing out of a multi-storied place. This is an archaeological strategy of restoration via sublimation; the burying of other traces for the privileging of a preferred historic account that is strengthened by its single accordance of historical depth and endurance.

Snip's own troubled past is figured as the deep roots that sustain her current situation, which would otherwise be a terminal state of surface and disconnection. Her attempt to dig down and unearth what is locked below an unhomely surface offers a way out for the disordered nation as in the ground, the text asserts, roots are located, stories of 'being here' that are both implicit in and obscured by a culture of shame and forgetting. Anxieties over a superficial settler identity are thus put to rest through the provision of depth and value to non-indigenous relations with land. Extracted from a morass of 'bad' memories, and with her family trauma named, packaged and given a single meaning, Snip can disconnect from what haunts and is fantastically untouched. Unsettled belonging is not considered a complex modality of living in the world, but as something to be overcome. It is not enough to be uncertainly in place. This was an attitude widely shared in the millennial years, including, especially, by environmental commentators, who drew explicit connections between ungrounded non-indigenous belonging and perilous environmental futures. As they lamented superficial cultures of inhabitation, Gemmell's novels resonated with a popular consciousness of environmental concern in Australia, as well as in the contemporary West. As I go onto explore in the following chapter, these intersected with questions of uncertain place and belonging that found expression through a language of environmental pressures and pollutants in need of redress.

NOTES

1. It is widely understood that there is no single generation of stolen children and the high current rates of Indigenous children removed from family care is often regarded in this context. See Claire Coleman (2018) as example.
2. The Apology was delivered at Parliament House, Canberra, in the presence of survivors of the Stolen Generations, and broadcast around Australia. Hundreds of thousands of Australians gathered in public places to watch this historic event.
3. See Peter Pierce (1999: xii) for a discussion of this kind of 'saving' trope.
4. Notably, *Cleave* was published under the title *Alice Springs* in the United States.

Chapter 4
Redeeming Environments for Belonging: Tim Flannery's Australia Day Address

This chapter explores the deployment of environmental imaginaries, and their related spatial forms, in the millennial discourse of non-indigenous belonging. Here, an awareness of the environmental impacts of modernity and an anxious desire to overcome shameful colonial pasts come together in the pursuit of idealized environmental relations. This idealisation is implicit to what is commonly posed as 'sustainability' (Potter 2012). In turn, degraded or unsustaining environments are seen to evidence the failing – sometimes posed explicitly as a moral failing – of non-indigenous Australians to inhabit these relations, and in turn, to adequately belong to the country. Rather than the triumphalism of colonial claim, asserting its rights over 'golden soil and wealth for toil',[1] this narrative is inverted: the spectre of the post-invasion past becomes a polluting source in itself, active in the toxic culture of an ungrounded population.

Writing from the second decade of the millennium, when the burning intensity of summers and the devastation to riverine systems is daily front page news in Australia,[2] it seems an abstraction to talk of environmental relations through the language of imaginaries and spatial forms. Yet, modes of thinking and speaking the world have resolutely material consequence. At the millennium, certain environmental imaginaries that have a long history in how colonizers have projected their way onto the land were (and remain) dominant. While, amongst progressives, a recognition of the environmental consequences of colonization were front and centre of a discourse that equated settler-colonial alienation from place with environmental malpractice, this also folded back into expressions of a familiar paradigm in which certain bodies are unwanted, and the non-indigenous subject is rendered central to the project – and purpose – of ecological remediation. Here, too, environmental well-being is aligned with a return to a precolonial and unpeopled environmental past that continues to perform and idealize erasure. Such a state of return is understood as crucial for not just Australian ecological sustainability in the long term, but also for national, and at the core of this non-indigenous, well-being in immediate terms.

This discourse distilled not belonging to its base condition of matter 'out of place'. As we have seen in Gemmell's texts, and the national debates into which these connected, a rubbished environment speaks metaphorically, and malnourished country means a malnourished culture. Refuse of colonial pasts scatter across the Tanami desert, now useless and polluting. 'Cleaning up' the country becomes euphemistic for cleaning up the past. So too does cleaning away the 'ungovernable waste' of polluting others (Hage 2017: 48). The non-fiction writing of Tim Flannery, one of Australia's most well-known scientists, exemplifies this discourse. His public reach during the millennial years showcases a significant intersection of environmental signifiers and postcolonial anxieties, and how these circulated in broader narrative terms. Flannery's poetic framing of his environmental messages to the nation, poised on the edge of a new millennium and with the growing realization of significant climate change, rehearses and also substantiates a spatial imaginary that crossed literary terrains. Modern Western histories of environmental thought, nationalist rhetoric and literary poetics intersect in a prevalent language of waste and pollution that came to stand for the disabling effects of bad colonial pasts. Again, it is not the Indigenous subject of these pasts that is most at issue here; instead, it is the non-indigenous Australian without appropriate environmental relations and thus unable to generatively cohere to the land, with negative impacts for all.

Messed-up nation

The critical positioning of colonial culture through a metaphorical language of ecology is resonant in Australia, with 'alien' and 'invasive' species analogic for the imposing outsider, overrunning the country without ever 'truly belonging'. We can see this in texts as diverse as John Marsden and Shaun Tan's picture book *The Rabbits* (1998), Indigenous author Claire Coleman's speculative fiction *Terra Nullius* (2017) and in the language of national biological security, where parameters of autochthony, pollution and ecological place or 'fit' interconnect to demarcate non-indigenous bodies, both human and non-human, as intruders in the land. Colonization is figured as a juncture of before and after, that remakes space temporally, as a 'year zero' after which 'nativeness' is redefined (Rose 1997b). Problematically, such a juncture is attractive to the claims of non-indigenous belonging, which can point to colonization as the moment of decline – a 'place of expulsion or return – one Before the Fall' (Robbins and Moore 2013: 4) – that, through various acts of environmental piety, may be recuperated. This is a kind of 'return' for non-indigenous subjects that re-enacts the fantasy of untouched space. As a consequence, belonging discourse in this context invests heavily in a language of environmental restoration that works redemptively through expressions of self-admonishment, loss and grief and ultimately, an assured ecological place.

Demonstrating this, the non-indigenous public intellectual Germaine Greer wrote in her 2003 Quarterly Essay: 'The country I love has been crazily devastated by whitefellas, and who even now insist on continuing in their madness [...] If we truly felt that this country was our home we could not despoil it in this manner. We are trashing it because it belongs to someone else' (2003: 117). Greer's ire targets the inadequate colonial subject, undermining its own future. Peter Timms' bushwalking memoir, *Making Nature* (2001) also acknowledges this as a self-conscious deficiency: 'We long [...] today, for some sort of return to nature, and we conveniently gloss over the fact that we haven't the faintest idea of what that might mean' (2001: 7). These connections are ongoing, overspilling the millennial years. More recently, Michael Cathcart lamented in the *Water Dreamers* that 'the ailing rivers of Australia betray a failure to develop a sense of stewardship, understanding and responsibility for country that is the sign of belonging' (2009: 247). In a similar style, Sarah Maddison's critical work *Beyond White Guilt* (2011) opens with a reflection on a rubbish-filled, sluggish creek that speaks as a clear signifier of non-indigenous dysfunction – in this case, an immobilizing and unproductive guilt-ridden stance in relation to the country's past.

Such imagery of polluted rivers and trashed country speaks to an established tradition of toxic consciousness in the self-reflections and self-critiques of subjects in late Western modernity. These Western subjects come to realize, with a shock, that they are 'defined by [their] garbage' (Deitering 1996: 198) as the ecological realities of a post-industrial world become apparent. Importantly, it is something which cannot be escaped. Whereas the pastoral fantasy held out the idyll of an enduring place of retreat in the disaffections of a dirtying world, the realism of toxic consciousness (commonly attributed to American Rachel Carson's landmark *Silent Spring* [1962]) refuses the fantasy of externality,[3] and through the recognition of our complicit enrolment with pollutants, reorients the conditions of ontology: we can no longer see ourselves as separate from our waste. This complicity is registered as both personal *and* collective. It is something that we all carry as subjects of Western modernity, the responsibility for which is devolved to the individual who, according to the logic of Western consumption practices, is deputized to manage her own waste as a civic obligation (Hawkins 2001: 5). The fantasy of waste 'disposal' is challenged by the omnipresence of waste in the world – management is now the only way to go. While state-imposed disciplining and monitoring tactics induce the subject into the self-management of waste, there is also a reliance upon moral judgement in mainstream environmental discourse that appeals to personal restraint, responsibility and economy as the ethos of practice. Beyond government intervention, an assumed 'autonomous rational will in the service of moral codes' (Hawkins 2001: 11) provides a subtext to the articulated imperatives of managing waste. This individualized ethos is supported by an environmental imaginary that consequently reactivates the fantasy of pastoral 'immersion': the well-functioning environmental subject fits into an ecological whole without disruption and on the premise of disruption's erasure.

Scholars such as Ghassan Hage (1998) and Veronica Davidov (2015) have theorized a correlation between nationalism and environmentalism, with the former arguing that the nation-building project itself is its own secular version of the Garden of Eden fantasy – a project dependent upon the final domestication of wild nature. Belonging, in this context, takes on transcendent qualities: a cultivated state of existence that brings with it insight into the polluting earthliness of the ground, and for the human subject, a 'perfect fit between humans and their environment' (Hage 1998: 171). Hage goes onto argue that modern ecological dispositions take this 'fit' to a point of affective abstraction. Rejecting (conceptually, at least) instrumentality and exploitative relationships – which would keep the human positioned outside nature – this modern eco subject centralizes feeling as a primary point of interest and ultimately connection with the non-human world. The imperative to 'feel' towards, and on behalf of, a beleaguered environment is activated across interest groups that claim the 'right kind' of environment-human relations and a particular set of dispositions that constitute ecological subjects.

Expressions of grief and self-castigating loss in the narratives of non-indigenous alienation amidst environmental disarray call upon feeling in both the narrator and the reader (an implied fellow non-indigenous subject) as an impetus for change. Feeling is where action is catalysed in this discourse, centralizing emotional responses, in part at least, for their synonymity with 'depth', especially deep connections to place. This displaces a focus on structural harms that operate beyond the feeling subject (for instance, on the capitalist-colonial forces that underpin racial violence and climate change [Hage 2017]) and prioritizes non-indigenous experience as the cause most in need of redress. Notably, Shaw and Bonnett argue that environmental loss is something that the modern West has not assimilated into paradigms of feeling and put to rest. Presumably, its situated implications are too overwhelming and current. Unlike the 'passing' of Indigenous time, eco crisis 'shows almost no signs of being available for romantic recuperation' (Shaw and Bonnett 2016: 570). In an Australian context, however, Indigenous pasts/presence and environmental anxieties cannot be untangled, not least for the fact that attempts at the romantic recuperation of dispossession and genocide have been superseded by expressions of non-indigenous shame and guilt, and the backlash against these. Such reactions were mobilized by the pressing claims of Indigenous presence, rather than imagined absence. In the post-Mabo years, the 'return' of the lost indigene was irrefutable. But disentangling is also refused by the fact that colonization, dispossession and environmental exploitation are driven by the same logic of Western modernity, embedded into the very idea of 'nature': a passive other to culture, and an external resource to exploit for human benefit, without agency, or claims, of its own.

The promise of environmental immersion: Flannery's vision for Australia

The Australia Day Address, inaugurated during the millennial years in 1997, is benignly framed – much like the day itself, by its supporters – as an annual invitation to a distinguished Australian to 'express their unique perspective on our nation's identity and the diversity of our society [...] [to] reflect upon our history and our future' (Government of New South Wales 2019). Tim Flannery was the first environmental scientist to be given this platform, in 2002, in the wake of the huge public and critical success of his 1994 book *The Future Eaters*, an account of Australian history through 'three waves' of migration (of which colonization is the third wave) commencing 40–60,000 years ago, and the environmental impacts of these. It is the third wave that is the most environmentally problematic, his book argues – a theme that he continued in his Australia Day Address delivered in Sydney on 23 January, 'The Day, the Land, the People'. Despite the 'national' framing of the event, non-indigenous Australians were at the centre of its focus. This was the challenge of environmental reparation that Flannery tied indelibly to the quest for non-indigenous belonging. In his view, the two are inseparable. Environmental futures and national futures go hand in hand, he argued, shaped by the negative inheritance of colonization – the 'shadows that neither ebb nor lighten with the years' (Flannery 2002: 1). It is the 'bitter harvest' of an 'arrogant colonial vision [that] we [are] reaping so abundantly today' (2002: 2). We are 'liv[ing] as people from somewhere else, who just happen to inhabit – sometimes unsustainably, ignorantly and destructively – this marvellous continent' (2002: 1).

For Flannery, the alienated settler who dwells superficially bears responsibility for lost biodiversity, exploited water systems and degraded land. But they also bear a cultural and psychic burden as with them lies the project of shaping 'Australian' identity. By contrast, the experience of Indigenous people and their contribution to the national story is dealt with early on in Flannery's address (Australia Day marks the 'day that ruined the neighbourhood for the Cadigaleans' [2002: 1]). The ongoing issue, as he saw it, was a 'yet-to-be-formed Australian culture' (2002: 3) predicated on non-indigenous modes of occupation. This includes a policy response focused on restricted population targets and a critical eye on multiculturalism, which, for Flannery, potentially conflicts with the principle of adaptation required for sustainable environmental futures: '[N]o culture can exist unmodified in a new environment' (2002: 3). Flannery's vision of multiculturalism as a jostling of distinct yet related cultural groups does not manifest the kind of ecological relations that he determines as crucial to an ideal and sustainable 'Australian-ness'. Such relations are forged in the 'realis[ation] that we have no other home but this one, and that we cannot remake it to suit ourselves' (2002: 5). Modes of inhabitation require coherence, he argues, which requires overcoming practices from 'elsewhere', a clearing away of 'ungovernable waste' (Hage 2017: 48). This is the kind of domestication of multicultural difference that Hage identities in the determinations of settler-colonial sovereignty: a 'true', cohesive, national identity lies in the subjection of all to a single vision and 'mode of inhabiting the world by occupying it' (Hage 2017: 94). National 'disorder' and environmental malpractice go hand in hand, and Flannery castigates urban non-indigenous Australians over their misplaced preference for 'beloved Europe-green lawn, English roses and London plane trees' (2002: 3).

Correct environmental relations are thus the key to finally overcoming colonial anxiety and finding a settled belonging. They are the key, too, to social cohesion and the future of national well-being. Without these, we flail. Immigration policy must be yoked to this vision of environmental order. An altered, 'unsustainable' environment cannot hold the nation sufficiently or securely. Resonant with Gemmell's poetics, and the concerns of multiple critics and writers explored in this book, such security is understood as crucial to belonging. In this focus on ecological crisis Flannery embeds an ontological one: the condition of the settler-colonial Australian subject. His focus of a speech aimed at the nation entire is non-indigenous Australians whose disconcerted belonging is given not just as a symptom of environmental malpractice, but as the primary hindrance to its restitution. To be ultimately at home in the land is to 'surrender our "otherness"' to it, and 'thereby find our own distinctively Australian way' (2002: 5). This argument turns towards the idea of national unity ('Australia is the only thing we share in common' [2002: 1]), and the absorption of difference, in which bad pasts are cleared away, as the path to environmental well-being.

Flannery's national imaginary, in turn, models his view of best environmental practice. He insistently correlates the 'inner' virtue of the individual subject, expressed through self-restraint and a capacity for cooperation with other subjects, with the 'outer' health of the external environment. Individual 'patterns of consumption' hold the key to 'what environmental sustainability really means' (2002: 3); likewise, 'a kind of interdependence fostered by adversity' (2002: 5) underpins a functional nation and ecology, as well as a suitable mythology of 'who we are'. The part must give way to the whole. Connected to this, Flannery identifies globalization as a final unsettling factor in the cause of a unitary and settled culture. Here, the ecological relations that he champions offer a way of fighting 'the battle to preserve the defining values of Australian society' (2002: 5), instigated by a globalizing world. In this configuration, the actions of each individual towards the land are accountable to create or destroy a cohesive society and a sustainable environment. There is a need for common values in order to live with 'depth', and therefore with the right kind of unifying environmental relations. Environmental responsibility in Flannery's terms therefore means more than routine pragmatic duty, fulfilling the criteria of a well-ordered and sustaining ecology. It takes on – like the domestic activities of waste management – the shared values that make a civil society.

His concern for the future of 'our' children, 'our' identity and 'our' land is based on the desire for stability in what 'we' have and are. The treatment of the environment 'unsustainably, ignorantly, and destructively' (2002: 1) mirrors our own cultural degeneracy, while a regulated, but 'naturally' interdependent, environment can enable the settling and certain belonging of non-indigenous Australians for the benefit of the nation at large. Yet, what he also implies is that, despite his fears for a discordant nation, there is already a common ground of value that links Australians together. For if the national subject is to respond to Flannery's appeal, he/she must already belong in this way. A pre-validation of shared values is thus a prerequisite for a sustaining, stable environment. This is the immersive ecological being that Flannery calls for, a 'surrendered' otherness that is offered against the dualistic vision of the colonial eye that enforces sharp divisions between self and other and sees difference as deviancy. Colonial consciousness needed to project a rationalist narrative onto the land, where perceived 'disorder' was necessarily held at bay. Consequently, the unifying suggestion of 'immersion' and 'surrender' promises to overcome these divides, and two ontological and ecological alternatives emerge: one defined by separation and exclusion, and the other by holistic interconnection. And as a divided ecology occasions environmental and cultural destruction, a smooth, unified one means health and security, signifying sustainable futures. Therefore, in these spatial models on offer, Australians are either sutured together or wrenched apart.

Climate emergency

When Flannery delivered his address, climate change was a building public concern that sat alongside 'several global environmental issues' to form a picture of modernity's blighted environments, and their threat to Australian life (Flannery 2002: 5). Within a few years, however, climate change would become a common, overarching reference for human ecological impact, a concept that rapidly communicated entrenched cultures of environmental exploitation and instrumentalization, and also the interconnection of effects – essentially, it was now a shorthand for connecting drought, or species decline, for example, as part of a whole of system response to certain human environmental practices.

By the time Flannery published his best-selling non-fiction book *The Weather Makers* in 2005, followed by his 2008 Quarterly Essay, *Now or Never*, his concern for postcolonial Australian alienation had become embedded in a broader landscape of issue: the wholesale dispossessing force of climate change for human life. Of particular interest here is the synthesis that Flannery finds between these two effects – thwarted non-indigenous belonging and humanity's 'unhoming' by climate change. In these works, the profound non-indigenous 'misunderstanding' (Flannery 2008) of Australian environments, resulting in an ongoing estrangement and the threat of even further ecological collapse, and the looming 'dark age' of a climate ravaged future 'likely to destroy our civilization' – 'wherein a few survivors (perhaps just one out of every ten alive today) will cling to the few remaining habitable regions' (Flannery 2008: 16) – belong to the same quandary. This is Western culture's exploitative drive to claim and consume, refusing to see itself as 'a part of the Gaian whole' (2008: 6). The redress of this underlies the pursuit of sustainability. Positioned in this way, the challenge of non-indigenous belonging becomes generalized and also de-historicized, despite Flannery's concern with 'dark' colonial pasts. It becomes a challenge, instead, of abstracted human failings, with the daily intimacies of what it means to inhabit a place, constituted of multiple histories, ignored.

This is a replay of anxious non-indigenous belonging and environmental alienation in modernity as conflated tropes in postcolonial ecological commentary. But here, the particular *future* threat of climate change's dispossessions is significant, as climate change galvanizes the generality of insecure belonging for all of humankind. It is implied in the discourse of prediction that attends climate change discussion that the future must necessarily be one of reattachment to what has become so removed. The mitigation of the coming catastrophe means re-establishing the right kind of relations between human subjects and their more-than-human worlds, relations that ultimately transcend all concerns other than that of restored ecological harmony. And so, we see in Flannery and other's calls to arms against climate change (and it is a 'war', Flannery insists [2008: 17]) a recurrent poetics of reunion and retained stability through the reparation of perceived breaches between humans and their non-human living world. Government policy in response to climate change is indicative of this thinking, as it focuses on forestalling displacement from the familiar (Australia's 'way of life', for instance) by encouraging us to continue to live as we have in technologically modified form, through domestic energy efficiencies, water savings initiatives and carbon trading schemes. In the *The Weather Makers*, Flannery asserts that 'we cannot wait for the issue to be solved for us. The most important thing to realize is that we can all make a difference and help combat climate change at almost no cost to our lifestyle' (Flannery 2005: 6). In this sense, stability seems to mean minimized disruption to the (sustained) status quo, echoing descriptions of optimum climate futures circulating elsewhere: 'Delivering a stable climate is a security, prosperity and moral imperative', according to the UNHCR (in Hulme 2010: 270).

The focus on sustainable environmental practice is ultimately global rather than local, despite its emphasis on the individual to initiate change, as the specificities of Australian environmental malpractice speak of a whole-world concern. 'We Australians bear a special responsibility in this world of Gaian imbalance', argued Flannery, referring to Australia as the source of so much fossil fuel consumed around globe (Flannery 2008: 62). This configuration of the nation as (re)active to, and signifying within, a global system of environmental forces and futures was reiterated in a commensurate discourse of 'deep time' that found favour amongst environmental historians, and with whom Flannery was aligned. The concept of deep time situates specific events, cultures and histories in large-scale, even epic, narratives and temporal structures that take in many millions of mostly prehuman years. A singular event is positioned in, and thus is made meaningful to, an ancient continuum of time stretching both backward and forward.

Writing in 2000, environmental historian Tom Griffiths reflected on this 'millennial moment' context – 'when our bookstores are suddenly full of historical and philosophical texts on time' (2000: 1) – to explain a growing attention to 'deep time' and its significance for how we think about Australian pasts. Australian history, he argued, and moreover, Australian *space*, are inextricable products of 'global time', folded within the 'slower moving structures and cycles of centuries' of planetary history. The turn to deep time posed 'deeper currents' of experience against a 'history of short, sharp, nervous vibrations' that might preoccupy a local, surface-oriented culture. By 'rejecting a short time span' (2000: 2), locally tethered concerns – theoretically, the violence of the state, the pathologies of the colonizer, the dysfunctions of multiculturalism – give way to 'human commonality beyond the categories of "nation" and "race"' (2000: 2).

Griffiths saw this as offering much for environmental futures, too, but how deep time is invoked can be problematic in a postcolonial context such as Australia's. As environmental history is reoriented by deep time, it opens up 'the exponentially different timescale within which we now have to imagine life on Earth' (2000: 3), with implications for how humans, and postcolonial Australian humans in particular, understand and correspondingly imagine their environmental place. Deep time, understood in an Australian environment, opens the door to a continuum of environmental change in which the colonizer is situated at a particular point in history. It repositions their destructive environmental practices within a long past of more-than-human agency. This 'dwarfs' the colonizer's significance, but also potentially depoliticizes non-indigenous subjectivity as a continually enacted presence in specific and contingent temporal and spatial relations. To relativize non-indigenous Australian history in a continuum of more-than-human time abstracts critical focus from the very local and immediate ways in which postcolonial relations are organized, experienced and have effect. Deep time, of course, too, positions everyone as a newcomer to an ancient continent such as Australia and within the billion-year timeframe of the Earth itself. From this position, all human history and cultural practice is open to critique from the same baseline: that of a 'drop in time', an anthropologic blip prone to the same self-interest and blindness, capable of significant environmental impact. Citing Flannery's *The Future Eaters* as productive of a deep time perspective, Griffiths acknowledges the 'provocative' generalization of Flannery's take on 'Aborigines and settlers as humans', all capable of 'mistakes and misjudgements' in the process of living in the Australian environment. Ultimately, he sees this as a 'parable of hope': if Indigenous people could make mistakes but ultimately get things right, he thinks, then 'new settlers might, over time, learn to do the same thing' (Griffiths 2000: 6).

Flannery's position on Indigenous 'mistakes and misjudgements', outlined in *The Future Eaters*, was certainly contentious, with Indigenous critic Marcia Langton (amongst others) publicly rebutting Flannery's claims, in particular his assertion that Indigenous environmental practices were responsible for the extinction of Australian mega fauna. Langton challenged Flannery's evidential base ('slight and miscellaneous fragments of evidence from vastly different periods across many thousands of years' [Langton 2013: 25]), a hypothesis presented as 'settled' science (a smooth narrative shaped from the fragments) and cited peer-based critiques also aimed at Flannery's speculative conclusions.[4] For Langton, Flannery misrepresented theory as history, with significant consequence for its reception by a non-indigenous audience. The image of parity that Griffiths saw as hopeful in Flannery's 'deep time' assessment of Indigenous and non-indigenous environmental mistakes, for Langton, provides opportunity for non-indigenous racism and ultimately a colonial drive to erase difference and dissonance in a national narrative. In the logic that Langton critiques, prehistory is suggestive of Eden, after which, with the arrival of humans, comes the fall. If the real time of Australia starts with 'good' environmental practices, as Flannery seems to suggest, it also lies in a postcolonial future, with 'all' Australians in it together. The specificities of history and culture become part of the problem rather than something productive.

In the timescales employed by climate change discourse, the 'Anthropocene' comes to emphasize the extremely short period of human environmental impact relative to the prehistorical scope of deep time. To this extent, then, Indigenous people are included in 'human' experience, but then are also excluded as forces of and in modernity, consigned to an impossible position of poor environmental managers (because their cultural practice is seen to come at an environmental cost) *and* environmental anachronisms, who once knew how to live symbiotically in country. 'They had it right' (Flannery 2002: 5), Flannery claimed in his Australia Day address, despite his previously published assertions. Tellingly, though, it is at the point of absorption into the national body that Indigenous environmental practice is revered: living sustainably in the environment, Indigenous people become the first 'Australians' to demonstrate what it means to act as 'a truly Australian people' (2002: 2).

Flannery's Australia Day address allows for the incorporation of Indigenous Australians into the nation if they also adhere to the 'important management role' (2002: 4) that he identifies for them, predicated on precolonial practices, and when they provide, symbolically and pedagogically, the historical depth and continuity of 'good' environmental relations that non-indigenous Australians are seen to lack. With this grafted onto the non-indigenous subject, Australian identity can be indigenized. Further, where Indigenous approaches to land are couched in a value system that predates non-indigenous settlement, the national form can be justified as having existed for tens of thousands of years, thus countering settler anxieties about a too-young and immature national culture. While this rhetoric of continuity is a useful salve to non-indigenous 'surface' anxiety, adding temporal depth to their place in the land, it puts into relief the legally imposed disparity experienced by the majority of Indigenous native title claimants, whose imperative to demonstrate unbroken links with country, over time, is made impossible by colonial history. Flannery's emphasis on pre-contact environmental practices fits with the legal requirement that Indigenous continuous connection be demonstrated in order to prove and claim native title, something that colonization has made difficult, and even impossible, for many. Multiple displacements are thus channelled into a single dispossessing force for all Australians: estrangement from an original, 'lost' environment or place.

Resetting the future, realigning the ground

There are signals in Flannery's rhetoric of what Robbins and Moore, in a US context, term the 'Edenic sciences' – disciplines such as restoration ecology, conservation biology and invasion biology, dedicated to the recovery or recreating of 'fallen' environments, ambiguously in the wake of colonization *or* in a time before human contact entirely. The different baselines for an 'original condition' employed within the field indicate what Robbins and Moore describe as the essentially epistemological project that informs it. This is 'a "native" condition [that] can and should be known or restored' (Robbins and Moore 2013: 4). Such epistemological commitment illuminates the politics caught up in these scientific practices. Their concern with ecological restoration imposes contingent value on particular environmental coordinates, suiting a certain narrative of systemic health and well-being that easily slips between registers of meaning. As the Edenic sciences seek to reset the past, they participate in a charged historical imaginary that can be leveraged far beyond the supposedly neutral purpose of scientific enquiry.

This is where Flannery's poetics really come to matter. As he reads Indigenous environmental practice through the non-indigenous discourse of reunion and reconciliation, Flannery's vision for sustainable futures becomes inextricable from the favour and comfort of a non-indigenous majority, to be ideally redeemed and resettled comfortably into their place. His environmental imaginary, framed as scientifically informed and defended, is entirely in keeping with broader Western responses to the alienated modern subject estranged from its original 'home', shadowing a notable movement in humanities-driven ecological thought since its burgeoning in the 1960s and 1970s. This is the decentring of the human 'I' and a kind of ontological re-absorption, the subject no longer the commander on a stage at the centre of action but instead desiring to become 'the voice of nature in its totality' (Hage 1998: 171), sublimated to its part in a 'right' fitting ecology. In Flannery's address, echoing other discourses of the time, environmental reconciliation is conflated with the project of national, historical reconciliation, offering the promise of overcoming the 'metaphysical emptiness' (Carroll 2001: 9) at the heart of non-indigenous Australia. This is to 'not only [...] repair our damage to the outer world but to repair the deep splits on the inside, to work towards inclusive rather than exclusive concepts of self and identity' (Tacey 1995: 152).

Further, for the cause of reconciliation imagined as the reunion of divided parts, the transposition of Indigenous environmental knowledges onto non-indigenous Australians conceptually removes a sense of 'alternative and competing claim[s] to the national landscape' (Moran 1998: 109), stabilizing non-indigenous anxieties generated by the spectre of Mabo. The Australian nation itself becomes the sole occupant of the Australian environment, as difference is contained and homogenized within its boundaries. Concepts from natural science feed these imaginaries. Flannery's emphasis on correct relations and the 'right fitting' relational matrix that constitutes national belonging closely models 'Darwin's wedge', an idea within evolutionary theory that 'the face of Nature [*sic*] may be compared to a yielding surface, with ten thousand sharp wedges packed close together and driven inwards by incessant blows' (Darwin 1998: 117). Darwin saw 'the outside' of an ecology as shaping its internal relations, which work together, profoundly interdependent, until altered by competitive attack from outside. Then, an ecological member must be displaced or wedged out as its tightly fitting place is taken by another. The analogic potential of Darwin's wedge means that it is widely employed across fields from population debate to market economics and Flannery brings an evident wedge poetics to an appeal for population control ('the great multiplier of environmental impact' [2002: 4]) and against multiculturalism, where alien wedges disturb the balance of a coherent community.

In a system of properly aligned wedges, according to this view, different parts of the whole work in accordance with each other's interests, constituting ideal environmental conditions. In Flannery's concept of 'surrender' which, like 'immersion', can be seen to represent the total dissolution of boundaries between self and environment, lies an image of a perfectly fitted ecology with all its components in their rightful positions. The individual is no longer a jarring or abstracted presence but is grounded, existing in unity with its environment. 'Surrender' is consequently dependent upon the maintenance of an excluded, and regulated, outside. Ecological contaminants, materializing bad pasts and their destructive effects, defer belonging, and have no place within a wedge-constituted structure.[5]

The antagonism frequently shown towards feral or introduced animals and plants in the Australian environment, which exceed the bounds of safe domestication, speaks of the same poetic framework. Successfully adapted but illegitimately present, such species represent an uncertain belonging, despite their capacity to 'overtake' in a wedge arrangement. Their threat to the 'original' wedge reflects their perceived challenge to an imagined, stable national identity. Ultimately, Flannery imagines a unitary space created through unitary values: an emphasis on the communal that still, even while it professes to decentre the 'I', centralizes a clean, renewed subject as the 'good' national ideal. For a future of homely unity, with ecological elements sustainably in place, the Australian citizen is charged with the task of curtailing both ontological and ecological disruption to a standard of inflexible and exclusionary cultural values. A call to collective action, premised on singular ideas of natural order and positioned as morally virtuous, belies a politics and a poetics of division and retained cultural privilege. A liberal concept of the nation as comprised of self-regulating units, and of the nation operating in the global as a unitary entity, informs this.

As the maturing nation comes into its own on an international stage it is considered both self-sufficient *and* accountable to the forces of the global collective in terms of the right kind of self-regulation. Flannery is not entirely comfortable with this, however, and his appeal to the 'national interest' (2002: 4) in his ecological view is couched in the imperative of security for Australian subjects. In light of 'a very [...] large and sometimes threatening world' (2002: 5), the local (as national) takes precedence over any celebration of global commonality. Thus, he concludes, it is necessary for non-indigenous Australians to realize in their current state of uncertain belonging that there is no home but the nation. And yet, despite Flannery's resistance to modernity's forces, his concern is fundamentally for a future Australian environment and its populace, and the progressive push forward that he condemns as too materially driven, too superficial and devoid of holding capacities, is replaced here in discourse that attributes damage to the past, and sees the future as promising potential for ecological remaking. Here, the present is overlooked, consigned to represent chaos alone as a saving future is pursued. Flannery's reference to Australia's 'dark' past and its damaging consequences are framed in precisely such a way: for 'a long-term future' (2002: 3) and a 'new beginning' (2002: 1) for the nation, its disordered past must be overcome.

Climates of belonging

The investment in the possibility of 'correct' relations providing a salve for non-indigenous belonging ultimately activates an environmental imaginary that reflexively sustains the terms of an ideal (non-indigenous) sovereignty – securely grounded, bounded and divested of unsettling forces. Correct relations rely on the myth of inviolate externality, the idea that what haunts us can be put and kept firmly outside. Theories of postcolonial belonging that look to related models of 'correct' relations (for instance Linn Miller's work utilizing an existentialist frame [2003]) exist in tension with this inevitability. Poetically, correct relations model a particular world of spatialized power: if belonging is something that 'makes us feel good about our being and our being in the world; a relation that is fitting, right, or correct' (Miller 2003: 218), then it must be a realizable state: a point that is reached, and within which the subject is settled, feeling good and in a rightful place. Miller asserts that 'a minimum conception of belonging might be understood as standing in correct relation to one's community, one's history and one's locality' (2003: 218). In this modelling, the affective agency of all these things – essentially, other subjects, the forces of history and a living environment – have no capacity to inform belonging other than by their finalized placement in a certain narrative of the world. The world outside the self is, in this sense, pacified. We flip back to the colonial subject striding his stage.

Miller, like Flannery, considers the disconcerted belonging of non-indigenous Australians as a 'crisis' that invariably triggers a host of socially and environmentally damaging effects. Climate change, as I have argued, offers another manifestation of these forces, and is accordingly treated as a 'sign' of human deficiency, including – or indeed concluding in – inadequate, and destructive, environmental relations. For environmental thinkers such as Bill McKibben, climate change signals 'the end of nature' (meaning the idea of external, transcendent nature) because human agency is totalized, absolutely filling the ontological space. Humans have marked 'every inch and every hour of the globe', McKibben writes: '[N]o longer is nature a separate and wild province, the world apart from man to which he was adapted, under whose rules he was born and died' (1989: 41). This is an argument about a lost relationship, the dissolution of implied correct relations. To isolate the recovery of correct relations as the answer to climate crisis, however, keeps the imaginaries on offer in the limited terms of human sovereignty rendered as a stable and secure place in the world, with its outside relations ordered and clear. Indeed, the language of crisis or emergency itself, attached to the rhetoric of endism and of national ultimatums, offers a real opportunity for this model of sovereignty – which, in an Australian context, is the preferred model of the colonizer – to reassert itself.

In philosopher Giorgio Agamben's understanding of sovereignty, the 'emergency' initiates a political state of exception that legitimates a sovereignty authorized to suspend certain political rights and claims. This state of exception occurs because the sovereign power names it as such, and the declaration of emergency, therefore, is a powerful political tool under the conditions of which previously unacceptable or illegal practices are authorized. For Agamben, the exception has increasingly gained normalization as a technique of governance, including in 'so-called democratic' contexts. This means that the 'voluntary creation of a permanent state of emergency (though perhaps not declared in a technical sense)' (Agamben 2005: 2) inaugurates the constant possibility of crisis that leaves the door open for a reassertion of exclusive sovereign power. Agamben is particularly concerned with the biopolitical nature of the state of exception: here, in his elaboration, the state of exception reduces its subjects to 'bare life' (described as 'the simple fact of living common to human beings' [Bull 2007]) excising political rights in reaction to a perceived threat to its power. This leaves the subject (no longer citizen) vulnerable to what Catherine Mills calls 'abandonment and nihilism' (2008: 59). For Agamben, this is deathly (Agamben 1995: 90). In the climate change context, 'the emergency' appeals to the cause of sustaining life, but its potential alignment with a material and symbolic affirmation of non-indigenous dominion threatens to foster the same repressive capacity of sovereign power, asserted in the act of naming what threatens.

A history of non-indigenous Australian insecurity has given rise to various periods of 'emergency' that have generated and legitimated exceptional legal treatment for groups perceived to threaten a particular national or ontological order. The legalized removal of Aboriginal children from their families; the White Australia Policy (1901–1973); and the recent Northern Territory Emergency Response (2007),[6] also known as the 'Intervention', are examples. While the climate change emergency has no specified 'outsider' that threatens non-indigenous dominion – except the environment in the abstract – the (re)assertion of non-indigenous sovereignty as a remedial response perpetuates racially determined disadvantage. It re-enacts Indigenous dispossession as it overrides Indigenous peoples' claims to sovereignty, reiterating colonial logic and perpetuating environmentally devastating cultures of occupation. Indeed, as Lars Jensen has argued, climate change and racial privilege have a complex relationship. The failure of the world's wealthiest countries to reach consensus on international climate action, according to Jensen, 'demonstrate[s] the ability of white nations to close ranks when their world order [is] threatened' (2011: 85). Remote Indigenous Australian communities are anticipated to be amongst some of the worst affected by the environmental conditions brought by climate change in this country, facing a double dispossession as traditional lands become increasing uninhabitable.[7]

As the emergency curtails the claims and rights of some at the expense of others, it suspends history too, disconnecting from past 'wrongs' (such as the dispossession of Indigenous people and the mismanagement of environments) and resetting time, whereby the security of non-indigenous Australians in place promises sustainable futures: a well-worn tactic of colonization. The discourse itself of emergency or crisis also enacts a forward-focused logic trained on moving on to a future where order is restored and crisis allayed, thereby perpetuating the forgetting of immediate conditions. Caught between the future and the past, and looking to these only, what is happening in the space of living, right here and now, is obscured, with 'crisis' configured as an aberrant and transitory moment. The militarized language surrounding climate change (as Flannery indicated) performs this paradox, where climate change is an unfolding daily reality, an often unnoticed, disordered and untimely myriad of transformations. Crisis is the new normal (Houston 2015). At the same time it is rhetorically something to move beyond.

Such a desired 'correct' relation sought as a way out of a national disorder seeks to position the historical subject once and for all as safely away from its 'waste'. This waste is held in abeyance, now and in the future, through the reproduction of an environmental imaginary in which the transcendence of pollution and 'mess' promise ontological security. The danger here, despite intentions, is that as the land is smoothed over and made pristine once more, marks of violence are cleared away. Colonialism's mess is the environment's disorder and it must be restored if an optimum non-indigenous belonging is to be achieved. Closed off from meaning and pushed out of a national self-image, this 'bad stuff' is refused any kind of relation with those who pass through the landscape, and endorses the push to abstract from the immediate every day. This re-enactment of colonial tactics, conceptually and literally, predicates a 'good' and sustaining model of human engagement with an environment on the basis of externality – on the belief that rubbish can be ultimately cleared away. What is considered useless, or without value, for a desired environmental state is excluded from ecological relations.

In the next chapter I explore the depiction of a postcolonial Australia in which environmental and social degradation undo any possible grounds for 'correct' relations in Thea Astley's *Drylands*. In the absence of this, however, the novel begins to offer different imaginaries that complicate a straightforward declentionist reading in which everyone is dispossessed of home. Here, ambivalent poetics make way for new possibilities.

NOTES

1. This is a line from the Australian National Anthem, https://www.pmc.gov.au/sites/default/files/files/pmc/Honours/anthem_words.pdf. Accessed 27 January 2019.
2. In mid-January 2019, Australia experienced its hottest recorded temperatures across the south-east of the continent over a run of scorching days. At the same time, hundreds of native Murray Cod fish were found dead along the Lower Darling in one of the nation's major river systems, the Murray Darling. The fish had been killed by low water flows due to over-allocation of water for agriculture and high temperatures resulting in algal bloom. Murray Cod populations may never recover.
3. Barbara Ehrenrich describes the logic of capitalism in terms of this externalizing fantasy – a willful 'dematerialization' of the impacts, effects and entanglements of mass production and consumption. This is our Western desire 'to be cleaned up after [...] to achieve a certain magical weightlessness and immateriality' (in Plumwood 2008: 142) despite our resource- and polluting-heavy lives.
4. Recent works of scholarship that explore the complex environmental stewardship of Indigenous people precolonization, implicitly contesting Flannery's view, include Pascoe's *Dark Emu* (2014) and Bill Gammage's *The Biggest Estate on Earth* (2011).
5. Antipathy towards asylum seekers in Australia (and throughout much of the Western world) over the last twenty years utilizes this logic, with immigration represented as a threat to local prosperity, security and identity. See Marr and Wilkinson (2004).
6. The Northern Territory Emergency Response (the 'Intervention') was announced on 21 June 2007, after revelations of sexual abuse and family violence in remote Indigenous communities in Australia's Northern Territory. The 'response' was legislated in August that year and involved a raft of financial and physical community control measures, including the deployment of Australian army members to implement these. The Intervention has been widely criticized for its militarist paternalism, entrenchment of colonization and failure to improve conditions for remote community members. See Waanyi author Alexis Wright's 2011 open letter to Green politicians in opposition to the Intervention (https://www.abc.net.au/news/2011-03-30/talking_about_an_indigenous_tomorrow/45734). Wright's celebrated 2013 fictional work, *The Swan Book*, takes the Intervention as its context in a depiction of a future Australia debilitated by colonial violence and climate change.
7. See Department of Climate Change and Energy Efficiency (2010).

Chapter 5
Desiccated and Infective: Writing in Thea Astley's *Drylands*

Drying up

Thea Astley's 1999 novel *Drylands*, consciously positioned at a millennial moment of 'endings', does not make explicit reference to climate change. Nevertheless, the symbolic threat and physical unfolding of a rapidly warming world are everywhere in the text. Named after the book's fictional setting, the small Queensland town of Drylands, the novel's title plays with an obvious double entendre as it presents a bleak and desiccated world both environmentally and culturally falling apart. Astley's cast of characters, all but one non-indigenous, are pushed away from Drylands over the course of the text. None are more immune than each other. The weather is repeatedly positioned as a driving force in this, beating out the life out of things with 'rainless air' (Astley 1999: 112) and the unrelenting combination of 'heat dust poverty' (1999: 135). The text does not externalize these effects however: this is not a story of nature against culture. Humans are absolutely complicit in the fallout around them.

Astley takes a spotlight to the multiple dysfunctions of non-indigenous society connected to exploitative colonial and patriarchal cultures. On display is what Stephen Turner calls 'the malignant cultural body of the settler [Australian]' (1999: 23) turned rotten with secret and unresolved pasts, including environmental ones. In line with Flannery's critique, the text makes evident analogy between this state of environmental alienation and the community's endemic violence and failure of sociality, which provides the back-story to all of her characters. Human and meteorological conditions in the town are thus strongly interlinked. Evoking a moral discourse of the millennium years that reflected on a nation emotionally hardened and divided, this is a place without hope, drained of good will and full of weary, melancholic individuals disconnected from each another. And it just keeps getting drier.

The text takes the paradigm of the dispossessing colonizer and inverts it to presage Australia's possible future in a state of continual crisis where the new normal is a shared vulnerability to a loss of place. It is from this perspective that the novel offers a complex response to the various unsettlements of a postcolonial nation at the millennium. At the metaphoric centre of the text (but not literally, as her focalization is woven throughout) is Janet Deakin,[1] a non-indigenous woman who has sought fantastic solace in a romantic view of country Australia. When we meet Janet her illusions have already been exploded, and it is her response to this recognition, distributed amongst the narratives of six other Drylands' residents who she observes at a distance but is also aligned with (even folded into), that drives the narrative. Evincing a millennial mix of insecure place and what Mark McGurl terms the 'ordinary doom' of relentless modernity (2010: 329) – the inhabitation of crisis as an everyday condition – Janet looks to her writing as the only possible site of redemption. It is through her novel, which we are led to believe is the text we are reading, that she seeks to stabilize the ground and hold back 'the inevitable end' (Astley 1999: 288).

Ironically subtitled a 'book for the world's last reader'[2] (Astley 1999: title page), Astley's novel references a cultural investment in storytelling as a means of securing place and belonging. This investment is erroneous the text ultimately concludes, even while the devaluation of stories and the pre-eminence of a brutal and exclusionary imaginary is implicated in the political and moral deficiencies of contemporary Australia. Janet, like the other characters, is exposed and even ridiculed by the novel's end, her ambitions made hollow and her place never secure. At the same time the realizations that Janet makes, undoing her grandiose vision of the literary author seeing and controlling meaning in the world, brings a generative ambivalence to the text. In this regard, it responds to the dominant discourses of millennial Australia that met insecure tenure and illegitimate sovereignty with the desire to dig down or to find belonging in immersion or positioned its opposite as dissolution and collapse. The end of externality, made palpable by climate change as a growing force and point of awareness, speaks to Astley's invitation to reconsider literary work and its role in a fractious and anxious nation. Without the possibilities of survey or immersion, a counter-poetics of entanglement working alongside division and hard-edged repulsion offers much as a spatial form towards alternative postcolonial imaginaries.

We meet Janet at the end of the twentieth century in the flat above her failing Newsagency, as she darkly surveys the dry lands before her: a world 'going to hell in a handbasket' (Goldsworthy 1999: 30). Like a weather forecaster, Janet summarizes the conditions of the Drylands' community while predicting an increasing spiral of social chaos. Her assessment of Drylands is presented with apparent authority for she is spatially and, in her own mind, demographically elevated above the town. A series of stories following her fellow Drylands residents are framed by Janet's focalization in the text, and in these her forecasts seem justified. Janet watches the sky as it misleadingly swells grey with clouds that never unload their rain over brown and thirsty lands. '[D]ying stocks and impossible debts' (Astley 1999: 244) inform the tensions behind the daily encounters of Drylands' townsfolk, 'a sluggish mix bubbling briefly, subsiding briefly' (1999: 17), and propel the exodus of ruined farming families in their beat-up cars 'rattl(ing) away along the gravel roads until their petrol ran out' (1999: 245).

Any hope for a change in the weather – a recuperation out of dissolution – recedes for the novel's cast of alienated characters, whose lives are battered as much by the harsh and wasted environment as by their own lack of possibility. Under the mind-numbing whirr of ceiling fans, beating uselessly at the heavy heat, the stagnant town and community continues in its demise. Drylands is 'worthless land' (1999: 111), 'a town to escape to, rot in, vanish in [...] run from' (1999: 16) amidst a 'landscape whose gullies and small streams had almost forgotten the pollution that clogged them' (1999: 32). Full of 'relict[s]' (1999: 6) and 'refugee[s]' (1999: 35), Drylands accumulates drifters and wanderers who match a dispossessing place of unprofitable farms and barren earth. Janet (like Gemmell's Snip) arrives in Drylands as a city-woman sick of urban alienation and full of hope for a tight-knit and supportive rural community. She swiftly discerns her move to be 'a step into the dark' (1999: 6). The newsagency in which she had once hopefully stocked the latest literary journals and literary fiction now sits amidst the decrepitude of the town's main street, a doomed enterprise in a streetscape of closed and run-down buildings. Janet's own livelihood dwindles as the population shrinks. Her books and journals become swiftly displaced by the 'unuttered demands of local taste' (1999: 12) for the '"men's" magazines [...] [and] the car and gun monthlies' (1999: 7). Absent or one-sided communication repeatedly characterizes this fractured community.

As the novel progresses, time seems to compress into an unbearable yet ongoing moment of failure and unoriginality: a kind of crisis time, reflecting, as Ruth Morgan reminds us in her discussion of 1990s climate change discourse, 'a broader trend in depictions of environmental crisis' as an inhabited slow burning state of collapse (2014: 51). In Drylands, Janet laments, 'there are no nails new under the sun' (Astley 1999: 5). This place is 'not quite hell' (1999: 16), but close enough to it. Even after ten years here she feels 'alienated from [the town's] life-pulse' (1999: 290) and sees herself as 'useless' (1999: 3), sucked into the responsively deadened repetitiveness of 'the day to day to day to day' (1999: 285). But these circumstances are not Janet's alone. Around her is a human climate of desiccation and fracture. Here, words 'thud [...] like small stones' (1999: 167), kisses 'drop [...] to the floor and fragment' (1999: 217), while '(e)mptiness puts its arms about you and gives a Judas embrace' (1999: 272). In the Drylands' community, 'spite has no end' (1999: 265), a 'grin isn't a grin [...] it's a slit in a cavern', and 'small spatterings of rain' are 'as offensive as spit' (1999: 287). A 'mournful tune of loneliness' (1999: 281) runs through the town.

The novel's atmosphere of doom and decay reflects the concerns expressed by the cultural commentators of the millennial years who lamented the death of sustaining collective narratives in Australia – narratives that would 'hold' a people, invoking unity and cohesion (and the erasure of difference as the flip side of this). As Dixson wrote conterminously to Astley, Australians were 'all surface, no depth' (1999: 8). Yet, rather than seeking the restoration of these, Astley's text exposes the virtuous and mythic foundations of the nation as perversely manifested and voided of meaning. Each of the stories in the text conveys a cumulative image of corruption, physical threat and social dissolution. Fear, persecution and exclusion blank out trust, care and reciprocity, while division and estrangement replace a cohesive and bonded collective. There is no redemption from hardship for *Drylands*' characters. 'False identit[ies]' (Astley 1999: 21) and shallow preoccupations dress a fragmented collective that meets primarily in the hard-edged space of violence and abuse.

There is a paradox depicted in this un-cohesive culture that demands sameness and rejects the unorthodox, while still singularizing and dividing. A monotonous hegemony of creed and opinion is demanded in Drylands, with difference met suspiciously or more often, persecuted. Franzi Massig, or the man who takes over his identity, is regarded with hostility when he first arrives in town, watched with hard stares by the men who cluster in proprietorial fashion around the Legless Lizard's front bar. Though he has come to Drylands to escape his past and find 'anonymity in anonymity' (1999: 24) and the life of someone else, Franzi can no more disappear here than he can blend with the landscape, barbed and littered with the failed refuse of industry. His first 'cultural mis-step' at the bar, ordering a pina colada, reinforces the rules of a place in which '(o)rdinariness is all' (1999: 42). Despite a doctrine of acceptance in uniformity – 'Agree. Melt in. Be dull [...] [so] the town forgets you are there' (1999: 42) – the regulation of normality depends upon an inviolable social outside. After four years in Drylands, Franzi with his suspect German name ('you're half a Brit', he is reassured. 'That's the main thing' [1999: 41]) is still 'a newcomer' (1999: 43), relegated to the edges of belonging.

Racism and sexism are deep-seated forces here. Evie, a visiting creative writing teacher from the city, is sized up as a meddling outsider by the patriarchal order that dominates the town. 'And who the fuck are you?', she is asked. 'Some two-bit bitch teacher from the city out to see how the other half lives' (1999: 90). In this 'two-cow town' (1999: 71), as Evie dismissively registers all the rural areas she has visited on her writing tour, her position on the outside of social codes is made clear. Shocked by a culture of domestic violence that appears naturalized in the town, Evie tries to reason with the women who have left behind their domestic drudgery for a day to participate in her class, but seem resigned to their socially subordinate place. Acclimatized to such abuse, these women regulate their own self-expression, keeping in line for fear of moving too far beyond 'those sanctions imposed by the conventions of thinking acceptable for small-town wives' (1999: 85). In class, they write 'pieces so polite, so tentative [that] they become mounds of indistinguishable dullness' to Evie (1999: 85).

The women's resentments and pain are kept unvoiced, registered only in the 'neat starched cottons, the shampooed hair, the vestige of makeup that reassured them they were not simply milkers, tractor drivers, cleaners and cooks' (1999: 87). While they are wholly aware of their disempowered place in this culture, Evie initially cannot bridge the divide that lies between the women and herself, and accept, let alone comprehend, a status quo of silent acceptance. When she expresses her disbelief that Ro could ever contemplate returning to her husband after his violent intrusion into their day, Evie is 'told [that] she didn't understand'. The women 'told her how small the town was. They told her the police wouldn't act. The police always took the husband's side in these matters [...] They wouldn't do anything to upset a mate' (1999: 93). The women's enjoyment at being engaged for the day in creative activities is underscored by a sense of 'hopelessness' (1999: 83) that closes in on them, even as they attempt, just for a time, to push it away.

Evie feels like an 'intruder' (1999: 80) as she walks along the sagging streets of Drylands and the 'indefinable terror' (1999: 80) she senses when she first arrives finds its form in the violence she witnesses and eventually experiences. There is an 'ingrown self-sufficiency of secrets' (1999: 80) here that mirrors a sense of menace coming from the landscape, again homogenized in Evie's mind as she recalls the last rural town she visited and how its 'regiments of indifferent trees', frightening with 'their bony limbs' (1999: 80), sent her running wildly away in a spin of fear and panic. Evie's feelings of disequilibrium are left unexplored by Astley's narrative that ominously translates this unsettlement in relation to the environment through the hard-edged realities of explicit social damage. Astley plays with the mythology of a threatening Australian landscape – what Benny Shoforth calls 'scrub-scare' in the text, a landscape viewed as 'alien, spiky [and] unwelcoming' (1999: 182) by settlers – and critiques an urban view of any land outside the cosmopolitan in these terms. The text parodies representations of the outback as providing spiritual 'depth' and enlightenment to non-indigenous venturers. Drylands' only tourist attraction is a 'weird escarpment' upon which, 'at certain hours of the day in certain angles of sun and shadow' (1999: 46) an outline of the Madonna and child appear, suggesting Jean Baudrillard's 'divine irreverence of images' (1983: 5) in a shallow cultural landscape.

Far from being shadowed and ambiguous in its 'secrets', Drylands is configured as a surface place, with violence and pain exposed in the 'eye-blindly bright' (Astley 1999: 80) world of unsubtle actions and devastating, irredeemable consequences. When Win and Ro's husbands intrude into the class' lunchtime, a 'flattened moment' overtakes the 'bright air' of the day (1999: 89). The abuse that flies from the mouth of Ro's husband in words like 'chunks' (1999: 89), 'soured from failure and a need to bully' (1999: 89), represents the withering of discourse as Ro stands almost peacefully, 'a willowing saint, enduring abuse like a terrible balm' (1999: 89). His words are heavy and non-dialogic. Ro 'was not dodging but receiving' (1999: 89), unable to negotiate this humiliating monologue. Male violence recurs throughout the text and is figured in terms of hunting and conquest. When Joss, whose narrative is the last to be told, is chased by two local men aggrieved by her 'rejection' of them, they smirk: 'She's a stuck-up bit, all right! Thinks she's something else [...] Kinda asking for it, aren't you?' (1999: 263). The notion of 'reckoning' (1999: 86) in terms of sexual scores to be made and accounts to be tallied comes to characterize male attitudes towards women in *Drylands*.

Through each of its narratives, the predatory tone of *Drylands* conveys an unsafe world always on the verge of violence, enabled by a poetics of hard, unyielding exchanges and devastating encounters. Jim Radley's story emphasizes the depth of resentments that mark the town. Worn out by years on his unprofitable farm, Jim attempts to resurrect both his hope and dignity in the fruition of his long-held desire to build and sail a boat of his own. His dream is vandalized, however, and made more terrible in its nearness to realization, by the self-obsessed Toff, the son of Drylands' most wealthy land owner. As if demonstrating the perversity of inheritance, Toff is educated by his councillor father, Howie, in corruption and 'the finer points of rorting and living well' (1999: 140). Setting his sights on Jim's persecution for the single pleasure of expressing his own 'vile sterility' (1999: 145), Toff lights Jim's boat aflame, ecstatically watching it burn.

Arson becomes a ritual of sorts as Toff performs a 'dousing [...] [a] baptism' (1999: 145) and the sadistic nature of this behaviour is thus additionally laden with the impossibility it signifies for Jim's own redemption. His future's desecration is Toff's 'baptism'. As the boat tosses and rides its flames, making Toff's triumph extreme, the image of a rising phoenix is employed ironically (a motif that appears throughout the text), emphasizing the destruction of any hopeful desire that characterizes Drylands. Jim's 'glowing hulk would never rise from its ashes' (1999: 146). A narrative of inheritance is affirmed in Jim's reminiscence of the first and only raft he ever owned as a child being smashed to pieces by Howie and his gang. Toff's mean 'raking' eyes (1999: 136) mirror his father's as a child, 'watching' (1999: 124) Jim's raft with the same kind of malicious envy and waiting for his moment to destroy. Thus, the perpetuation of some narratives and the exhaustion of others is realized in this story. Jim's hope is '[e]clipse[d]' – 'Finished [...] Finished' (1999: 147) – and his exit from Drylands is marked with failure and resignation as he heads for the place of his spent desire, the now 'inevitable' (1999: 147) rather than promising ocean. For Toff, there is no exit out of the cycles of violence and the behaviours learned in narrow isolation that consume his young life. Prejudice is, perversely, the only binding force in the town, which also divides and displaces.

Failed resurrection is a theme of the text, and in several instances, characters profess a baptismal fantasy that is swiftly annihilated, in contrast to Gemmell's *Cleave*. Benny Shoforth's story brings to light the anxieties that motivate the bigotry of Drylands' inhabitants. With both non-indigenous and Indigenous parentage, Benny is another character on the outside of the community, his background and indeterminate colour generating disquiet in a dominant culture that demands identity be certain and cleanly differentiated: 'You'd have to peer closely to spot that touch of tarbrush [...] Was he one of them, the skin-privileged, or did he deserve dismissive contempt? The very unsureness gave offence' (1999: 158). Benny is alienated for this ambiguity. The perverse nature of prejudice is demonstrated when Benny's unsettling difference is read into his equally 'offensive' neighbourly behaviours. His goodwill and gentle nature are mistrusted in a distorted perception of selfless generosity. 'How the hell do you deal with that?' (1999: 159), someone asks, referring to Benny's reluctance to accept payment for the odd jobs he does around town. The non-indigenous men of Drylands deal with this uneasiness by forming a 'tighter blokeship club' (1999: 158) within which they affirm social superiority.

Hard edges, flat surfaces and non-dynamic forms of exchange communicate bigotry and intolerance. The police who approach a group of Indigenous men with whom Benny is conversing, are 'casual over the inner threat' (1999: 161) that lies in their interrogating questions and racially privileged authority. Similarly, the white overseer of the property on which Benny's Aboriginal mother worked speaks to Benny in a tone '[n]ot friendly [...] [n]ot unfriendly' while still effecting a 'warning-off sound' (1999: 163). Benny's youthful challenge to this culture infers a primary settler anxiety of an uncertain claim on the land that shapes non-indigenous relations to Aboriginality. When he rewords Dorothy Mackellar's iconic poem of Australian identity – 'I love a sunburnt country. The land belongs to me. I'd like to see the whites strung up/From every gidgee tree' – and although his teacher is '[s]ecretly impressed by the neatness of his parody' (1999: 169), Benny is caned in front of his classmates.

Benny's capacity to remake his home, time and again over his years of moving on and persecution provides an unsettling contrast to the efforts of non-indigenous characters, who continue to 'lose' – in a classic colonial trope of failure – against the land. The home-in-a-cave far outside Drylands that Benny sets up, complete with lounge suite and bookcase, is read as an affront to non-indigenous Australian security, parodying suburban domestic culture in an 'uncivilized' context. Yet Benny's ease in the landscape is conveyed as neither simplistic nor romantic, and his move to the cave is prompted by eviction and poverty rather than a desire to be there. He is slowly beaten down, we are told, from the repetition of 'the way things were' (1999: 186); 'too old for fighting the system' (1999: 183), his resettlement in a National Park represents a permanent state of exclusion, for even here he is forced to move on. Howie Briceland's determination to evict Benny from the Park is reminiscent of settler endeavours to hound out Indigenous people from the land, creating a 'wilderness' via dispossession. Hunting provides 'purpose' (1999: 189) to Howie, yet it is for more particular reasons that he seeks the persecution of Benny. Knowing and 'pressing down the truth' (1999: 195) of their shared parentage, Howie's unease is glaringly loaded with the need to erase the evidence of this knowledge. In his glee at running a peaceful man out of town, Howie protects himself with white authority and power, and a wilful habit of forgetting that has been entrenched through settler-colonial generations.

Benny's white father's ability to erase the traces of his illegitimate son from his life, and by the same token, his own sexual crimes committed against Benny's mother, demonstrate the silencing capacities of non-indigenous privilege. The 'family' values endorsed by Australia's conservative mainstream, and the celebrated rural tradition of strong community bonds, are exposed as hollow in actual social experience, made all the more hypocritical in light of a culture that practiced the theft of Indigenous children from their parents. Despite the contact Benny initiates with his mother, it eventually 'seemed easier [for him] not to make the painful visit to the big homestead' since 'nothing was able to dissolve the tundra of years that had separated them' (1999: 172). Reunited with her, 'Benny had never felt so lost' (1999: 173). Narratives such as Benny's represent the 'sore places' of 'Establishment ground' (1999: 190), that for this reason are kept excluded by dominant cultural narratives. As if wearing the public silence of his story, Benny's understated behaviour – like the women in Evie's class – also testifies to his familiarity with these structures and his 'reclusiveness' is described as 'pulled around him like a cloak' (1999: 178). He is confined by unspeakable things, secreted behind harsh surfaces. For Howie, Benny's removal from the National Park is like '[a] clearance [...] [a] purge' (1999: 191) of what taints his 'master-race assurance' (1999: 189). What Astley articulates here is the paradox of settler indifference to, and acute awareness of, the past, the suppression of which results in prevalent forms of weighted forgetting, violent dichotomy and more ambivalently, pollution and mess, which I will focus on shortly.

Standing up at the council meeting chaired by his half-brother, Benny rails against his persecution in the community and its wilful exclusion of discomforting knowledges. As he shouts out his anger – 'I'm Kanolu tribe, you hear? His brother!' (1999: 196) – he is forced from the chambers, denied his long-desired confrontation with Howie. The doors of power and social belonging close behind him while his words 'vomit' (1999: 196) out into the night over lands as hard and resistant as the people inside, and as vandalized and tired as Benny himself. This duality of forms, cohabiting in the poetic rendering of the land, conveys the subjection *and* estranging force of the environment under colonial-capitalist exploitation, and that sociality in *Drylands* continually returns us to. The apparent unbreachable social and historical divides spatially conveyed in this scene, related to a hegemony of official silence, are a desiccating force in these lands, connected by shared histories of power and sustained by dominant cultural imaginaries. What Janet ultimately rails against are the estranging, oppressive and violent forces of colonial, patriarchal power, which in turn speak to a draining of generative and sustaining poetics from the world.

Saving narratives

Janet's alienation amidst this all is somewhat self-imposed, as she initially views herself in distinction from the other residents of Drylands, and more refined in her tastes. With the sun unleashing its heat day after day, she determines to make 'use [of this] place' and to take advantage of her position as 'a watcher rather than a participant' (1999: 14). She will, she decides, surrounded by interpersonal, environmental and narrative decay, regain meaning in her life through a reinvestment of value in the word and thus in the community. She will write a novel – like Astley – 'for the world's last reader' (1999: 6). Distance affords critical reflection, Janet supposes, enabling personal enlightenment through the work of her pen within a broader malaise of disaffection and violence.

The novel thereby raises as a central concern the question of literature's role in a socially dysfunctional, environmentally ruinous and culturally vacuous Australia, tapping into these conversations already at play in the space of national literary discourse. It also raises challenging assumptions, ironically handled, about the capacity of literature to bring meaning to the lives of its readers. There is a tension here, for while Astley seems to mock Janet's ambition, she also affirms her own belief in the worthwhile purpose of literary fiction, which the novel overtly pits against a cultural preference for electronic entertainment. Indeed, Janet's decision to creatively produce in response to perceived cultural and environmental collapse is in keeping with the redemptive investment in literary practice evidenced in discourses of non-indigenous belonging and the state of the nation at the millennium.

In the development of eco-critical thought there has been a notable trend for literary fiction to be celebrated for its assumed ability to model a range of contemporary and future environmental contexts; its speculative parameters have been seen to afford a realistic, and through this, affective, engagement with climate change scenarios. There is, within this, an identified linear correspondence between representation, feeling, knowledge and change. Relatedly, the idea that literature has the capacity to 'improve' the reading subject spiritually, emotionally and intellectually, and that the writer is consequently tasked with moral purpose, was critical to the development of the novel in the eighteenth century, and what Richard Kerridge calls 'the mission of English', which fed the evolution of the literary discipline itself (2012). This was strongly influenced by liberal humanist ideas that pitted a moral, social project against the alienations of industrialization and its elevation of rationality and commerce over beauty, transcendence and the ephemeral. Influential here was the idea that 'inward' improvement was the way to social change and human happiness, put in blunt contrast to the externally oriented, prosthetic pleasures of consumerist culture. Inward cultivation was thought to generate feeling (sensibility) which, in turn, would inform or impel conscious action. At the turn of the millennium, this capacity to cultivate the reader and generate impactful feeling was invested in by a discourse of literary value that sought to make a case for the work of literature in a time of emergent climate change.

Exemplifying this is the literary study *Hearts and Minds: Creative Australians and the Environment* (Pollak and McNabb 2000), which makes the case that generating affect through poetic techniques is the work of the environmental literary text. As the collected essays assert, literary texts offer empathetic and affirmative ways of positioning the human subject of environmental crisis in the world. 'If a[n] environmental horror is described in a novel', Pollak and McNabb argue, 'complete with the human element and the emotional consequences, a reader is touched – and takes to heart what is at stake' (2000: 12). They address the privileging of reason over feeling in modern Western thought, resituating the imperative to respond to environmental challenge in the 'heart' rather than the 'mind' as a radical and restorative gesture. As a conduit for feeling, they contend, literary representation allows for 'a parallel rejoicing at [environmental] splendours and anger at [their] vandalisation' (McGregor in Pollak and McNabb 2000: 29). Anthropologist Nonie Sharp made a similar argument five years later that literary poetics enable an 'attunement' to environmental conditions that can generate a 'defense of nature', necessary as threats against it multiply (2005: 354, 362). Only when 'people's hearts were with Australian places' (2005: 355), Sharpe asserts, could generative place responses grow. She cites the Jindyworobak poet[3]

Rex Ingamells on this point: 'The real test of a people's culture is the way in which they can express themselves in relation to their environment' (2005: 358). The 'people' under discussion here are non-indigenous Australians.

This perspective on the capacities of literary work to move and impel a reader to action strongly echoes the 'information deficit' model of environmental communication that aligns public responsiveness to the challenge of climate change and other threats with the provision of accurate information, communicated in targeted and nuanced ways – ways that foster the right kind of feelings and responses. The form and mode of communication matter, in this argument, because they bear responsibility for how information, or data (which itself directly relates to the real and is thus considered unbiased) is received (see Potter and Oster 2008). The poetics of communication are considered crucial to the reception of facts, in a similar vein to poet Mark Treddinick's concept of the activist 'lyric witness' (2003: 36), able to generate connections and agitation through poetic expression. From this perspective, then, literary practice is tasked with enabling the imagination of what would otherwise be an alienating, or overwhelming, dataset – serving the empirical but, as eco-critical scholar Louise Westling writes, also 'mak[ing] "visible" [...] the "invisible" environmental dangers that [...] readers could not have imagined', enabling them 'to live vicariously in potential worlds our science might bring to pass' (2012: 84).

What is apparent in these discussions is the positioning of literary work as a medium well-suited to opening up the realities of climate change (be these already here or yet to come) because of its fictional remit and imaginative capacities. In such assessments of the value of literary contributions, the text is configured as a uniquely equipped conduit for climate change possibilities. Ironically, too, for a textual medium, this vision bestows it with the capacity to materialize and make perceptible the famously ineffable qualities of climate change's complex unfolding. The writer appears as both say-er and see-er in this discourse, implicitly tasked with purposeful work. These 'special' capacities of literature to access the feeling subject and illuminate, as well as presage, truths, are vital to the writers' perceived responsibility at the turn of the millennium, as the world rapidly warmed.

From her room in Drylands, Janet gives voice to resonant ideals. Her writerly motivations appear correspondingly redemptive, and, as the novel makes a symbolic connection between blasted environments and embittered, emotionally bereft communities, she makes repeated contrast between the emptied cultural life of the town, contextualized in environmental ruin, and the meaningful promise of her ambition to write. Her vision of Drylands, like that of the novel, draws poetic links between hard, estranging surfaces of social relations and a drought-ridden land, and the alienations of modernity, with its fast, unrelenting pace towards an idealized future, abandoning community in its wake. With individuals connected globally through satellite discs and Internet cables there is no space for retreat from these modes of 'connection' as the polyphonous narrative of millennial modernity is recast by Astley in a population tuned in, zoned out and beamed-into twenty-four hours a day. This relation, like the violent encounters between individuals in Astley's text, is sharp and un-generative. The ethical challenge of a medium that distances disaster and fabricates proximity in the space of the private, while unremittingly exposing its objects of focus, is not lost on Janet as she considers the sight of broken farming families broadcast to the nation and 'the cruel television coverage that stripped them naked' (Astley 1999: 245).

Conversely, the realm of art and feeling is figured through a spatiality of depth with immersion conveyed as an experience of imaginative truth. 'A story should fester', Janet proclaims, it 'should spread its attractive bacteria until it absorbs the whole body' (Astley 1999: 16). In this context, the metaphor of total infection speaks to an idealization of literature's transformative capacities – an astonishing power, as Janet tells it, to generate effects from a modest materiality: 'The miracle of it! Flyspecks on white that can change ideologies or governments' (1999: 6). These assertions of the value of literature predicated upon the text's capacity to connect to particular truths and participate in a reparative way in an ontological project of unification and repair, sit in tension with the post-structural tradition that widely informed literary practice and criticism in the late twentieth century.

Post-structuralism's emphasis on unstable and multiple signification and a dematerialized politics of meaning rejected the idea of fixed truths and the possibility of certain interpretation or authorial power. The persistence of these latter ideas in a broader environmental politics, however, evident in the prevalence of redemptive environmentalism (the idea that an environment can be restored or 're-wilded' to its pre-industrialized or pre-commodified state) and the frequent appeal to human sympathy and connectivity in environmental communication, continues to inform eco-critical thought. In some quarters, this has involved an explicit response back to post-structuralism and its political limits in the face of climate change and other 'global' concerns. This is evident in Astley's novel, where postmodern literary and media culture is aligned with the social and environmental degradation that concerns the text.

While *Drylands* can and has been read as referencing the rise of Pauline Hanson's One Nation in the mid-1990s and the concerns that motivated her supporters (Kossew 2000) – for instance, the divisions between city and country; the economic burdens carried by rural populations while economic and social policy favours urban dwellers; and a resentment towards difference and cultural change in favour of homogeny and 'traditional' Australian values – there is a further force of change that clearly preoccupies the text. This is the post-industrial iteration of Western modernity, expressed in the 'meaningless' noise (Astley

1999: 287) of a digitally dominated, globalized culture. The battered stretches of rural Australia are redefined by Janet not as a space outside modernity and its cultivating effects, but as also paradoxically oppressed within, and violated by, it. The incongruity of a town 'half-way to nowhere' (1999: 4) yet connected to a global media landscape highlights the tension between a nostalgic view of the country as somehow untainted by the cosmopolitan, and the processes of techno-transformation that, in Janet's perception, standardize global culture. Damaged lands and a frayed community are juxtaposed with a 'blurred world of technobuzz' (1999: 9), as the town's entire population is 'tucked for leisure [...] in front of television screens [...] Internet adult movies or PlayStation games for the kiddies' (1999: 5).

Flattening out

Looking out over Drylands, Janet imagines a globe 'full of people [...] glaring at a screen that glared glassily back' (1999: 9), and the disavowal of the literary text in preference to the shallow simulacra of hyper-reality is her main point of attack as she protests against the death of the novel at the expense of 'the half-second grab of television, the constant flicker-change of colour and shape against a background of formless noise' (1999: 16). Her anxieties give voice to the terminal condition that Baudrillard identified in Western modernity – the privileging of image over word, historical 're-enactment' as the only relation between humans and the past, and a reality-as-simulation that is 'unendurable' (Baudrillard 1983: 72): without depth or shadow and totally enclosing. 'To simulate is to feign to have what one hasn't', Baudrillard writes (1983: 5). There is nothing substantial in this age of simulation, no anchors to truth or reality. In the too-bright light of Drylands there are no subtleties of meaning and everything is revealed while perversely deferring any purchase on the real.

The relentless nature of modernity, she suggests, has left language evacuated of meaning. 'Illusory ideologies crumbled and [run] away like sand' (Astley 1999: 293). The power of words, undermined by 'television boom' (1999: 203) and sapped in a climate of introversion, is further debased in a contemporary political landscape that devalues and silences social debate. This is indicated by Benny's knowledge that 'words mattered' (1999: 172), even while his protests against imminent eviction and the voicing of his hidden relation to the non-indigenous mayor of Drylands go deliberately unregistered at the local council chambers. As discourse dries up and global media moves in there is nowhere to hide. Technology is given the power of revelation but also of forgetting: a signature attributed to late capitalist culture and its substitution of the 'real' by commodification, spectacularization and technical reproduction. The striation of global media across the land operates as a sign of the nation's symbolic fragmentation and the alienation of its population – out of touch with the ground, propelling rather than settling, and estranged from depth in a superficial place. Janet's fear of recidivism, her own anachronism *and* the evacuation of the past/tradition come together in the spectre of techno-determinism and its consequences of profound human disconnection and alienation.

In this, Janet seems to take on perspectives of both modernity and its ambivalence, concerned as she is for the rejection of tradition and (what she understands as) inclusive community. Her yearning for beginnings is structured by a nostalgia for the past that constantly seeks out the traumatic point of initiatory estrangement. Janet's motivation is this realization, in what she perceives as the empty shadows of contemporary techno-culture: 'Surely the world's last reader would crave narrative, but how to seduce an eye and a brain that had fed for two decades on the [...] constant flicker-change of colour and shape against a background of formless noise?' (1999: 16). Technology from this perspective estranges the subject from its bodily and locational referents, and is implicated in the loss of, or disregard for, tradition and a spiritually lacking or historically and emotionally 'shallow' culture/nation. Enforcing a chain of presents, forward-looking and reducing the past to waste, techno-modernity is signalled by shadowless ground inhabited by alienated and disconnected subjects.

Astley's text thus positions anachronistic literary 'depth' against a barrage of vacuous and superficial digital technology that has won out: meta-narrative is dead. Franzi, already wise to a shallow urban world in which corruption and the deferral of responsibility is not only normative but rewarded, refers to the pub's customers eating 'with eyes glued to the sports channel, hands moving forks automatically to gaping mouths' (1999: 47). Now '[e]veryone watched' (1999: 10) but were turned from the things that matter. Yet the self-satisfactions of postmodernism, with its rejection of totalizing narratives and hierarchical power (scornfully noted by Janet) are also hollow, as self-interest and competition aimed at silencing the other proliferates. Janet's vision of cultural degeneracy culminates poetically in the image of the silent youths who circle her, indicative for Janet of a society spiralling downward as control passes into the hands of the next generation. These youths enact a kind of tribal scene, connected by and privileged in their undecipherable knowledges, and heralding a future from which she is excluded. The unordered mobility of their young bodies, spatially and audibly dominant in Drylands' main street, attests to something strange and threatening for Janet. A new division thereby emerges in the nation as the product of a broken-down sociality, intellectually demeaned and extra-nationally defined, and in which there seems no hope for Drylands' recovery.

Astley's portrayal of youth culture participates in what Mark Davis describes as the 'overwhelming rhetoric' (1997: 5) of destruction concurrent with postmodernity: a claim to 'all those things being taken away' (1997: 5) that resonates with Dixson's warning for the globalized nation heading further into 'crisis'. As an icon of cultural anxiety '[y]ounger people, it seems, are some kind of trouble' (1997: 11), irreverent pall-bearers of a contrasting past now signified as redundant. This discourse of generationalism and Astley's 'spectre of the "teen gang"' (Davis 1997: xii) – a well-worn media cliché associated with social degeneration – is laced with an apocalypticism familiar to both techno-phobic pronouncements and the 'end of nature' discourse that increasingly permeated the millennial years (McKibben 1989). McKibben's assessment that climate change terminally collapses the demarcation between 'human' and 'nature', inaugurating a profound metaphysical void, is recalled by Astley as both texts evoke long-standing fears of technology's assault on the spiritual realm.

Astley's novel, at the end of the 1990s, is entirely unconvinced of a cohesive and meaningful future for the nation, as the climate warms and culture degrades. Characters leave and do not return. 'Nothing was okay' (Astley 1999: 209). With the local exploded by the global, its wasted fallout spread across the landscape, the triumph of a competitive capitalist ethic – survival of the fittest – sees the dream of a harmonious interconnectedness irrevocably displaced as 'illusory ideologies crumbled and [run] away like sand' (1999: 293). *Drylands* describes the paradox of everything and nothing brought into the light. While surface is privileged, laid open and bare, depth and connection is mocked and reduced. The empire-building Briceland's will be the last ones standing in Drylands' apocalypse, reaping success from other's failures. Astley's persecuted and victimized characters endure the public ridicule of what are personally valued knowledges – Jim Radley's boat, for instance, or the writing group's desire for independence and expression – or when, like Benny Shoforth, they challenge a nation's view of itself.

Janet's response is to wrest back narrative control from the pervasive technology that has flattened and disjointed social relations, and reinvest in the capacity of words to speak to a stable, external truth. Her dislike of postmodernism's 'endless reactions, and possibilities of reactions [...] like some never-ending story' (1999: 4) reflects her dismay at the disordering of textual authority and its infection with the inconclusive and the impure. Her desire to encapsulate 'the themes of a lifetime [spent] reading' (1999: 10) in her novel rehearses the illusion of a unified ontological and epistemological base for knowledge and the production of meaning, 'the one' from which everything emerges. Janet is thus determined to 'achieve the voice of her times' (Astley 1999: 10) as she tells the story of this town 'being out-manoeuvred by the weather' (1999: 287). Her spatial position references an ideal authorial stance that also evokes the colonizers' preferred modality: elevated, all-seeing, with the gaze taking control of a pacified vista. Her self-professed role is both prophetic and custodial for the culture at large, protecting the future from the creep of pedestrian entertainment, associated – like popular fiction, too, Janet tells us – with homogeneity and banality.

While this might be Janet's vision, however, it is not Astley's. Ultimately *Drylands* refuses Janet her desired authorial power, and the redemptive capacity of literature that she so invests in. Her literary ambitions are exposed as hollow and without value by any external measure. Astley repeatedly undoes Janet's claims to any kind of special insight or authority and amplifies Janet's own recognition of her failing project with a broader undoing of her narrative position in the text. Notably, Janet's eagle-eye is demonstrably fraught. Looking out from her window she is '[e]mbarrassed' (1999: 200) to see a waving hand down below 'give her the finger' (1999: 200). It is common knowledge in the town that Janet watches and writes what she sees – she is no all-seeing and detached narrator. Win Briceland makes reference to Janet 'writing away' and '[p]utting it all down'; she is implicated in the town's chaotic composition, no matter how her self-image sees this to be otherwise.

Astley's sense, as Kossew terms it, that 'even the watcher is being watched' (2000: 178) unsettles the clear meta-narrative that Janet's voice purports to offer and is playfully emphasized by Evie's decision as she leaves Drylands to 'write a story [...] about a woman in an upstairs room above a main street in a country town, writing a story about a woman writing a story' (Astley 1999: 99). Janet observes Evie as she scurries for the train station, intending to leave town, but equally Evie has her eyes on Janet, framed in her window, from the street below. Narrative control, and with it implied authority and authenticity, are thus opened to question in Drylands' crumbling social landscape. Franzi Massig too, professes to be 'the watcher' (1999: 45) in his narrative but, like Janet, his position is destabilized when we discover that he is also being watched, shadowed by the man whose identity he has purloined. Issues of authenticity are again raised here as the 'copy' (living this identity for four years), and the 'original' (having been 'lost' and untraceable for a length of time) confront each other.

Janet's vantage point becomes vulnerable on the several occasions her newsagency is broken into: the crash of a body in the yard and the sound of disappearing footsteps convey the threat of perceptible, but unseen and unarticulated, danger. Her secluded elevation is exposed as compromised – she is caught up with everyone else, joining them in a 'peculiar sense of belonging' (1999: 153). When Janet confronts a group of youths in the street, driving her 'crazy' with their 'meaningless' (1999: 287) noise, they laugh in her face and 'dance [...] about her chucking the ball from one to the other', leaving her feeling 'giddied and befuddled' (1999: 287). The possibility of textual authority is thus constantly undone. The 'deconstruction' of Janet's novel, its pages left 'shuffled out of sequence' (1999: 293) by anonymous hands when her flat is broken into, parodies her attempt at narrative certainty and the search, either textual, cultural or geographic, 'for the ultimate Eden' (1999: 294). There are, she concludes at the 'end' of Astley's text, 'no endings no endings no' (1999: 294). In contrast to the expectations for literature to 'save' and reverse declentionist trajectories, there will be no resolution to this story.

Thus, while Gemmell returns to origins in *Cleave* and *Shiver*, it seems Astley mourns something *original*: a space outside capitalist culture within which to cultivate a unique sense of self and from here speak truths in literary form. The reduction of subjects to replicants of commodity logic reflects a transformed temporality brought about by technological change and shifts in consumption, work and mobility patterns. Janet's regret for the loss of community responsibility and care can thus be tied to an explosion of commodity fetishism that looks only to the immediate and the disposable in terms of satiation and meaning. 'Because we have no idea how commodities come into being', Hawkins notes, 'their life after we've finished with them is also of little or no interest. The magical quality of the commodity can obliterate their origins and their final destination' (2001: 9). History is apparently evacuated in the ever-present moment of temporal satiation, and with it, political purchase. From this perspective, Astley seems to condemn the interventionist possibilities for literary fiction in the face of a fractured and disaffected millennial Australia, fearful of both the past and the future. Janet's privileged view of the novel is ridiculed; her attempts at a totalizing realism ('the voice of her times'), as the ultimate goal of creative production, fail. The ground of who and where we are is far from given, Astley suggests. The novel is (paradoxically) shown to be impotent and associated with either passive, or potentially active, violence. The bourgeoisie, who Janet at once abhors but is aligned with, are busy alienating and suppressing difference and dissent.

At the same time, there is a counter imaginary at work in the text that, through alternative forms, models a different register of relations for living in a postcolonial country. Rather than a problem of the novel per se, what Janet evidences is a problem of an imaginary that sees the world in terms of temporal junctures, clean distinctions and hermetic experience. This is the dominant imaginary of global capital, and in turn, the colonial project and its legacies. While the novel, like any artwork, and perhaps more than most, is constrained by aspects of its formal conventions – such as chronological pages (in a printed and bound text) and the reading subject who generally starts from page one and moves through the text sequentially – these can also be upset and challenged within the form itself, which the disarrayed page sequence of Janet's novel by visiting vandals sardonically suggests. Levine's point that multiple forms overlap in the world, in diverse contexts, speaks to this. Coexistent with textual modes are the forms active within and across the space of the text, with different affordances for thinking and doing. Diverse imaginaries are possible, Astley suggests, even in a conventionally bourgeois context such as the novel. While anxieties of belonging continue to operate in this other poetic space, the text demonstrates that these are not inevitably linked to a pathological obsession with secured ground and historical wipe-out as a response to perceived alienation. There are other possibilities apparent, advanced in alternative spatialities and configurations of subject and ground.

Revisiting the Drylands

Astley's refusal to allow Janet's fantasy of spatial and imaginative separation to be sustained offers a complex layer to the book's engagement with literary work in a time of crisis. Astley's insistence on Janet's complicity in the world she views and writes about does not reposition her as the primary agent in the text, despite the repeated return to her voice. Her hubristic self-positioning as an eagle-eye surveying all that is before her is undercut by the text's coexistent emphasis on entangled subjects and dynamic relationality (despite the prevalence of monologic discourse) that informs its position (and despite Janet's crisis-view of literary fiction) on the work of writing in the world. The folding of characters into each other, and into and across the stories that Janet supposedly composes, contributes to this. Subjected to an attempted rape by a visiting salesman, Evie is brought into relation with the verbally abused and threatened women she earlier sought to instruct. When she finally reaches the train after wrenching herself free from her attacker, there is little difference between Evie's urban self, stumbling and bloodied, and the rural woman represented by Ro who also sits on the train 'huddled' and 'bruised' (1999: 98). While Evie sees herself, like Janet, as an observer of 'the underprivileged outback' (1999: 70), she cannot avoid implication in it. 'Two of a kind' (1999: 99), Astley writes, as Evie flees Drylands on the same train as Ro, with a sense of indistinguishable futures: '[B]eyond the shaken windows' (1999: 99) of the train the landscape is blanketed in darkness, 'black on black' (1999: 99). No one is exempt from the conditions that generate Drylands' devastation.

Janet is a 'player' (Astley 1999: 244), too, repositioned as caught up in this world from which her writing cannot be extracted. Here, the text suggests, words won't capture the real because they contribute to its enactment – they will always be partial and incomplete, even as they impact and give rise to change ('there will be no endings no endings no'). This can be understood in line with new materialist thought that denies language special access to the real and instead sees it as a relational practice that participates in its making (Barad 2003). Language and discourse have no archaeological function, instead they contribute to producing our conditions of living: what we can see, know and make. They seed and continue to inform imaginaries. This is where Janet's position as a 'forecaster' of Drylands future is also reconsidered. Caught up in an ecological network, she will always speak from a relational position and never outside one. This enables insight but refuses totalized accounts. It indicates a shift from forecast as a commanding empirical mapping to one of situated prediction. No longer 'the poetics of a first-person narration versus the empirics of an encompassing survey' (Gibson 2014: 255), such distance is collapsed. But what is enabled is not the fantastic immersion sought by Romantics and colonizers. Reality is not something that can be observed or captured from a distance. Forecast, as a technology of prediction, is a practice that also enacts. It generates realities.

We see here the possibility for literary work, and its interventions, in the context of Australia's postcolonial 'rivenness', as literary critic Lyn McCredden puts it, caught between 'guilt-ridden and sentimentally static' and 'reactionary and essentialist' sentiments (2007: 17). McCredden's fictocritical exemplar of Jennifer Rutherford's *The Gauche Intruder* (2000), an innovative scholarly work that performatively reflects on non-indigenous Australia's impulse to at once 'do good' while manifesting a 'sustained aggression to alterity' (Rutherford 2000: 10–11), identifies the precarious position of the author (Rutherford) as solicitous of new readerly *and* political stances. Rutherford's hybrid autobiographical-critical writing, 'opens up the authorial position as potentially vulnerable, still "making itself", and as distinct from authority-driven modes of critical practice'. This, McCredden asserts, resonant with a view of poetics as generative beyond representational terms, is 'a set of practices that invite, rather than close down, continuing dialogue about Australian identity' (McCredden 2007: 18).

If we return to Janet's reflection on the power of words in light of this – 'Flyspecks on white that can change ideologies or governments' – a slippage occurs. Rather than human agency enabled by writing, we can understand writing as participant here, as a force in the world that materially intervenes. This puts Janet's own writing in a different light, too. With her eagle-eye undercut, Janet's 'observational' powers are suspect, and we can read this, as I have discussed, as a cultural impotence rendered by socio-economic and environmental forces. From a perspective of decentred agency, however, Janet's participatory stance, caught up in the weathers of Drylands, repositions what her writing can do. What we eventually see is not Janet's words documenting Drylands and the world that it signifies as it collapses around here, or as evidencing her alienation, or even victimization, in such a place. We see Janet's writing as active in the place-becoming of Drylands instead: her words feed narratives that make it uninhabitable, and that push her out, back on the road. They contribute to imaginaries that dispossess because they reiterate the self-image of the colonizer – a closed circuit of projected fears and ambitions – in the 'rainless air' (Astley 1999: 112). The multidimensions of the world are refused in preference to planarity. Despite what she senses as the possibilities of words and their network of effects beyond the authorial mind, Janet cannot countenance this outside the failure of ontogenetic meaning:

> If she could open up one word only and watch it expand from bud to fully formed [...] A bud could have a whole fiction buried within [...] One word, monosyllabic, or polysyllabic [...] opened up a wordscape of ideas [...] She thought this, she thought about the shadows of the shadows of words – and hopeless! – and slammed the cover back on her typewriter [...].
>
> (Astley 1999: 199)

These shadows, however, suggest the literary text as an agent that generates connections and effects, not a device of authorial or readerly power and meaning. This is something that post-humanist ecological thought encourages us to see. Timothy Morton, for instance, has called for literary texts to be recognized as non-human actors in his account of object-oriented ontology, in which the object retains non-relational agency as a 'weird entity withdrawn from access, yet somehow manifest' (2012: 208). Yet as Jane Bennett contends in response to Morton, from her new materialist perspective, relationality does not mean full disclosure or subjection to another's power. Instead, it signals the affective entanglements of bodies, not all of them human, which do things in the world. The literary object, and its composition of words, page, reader, writer and ecology of production and reception – including atmosphere and sensations – are all 'bodies' in Bennett's terms (2012: 225).

Janet's enmeshment in the Drylands' community, and its desiccating, suffocating weathers, in this sense speaks of such entanglement rather than the abstracted value of 'failure' or a linear shift from creation to destruction. This is not the end of externality as pastoral immersion but as profound, unsettled relationality. To return to Jane Bennett's point, relations between bodies in a worldly network do not necessarily entail subjection or total revelation: not everything is exposed to the light, because relations are dynamic. Networks are always in process. Because of this, a reading of Astley's text (and Janet's, too) through an emphasis on assemblage, rather than an eco-critical perspective of literature's values-based work, refuses a terminal diagnosis. Assemblage thinking understands power and the capacity to act and be acted upon as relationally constituted, and as always emergent rather than operative through fixed formations and forces (Anderson and McFarlane 2011: 125). A range of agencies, both human and non-human, and including technologies, are active within these relational networks, and compose and recompose in situations that are spatially and temporally dynamic. Such assemblages give rise to forces and effects that have material consequence, but are only ever provisional, meaning that network arrangements and alliances shift and give way to other possibilities.

Astley's emphasis on broken community relations and dysfunction is not disavowed in this reading. Rather, assemblage as a form encourages us to see violence and damage as relational emergences that enact particular realities. These are ones from which the writer cannot be extracted as she tells her tale: '[T]here are no endings no'. Janet's return to her vandalized room, with her disordered novel scattered about the place, conveys these effects despite the intrusive violence of the scene. Arriving home, the 'yard door shifted slightly as if to greet her and a small quiver of unease crept round her stomach. The back door swung ajar [...]' (Astley 1999: 292). The motility of this moment, the charge in the air, conveys a distribution of complicity: the authoring mind cannot control the scene, and a different imaginary is advanced. Upstairs, amongst the mess, monologue gives way to discursive exchange, without survey or command. Affronted by the line scrawled across a page of her 'GET A LIFE!', and groping in her mind for 'the ultimate reply', Janet realizes that 'she would never find it': 'She looked around her own drunken room and her hand, drunk on the pen, hesitated to write beneath the scribbled admonition the words: "TOO LATE". Suddenly she began laughing. She couldn't stop' (1999: 294).

Appropriate for the end of externality brought about by climate change, where an 'outside' to the human (and the parameters of 'waste' and 'value') can no longer be confidently demarcated, there is no end to an assemblage ('no endings'), nor an outside stance possible within the network. Conveyed in Janet's failed dreams is the end of the authority of Western modernity and its narrative of reassurance that human supremacy, social hierarchy and economic rationality will forge the conditions of a desirable world. Climate change signals the absolute failure of this project. Its emergence and effects put pay to the fantasy of human control over a passive nature, and destabilize the foundations of Western metaphysics. Rather than signalling the end of creativity, however, this conceptual and material transformation reconfigures the epistemological and ontological ground of what it means to create, and as a consequence insists upon a reconsideration of literary practice.

Janet's concern for the lost originality in cultural texts – the substitution of 'signs of the real for the real itself' (Baudrillard 1983: 4) – and her apparent surrender to techno-determinism ultimately reorients away from endism. Technologies are attributed horizontal power with other materials, practices and narrative modes in the enactment of the real. 'Data', we might infer, is given no epistemological privilege over other forms of story-telling. The apparently dominant spatial forms of Astley's text – evacuation, erasure, exposure and division – give way to others: entanglement, infection, overspill and affect (indicated in Benny's 'vomiting' protests, and the radiating effects of Toff's puritanical vitriol); they are unsettling, not terminal, impacts. Janet therefore comes to stand for the limits of this particular historical subjectivity and its attendant epistemology. Rather than a falling apart or loss, her anachronism in the Drylands community is, from this perspective, her metaphysical investment in the promise of totality or unity in the face of difference, contingency and relationality, as well as real environmental limits.

But more than the death throes of modernity, what we also encounter in Astley's novel is an argument for the text itself – 'the book for the world's last readers' – as the 'text-body' (Bennett 2012: 232) to which Bennett refers; not an abstraction of signs (representation) alluding to a real world 'outside', this is an assemblage of agencies and intensities that are in and of the world. These include signs and modes of representation as well as bodies (the author, the reader, their communities and many others who move through and with the book through the world), technologies and forces of capital and other social arrangements. There are also non-human forces, too, including weathers, which assemble in the becoming of a text. It is from this entanglement, rather than from a certain and elevated place of feeling or perception, that the writer locates an ethical stance: a 'loose alliance' of more-than-human collaborators, to reference Stephen Muecke, 'in which [...] thoughts and feelings can balloon out and surge' (2010: 6). In this perspective, the text is not a conduit of knowledge and feeling but rather a force that effectively works in the world.

Here, Janet's bacterial analogy for the infective nature of stories resonates again: this is narrative as profoundly ecological rather than omnipotent, emergent from and operative within these material interactions that take place beyond the form of the human subject in the situated more-than-human assemblages of a warming Australia. Janet intuits this collaborative future, without transcendent value or metaphysical purpose, and still with the capacity to alienate or injure. This is not a utopia, but an inevitable transformation in how literary work, and the authoring subject, makes sense at the millennium. No longer the 'heroic', overseeing author, writing to save the world, Janet – and Astley – are participants in the relational network of story-making through which we make sense of things and (re)generate our imaginaries. The characters that assemble across the novel, folding into and out of each other in occasions of doubling (Franzi's impersonator, and the return of the real Franzi) and resonance (Ro and Evie and Janet's shadowing – 'writing a story about a woman writing a story') generate effects beyond what Janet can control, 'beyond the boundaries of what she knew and what could be' (Astley 1999: 244). The ground of an alternative imaginary to the hard edges of colonial spatial fantasy is consequently opened up, as a poetic practice and as a mode of living in place.

Thus enfolded, the 'narrative hunger' (Gibson 2014) generated by practices of erasure and a totalizing gaze gives way to the possibility of stories told in the midst of things, in the conjunction of technology, body, environment and place, 'immersed, and involved. Not critically distanced' (Gibson 2014: 262). A world wrapped in wires, as *Drylands* depicts, does not mean a conclusive end, an alienated reality or simulacra. What it realizes is a living condition that is always negotiated and entangled with more-than-human others. Technology, in this perspective, is profoundly relational. It is also active in the production of the real, rather than its concealment or abstraction. As both material and sign (data), technology is situated within the unfolding of what Karen Barad calls the 'intra-activity' (2003: 822) of the world, an intra-activity that, for other new materialist thinkers, is a kind of storying – 'configurations of meeting and discourse' that generate narratives and attendant imaginaries (Iovino 2015: 71).

Due preparations?

Astley's mobilization of infective forms asks that the text's take on the past and the future be rethought outside a paradigm of terminal crisis and collapse. In these millennial years, when endism refound popular appeal, the possibility of failed futures pressed close. The ambivalence of *Drylands* in response to this 'slow crisis' (Buell 2003: 95) is usefully seen, by way of conclusion, in light of a non-indigenous Australian novel published four years later: Janette Turner Hospital's *Due Preparations for the Plague* (2003). This novel, which concerns the psychological, relational and ontological fallout from a plane hijacking on a group of survivors, asks what can we possibly expect of the future in light of contemporary uncertainties? We can't secure the future, the text concludes, and neither can we secure the past.

More evidently than the ambivalent gestures of *Drylands*, Turner Hospital utilizes weather and its poetics to make sense of uncertainty and the ever-presence of a past that will not be put to rest. Atmospheres swirl and are impenetrable to view; they can be deadly – 'anthrax weather' (2003: 223). At the same time, they manifest the transformative, mobile qualities of space: '[I]n fog everything shifts with the light, everything floats' (2003: 46). Her concern with 'plague' is broadly deployed – it is both metaphor and reality; it references the specificity of chemical weapons and new viral diseases that are the outcome of human interventions into more-than-human matter. It is ideological warfare and it is the haunting of traumatic pasts. It is the existential anxiety of death's inevitability. It is 'our own nightmares' (2003: 265). *Due Preparation*'s characters repeatedly experience the loss of stable ground beneath their feet as they ostensibly come closer to the truth of the plane's hijacking yet remain unsettled in their knowledge of what 'really happened' and why. '[N]o footstep is safe because the ground is soft and gives way. Funnels of quick sand wait like wet-lipped mouths' (2003: 273). What knowledge they have does not keep them safe from the past, nor does it resolve the question that recurs throughout the text: '[H]ow do we ready ourselves for what may happen tomorrow? What possible preparations can be made?' (2003: 390).

In its critical reception, the geopolitical landscape attached to Turner Hospital's novel was, unsurprisingly, that of Islamic terrorism in the West, and the West's complicity in forging the conditions of what was the defining terrorist event of the era: the World Trade Centre attacks on September 11.[4] Likely because of this, the book has not been considered in relation to the political landscape of its author's homeland. Yet, its resonance with the millennial anxieties expressed elsewhere in Australian literature at the time is striking, anxieties that elsewhere attach explicitly to questions of non-indigenous belonging. Its concern with the proximity of the past, and its unresolved nature, brushes up against the conterminous debates over 'what to remember and what to forget' (Rose 1997a: 97) in Australia's violent colonial history, and its articulation as an unsettling series of encounters that can neither be predicted nor easily allayed. The text articulates a cultural concern with detritus and what it means to be unable to keep 'externalities' at bay. Its protagonist, Lowell, reminds his associate Samantha, who is also intent on finding out what happened, that: 'The past leaves its own mark. Do you know that we're sitting on landfill? This used to be the bed of the harbour. Feel that vibration? [...] The past leaves traces that eventually come to light. No one can stop them' (Hospital 2003: 383).

The tape recordings of the hijacked passengers last words – recordings captured in a sarin-filled bunker that make their way to the victim's families trying to make sense of the political espionage behind the hijacking – sit unplayed beneath the bed of one of the victim's children, 'a toxic blue bundle', 'practically radioactive' (2003: 213). The effects of a terrible event leak through time; voices from inside it push against 'the capacity of press and public for quick forgetting, and [...] the quiet erasure of events from government reports' (2003: 61). Bad dreams do not go away, and there is no solid ground on which to stand. Lowell is repeatedly described as dissolving; without the ground, he is at sea: '[H]e is beyond help and recovery, he is sea, he is salt water, he is oceanic ferocity itself' (2003: 153).

Astley, too, takes the ocean as a counterpoint to the hard-edged dispossessions of Drylands. Her characters yearn for the 'mesmeric sea' (1999: 208), to be 'lulled by the steady rhythm of water breaking on the sand below' (1999: 208). Unlike Gemmell's redemptive account of Bud's swim out to sea, however, Astley's ocean is not conclusive. Nothing is healed here. What is suggested, however, is a different disposition in relation to a past that cannot be controlled, and a spatio-temporal present that is always permeable, that always shifts our relations to others. Caught up *within* this, literary work offers no transcendent insights: it cannot 'save' us. But it can act within an always assembling network, moving and reconfiguring arrangements of onto-epistemology, and resulting political realities, through its forms. Here, 'the end of nature' – a discursive basis of crisis in the increasingly climate change-aware millennial years – signals the recognition that externality (tactically separating our mess and waste from ourselves) is no longer possible and with this, the limits of a pervasive Western imaginary. As I further explore in the next chapter, the certainty of ground is what productively gives way as imaginaries that come from this entanglement, rather than from separation or immersion, enter the discursive field of non-indigenous belonging at the millennium.

NOTES

1. The name 'Deakin' cannot be disconnected from one of Australia's most remembered Prime Ministers, Alfred Deakin (1856–1919), the architect of the infamous White Australia Policy, and a proponent of irrigated agriculture in Australia that commoditized and transformed Indigenous environments.
2. As reviewer Kerryn Goldsworthy quipped, '[i]f she really believed that the screen had horribly taken over from the page, would [Astley] have written a book about it?' (1999: 31).
3. The Jindyworobak literary movement of the 1930s and 1940s was an attempt by a group of non-indigenous Australian writers to 'indigenize' their work by referencing and drawing from Indigenous Australian culture.
4. In an interesting aside, Turner Hospital's writing of *Due Preparations* was already well under way when the September 11 attacks occurred.

Chapter 6
The Past is All Around: Chloe Hooper's *A Child's Book of True Crime*

Quarantining the badlands

As we have seen, the drive to secure a particular relation to the ground registered across narratives of non-indigenous belonging in a fear of 'surface' living. This fear privileged particular forms over others in the imagining of non-indigenous Australian belonging at the millennium. Containment, separation, forward movement, un-dynamic relations and skimming the land gave poetic shape to the anxiety of disconnection and unfulfilled belonging. But other non-indigenous narratives looked to surfaces for possibility, and through other forms. Here, spatial relations could be imagined differently, outside a paradigm of rooted belonging or terminal alienation. This surface differs to the smooth facades critiqued by Gemmell and Astley, which reference either a refusal or inability to attach to place for reasons of cultural insufficiency. Instead, surfaces also registered in the non-indigenous literature at the millennium as an expression of complex relations between people, history and the ground.

One of these is Chloe Hooper's novel *A Child's Book of True Crime* (2002) that offers this kind of approach to the surface of millennial Australia. Through the deployment of diverse spatial forms, Hooper's novel reconsiders the colonial obsession with stabilized ground, sought out for the unimpeded mobility desired on an imagined planar earth. The ground's surface is reapproached here as unstable, multidimensional, folded and folding, and continually 'trips up' positivist attempts to map, know and claim truth and the real. It is constituted not wholly of solid matter, nor is it purely ephemeral. Instead, it is composed in ongoing arrangements of matter and energy: it is rock, but it is also atmosphere; it is relational and it is always in movement, but it guarantees no certain futures, nor finalized relations. It can hide but also reveal – it is solicitous. And it suggests, through this, an experience of living in history, in the midst of things unfolding.

Child's Book references and plays with the spatial tropes of non-indigenous pathology that characterized belonging discourse in the millennial years, and that fed a prevalent related discourse of 'haunting' for an unreconciled nation. These tropes identified 'depth' as an idealized form for attachment to place, and aligned shallow connections with cultural inadequacy. But, also, depth suggested hidden and secret things covered over by veneers that work hard at cultural forgetting. Hooper's protagonists – both human and non-human (for there are animal narrators within the text) – are drawn to these classic gothic tropes to explain the world around them: surfaces are untrustworthy, hiding repressed forces below that threaten to erupt through. Rather than endorsing this spatial determinism, however, the text unsettles it, opening up to other forms that shape and make sense of living with the past. The novel therefore self-consciously waivers between its poetic investment in a narrative of postcolonial repression, perversion and denial and its pursuit of a different imaginary that breaks from a formal dichotomy of surface and depth.

This playful oscillation begins in the novel's (incorrect) declaration of its genre – true crime. Is this, we are asked to consider, the pre-eminent Australian genre, an obsession at once registered and denied in the non-indigenous mind? A love of bushrangers and detective thrillers covers over genocide and dispossession. Here, the Tasmanian location of the novel seems pointed. This is a place usefully understood through Ross Gibson's elaboration of postcolonial badlands: spatial containers that encyst a culture's refuse and confronting madness, and – because of this quarantining – condemn a particular place to repetitions of 'bad'. Drawn from a North American colonial context that referred to its 'wasted' tracts of land in these terms, Gibson localizes the concept to reference areas of Australia that become popularly synonymous with violence, unpredictability, excess and fear. Badlands are rejected spaces, areas 'where people are warned not to go' (Gibson 2002: 13), and charged with a mythic status of deviancy and horror. They are rubbish dumps on the outskirts of the 'good and lawful'. They are also, according to Gibson, spaces into which the anxieties always circling around not belonging are amplified, referencing, via their abjection, the 'dreadful sense of insufficiency felt by Europeans forging into the more "savage" parts of the "new" world' (2002: 13).

The colonizers' cohabiting fear of spatial estrangement (not belonging) *and* spatial absorption (becoming lost in the land) feeds into the 'no-go zone' (2002: 15) of the badlands, which, because of their encysting work (a version of the securing hold in reverse, desired by the modern national subject) take on the symptomatology of colonization. That is, the badlands, like Australia itself, are 'an immense, historical crime-scene [...] [with] old passions and violent secrets [...] lying around in a million clues and traces' (2002: 1–2). In the badlands, national scale is obscured. They take the focus of Australia's blood-soaked past, with their '[t]ales of murder and itinerancy' (2002: 14) finding localized reflection in challenging environments and isolated townships. Yet, as Gibson's fictocritical work *Seven Versions of an Australian Badland*, published the same year as Hooper's novel, argues, the badlands generate discursive excess as they are continually reimagined and reactivated in cultural narratives. Badlands haunt, and because of this they overspill their cordoned-off boundaries. They bring the past and the present, the local and the national, into active proximity.

Hooper's *Child's Book* presents a similar ground in which 'old' and 'new' crimes coexist and disturb in Australia's southern-most state, Tasmania: 'Imagine feeling like you're living on the very end of the earth, and also knowing that you are' (Hooper 2002: 64), posits the protagonist and narrator, Kate Byrne. Her fascination with a 12-year-old murder/suicide and her efforts to comprehend this brutal event are caught up in the traces of colonial violence that litter the landscape. Tasmania's violent past cannot be divorced from contemporary crimes. This does not represent a linear inheritance, a cause and effect narrative and a discrete origin for trauma, however. What the novel posits is a relation between past and present that can be understood as an ongoing assemblage of place in the (re)enactment of place stories. It reminds us that what's 'bad' cannot be easily quarantined away.

Where Gemmell activates the mythic qualities of Tasmania for her textual purpose, Hooper plays upon both a broad tradition of the gothic qualities in Australian landscapes and the particularity of this island state as an icon of violence and perversion. In the midst of the millennial years' 'History Wars' that tussled over the facts of frontier violence, Tasmanian writer Martin Flanagan recalled his first visit to mainland Australia where he discovers that, in popular opinion, '[w]e' – meaning non-indigenous Tasmanians – 'were the ones who had done the killing, we had shot out the blacks' (2002: 21). Conveniently, the island position of Tasmania enabled its role as a repository for the nation's horrors. For Flanagan, the mass killing and displacement of Indigenous people from Tasmania and the island's convict history, Port Arthur especially, with its peripheral stories of inbreeding, sexual disorder and cannibalism,[1] marked out his home as disquietingly shadowed, overhung with the 'strangely deafening silence' (2002: 40) of untenable events, shameful and shut-out. Unlike Gemmell who suggests Indigenous absence as a silence in this landscape, the silence Flanagan notes is occasioned by discomforting presences, the narratives through which Tasmania is mythically known. In a 'badlands' frame, this is Tasmania as a 'lair for evil' (2002: 13), a place in which geographic and historical conditions seem to affirm a landscape that generates and perpetuates violence, danger and extreme behaviours.

After shooting dead thirty-five visitors at Port Arthur in 1996, the explanation of perpetrator, Martin Bryant – 'A lot of violence happened there [...] It must be the most violent place in Australia. It seemed the right place' (Bryant in Wahlquist 2016) – rehearses this narrative, laying down yet another tale of suffering and death upon a spot, now 'itself [...] cast as a serial killer' (Gibson 2002: 30). Historic crimes condemn a place to a repetition of violence. Yet, as Maria Tumarkin argues in accordance with Gibson's theory of badlands, this uniqueness or 'freakish quality' invested in the Tasmanian environment becomes an act of minimization equivalent to quarantine. A continent-wide story of colonization and dispossession is thus circumscribed, making such damage an exception rather than a constituting force of the nation and its history (Tumarkin 2001: 205). The isolation of Tasmania as the foundation of this traumatic narrative is what *Child's Book* confronts; in doing so, it gestures towards what Paul Collins calls 'the great Gothic horror stories' of Australia's past (2002: 13) – those stories of lost children, bunyips and hauntings that I have referenced earlier – that feed a cultural fascination with haunted places.

The home is the classic site of gothic unsettlement in the Western tradition: the 'anatopia', or uncanny context, that arises out of an unsettling proximity to secrets, mysteries or repressed preoccupations. In the context of home, questions of inheritance, genealogy and property come to the fore that translate persuasively to the broader 'home' of national imaginings. Freud's own application of unhomeliness to the 'house of western civilization' (Vidler 1992: 7) following World War I speaks to this point. The collective residence of those identified as civilized Western subjects was, at both a national, regional and ontological level, 'infiltrated' and in ruins. In the Australian context, the unsettlements of the post-Mabo years, and the growing sense of vulnerability to global, non-human forces (climate change), represent a pressure point on the idealized 'Australian house', secure and firm on the ground. Yet, Australia was never a homely place for the colonizer. In a colony founded upon repressions, 'a locus of horror' (McCann 2000: 1) sat at its heart, giving rise to how Andrew McCann has described a specifically colonial-style gothic where the everyday condition of 'dangerous proximity' to violent pasts emerges in unruly and surprising ways. This is 'the "repressed" of colonization' returning. Here, '[w]hat appear[s] to be a stable, law-bound order turns out to be founded on crimes that must be expiated' (2000: 1).

Hooper's text seems to follow this logic, and with it, a set of forms. Endpoint, the apparently peaceful coastal town where the novel is set, stages its own version of a disorienting eruption as a murder of local girl Ellie Siddell, previously discussed in hushed tones, is brought to imaginative light by the out-of-towner, true crime writer Veronica Marne. For the gentrified citizens of Endpoint, enclosed and safe behind their 'forefathers' hedgerows' (Hooper 2002: 72), the publication of Veronica's book *Murder at Black Swan Point*, a true crime novel pursuing the 'facts' behind the grisly murder (apparently at the hands of an avenging wife), is a 'surprise [...] [and] betray[al]': 'Why couldn't she let the dead rest?' is the general sentiment, or more specifically, 'She's opened up a Pandora's floodgate of worms!' (2002: 48). The return of the murder to public consciousness is a threat to community self-perception, and indicates the permeation of curated boundaries by the bad things previously pushed out: 'Why this town? [...] This is a quiet place [...] This is a good place, we don't even lock our doors' (2002: 70).

Kate, the school teacher protagonist of the novel, arrives in Endpoint some years after the murder. She begins an affair with Veronica's husband, bringing her into tantalizing proximity to the murdered girl, who her own affair fantastically echoes. Kate willingly identifies with Ellie, and also positions her antagonistically, critical of the clichés of good and bad female behaviour that swirl around the crime and its rumours. Ellie was a nice girl, well brought-up; Margot was an 'incredibly kind woman, practical and generous' (2002: 70) who disturbingly transgressed these boundaries. For those who knew her, she seemed 'incapable of such a brutal crime' (2002: 69): a devoted mother and loyal wife, Margot 'had done everything right', performed and perfected 'every good-girl trick' (2002: 191). Things had simply gone 'bad'. At school, Ellie and Margot's paths were the same, as they were told '[n]othing would really go wrong' when they set out in the world. The road ahead was already mapped, clear of irregularities. At boarding school, Margot watches the girls who creep outside to smoke with boys late at night and wills herself to fall asleep in the assurance that 'she would get everything she deserved' (2002: 74).

Ultimately, Kate realizes, both Margot and Ellie – and perhaps also herself – are 'sacrificial lamb[s]' (2002: 168) to the desires of a predatory world, hidden behind smooth surfaces and fantasies of innocence. 'For young women', Kate relates, 'doomed girls are annoying. It's a reminder one should start locking the doors of a car. A photo of a schoolgirl with bangs and a dental brace stands for never walk home alone on an ill-lit street' (2002: 132). 'Good' girls monitor security while 'bad' girls tempt their fate. Descriptions of 'good' and 'bad' things move throughout Hooper's text, and the cultural currency of their sharp distinction is repeatedly argued. This is a distinction that sells. Despite the community's horror at the crime and its distasteful re-revelation in Veronica's book, *Murder at Black Swan Point* flies off the shelves: an 'attractive' story, we are told, 'because it was classic', a formula of love, seduction and betrayal in which the step from 'nice upper-middle-class girl' (2002: 57) to vengeful murderess is a leap across a shocking divide.

Consuming through reading, it seems, is a safe way to come close to horror. When innocence is violated, newspapers choose 'the prettiest photo' (2002: 132) of the victim to present as an icon of virtue in a dark and dangerous world. If more ambivalent stories of young women emerge they are hastily erased. After the daughter of the 'equivalent of Tasmanian royalty' has an illegitimate pregnancy, then shoots herself against the wall of the family home, her parents 'covered the stained bluestone with pretty pictures' cut from the 'pages from an old *Woman's Weekly*' (2002: 53). Juxtaposed images of the *Murder at Black Swan Point* crime-scene (Ellie's child-like room full of stuffed toys, make-up and sports clothes splashed with blood; her body when found in her pretty single bed, severed at the head) complement the dichotomies (light/dark, surface/depth) within which 'gingerbread house[s], iced lovingly, bordered by candy-boughed trees' (2002: 16) secret away sin and corruption.

The motivation to cover over the 'bad' and to sweep the landscape clean of crimes is Hooper's allegorical link between the case of Ellie and the '*Ur*-true-crime-story' of Tasmanian history where 'in volume after volume the bodies pile up' (2002: 97). In naturally beautiful country, picturesque and even picture-perfect (Hobart, we are told, is 'a city that still looked, from the top of Mount Wellington, like a nineteenth-century oil painting' [2002: 13]) the reminders of colonial violence – ruins, wilderness, stories – are threaded together by roads and highways whose edges are littered with the animal carcasses of roadkill. 'Behind every loveliness was something harsher', Kate reflects (2002: 38); '[p]ray for rain to wash it all away' (2002: 64). 'We live here because nasty things don't happen. We live here because people are good. We have homemade honey at the local store, and lovely bed-and-breakfasts' (2002: 77–78).

Tasmania's 'game board' of settler names – 'Wander [...] from Cape Grim to the Never Never to Nameless Lake [...] Suicide Cliff [...] Purgatory Hill' (2002: 72) – are on the tourist map, sweetened by gift shops and produce factories. A painted wheelbarrow sits 'full of miniature lavender' (2002: 42) outside the old prison warden's cottage in Endpoint, while at Port Arthur, within the 'old sandstone walls' of the convict women's prison, 'truffles were handmade' (2002: 86). As Kate explains, these smoothing-away gestures were not new, but historically repeated in a crime-ridden landscape. Sympathy Hills and Point Puer overlook the waters where convict children had once washed, having built the penitentiary's walls with their own hands. After the closing down of the penal colony in the 1870s, 'Endpoint's newly righteous settlers painted the convict's unmarked gravestones white' (2002: 36) to hide their 'convict stain'; '[a]nd this was the way we reinvented ourselves' (2002: 150).

Endpoint's history is therefore characterized by attempts to keep crime in its place, cordoned-off 'with wire and [...] yellow tape' (2002: 236) like the rubble of Point Puer's prison, too dangerous to enter, a threat to safety. The repression of presences and the covering over of surfaces enables a divide between beauty and horror to be maintained, despite their repeated juxtaposition. Kate considers this as she walks, shaken and traumatized after her car crash (her fan-belt mysteriously cut clean-through), past a site where public hangings once took place near the sheer cliffs and 'postcard' views of the coastal waters. Holding an apple taken from a bag left trustingly by the side of the road, itself a marker of homeliness and community (honest people would 'leav[e] money in the empty jam jar' [2002: 77]), she pictures the condemned convict brought to the gallows, 'jubilant, indeed triumphant, at having been granted an exit from this hell' (2002: 85):

> It was hard to believe that my grandparents' grandparents were in the crowd watching the man laugh. My grandparents' generation certainly didn't speak of it: they were still touched by the stain. My parents' generation didn't speak of it because they had not been told. And at school my classmates and I didn't find this history the slightest bit related to us; even if it was, we didn't really care.
>
> (Hooper 2002: 85)

Like Ellie who realized at school that 'history only happened in textbooks' (2002: 67), Kate is also caught up in a culture of forgetting, but one that is vulnerable and easily punctured. Emphasizing this, sounds of threat from outside her house (rustlings, screeches and other unidentified noises) and her own intruding thoughts of Veronica's maniacal revenge erupt through and disturb her sense of security. Kate's alignment with children (a school teacher) and Ellie's own youth, still a teenager when commencing her affair with Graeme Siddell, suggest a permeable veneer of innocence that is a motif in the Western Romantic tradition. Rather than maturation signalling induction into a dark world of experience, however, childhood here is destabilized as a place of sanctity and purity. The storybook tale that intersperses Kate's narrative, of native animal detectives seeking their own answer to the Black Swan Point mystery, plays on the novel's title, creating an (ironic) story in children's terms for the terrible events of Ellie's murder. This extreme baptism of fire for innocents for whom such narratives do not constitute a 'normal' part of childhood imagination, conveys a place of bedtime stories gone awry, a gothic landscape full of underground whimpers and 'hidey-hole[s]' (2002: 29). This is a vista in which beautiful black swans sing in mournful tunes, their sleek necks bent to make an 'ocean of question marks' (2002: 110). The animals' narration, we are told, will tell 'the truth' (2002: 79) of the adult world, as Terence Tiger, Kitty Koala, Wally Wombat, Percy Possum and Kingsley Kookaburra see out their years dodging bullets and cars, their friends and relatives decimated by feral cats, chlamydia and lost habitats ('the years since Ellie's death had not been kind to any of them' [2002: 182]), but ever still in the pursuit of restoring a world out of moral kilter.

The animals' protective attitude towards Lucien, Kate's prodigious student and the only child of Veronica Marne and Kate's lover Thomas, is mirrored by Kate's professed instinct to preserve Lucien's childhood from the adult torpor surrounding him. 'I suddenly wished Lucien and I could just leave and go somewhere safe together', she cries, 'away from these people' (2002: 179). In Kate's ambiguous eyes, herself slipping between the boundaries of adult and child, childhood is nostalgically rendered, a time after which, 'nothing will ever seem so green'. Yet as she stands by the side of the cricket pitch watching her primary school class play, she senses 'the menace underneath' this scene of innocence, a 'tiny rip develop[ing] in this sporting picture' (2002: 160); '[t]hey were statues on a well-kept lawn, in poses sketched by a noble to inspire other paedophiles' (2002: 161). The threat of crime latent yet slowly eruptive is made analogous with puberty and the sexualization of the child's body, brought with a shock into adult desires. 'Wouldn't it be lovely', Kitty Koala whispers, 'if there were some recipe to avoid becoming an adult' (2002: 225).

Instructively, the storybook protagonists turn with 'old-world dignity' (2002: 209) from their mammal cohorts engaging in flagrant sexual activities, the night sky full of the cries and screeches of 'worlds ending'. Kingsley's tree, 'his palace', becomes 'a bestiary' as '[e]ach branch strained and groaned' under the weight of 'simpering creatures'. Turning from this chaos, his 'bushland gang on the ground below [...] like displaced nobility' (2002: 208), Kingsley cries into the sky where, even there, 'cloud-lovers' tussled together: 'Lucien [...] Hide! Hide!' (2002: 209). Lucien's exposure to things beyond the 'normal' limits of childhood safety represents an uncanny shift, a disturbing fault line in a 'manageable' world with 'its scale of anarchy', as Kate expresses, 'to my liking' (2002: 47). Kate's flirtation with danger only goes so far.

Kate's classroom observations of Lucien's disturbed mental condition – 'What it meant for this child psychically, to have a mother obsessed with death and gore' (2002: 49) – suggests the breakdown of a state in which children are 'protected from things so strenuously that the slightest irregularity [...] could overwhelm' (2002: 66). A version of 'pristine' (2002: 57) crime with its clear right and wrong, watered-down or evading complexity and horror, seems preferable to Kate, kept within the reasoned limits of psychology and its understanding contained by 'pure science': the 'jigsaw puzzle nature of crime' that leads the bushland animals 'ever on' (2002: 82). Endangered childhood, juxtaposed with the raggedy collection of native animals, thus positions innocence and a 'natural' order against a badland chaos in an apparent morally inflected environmental tale. This points to a tradition of colonial configurations in which 'the lost child and indeed the lost world of childhood' (Thomas 1998: 53) infers a relationship between purgatory and the unknown Australian environment.

Kate professes an abhorrence of commodified innocence, and she identifies with both Ellie and Lucien as innocents debased by this kind of experience. However, her complicities challenge this, as – like Astley's Janet – she is an active participant in the culture she critiques. Her disconcertion over the veneer of Endpoint's goodly community ('I stood near some mothers, wanting to blend in. They talked in hushed tones without acknowledging me' [Hooper 2002: 174]) comes from her awareness of a pleasure economy, where, in the pursuit of adult's self-gratification, boundaries of safety waver. Kate's affair with Thomas demonstrates this, and the currency of excitement, as well as horror, that is exchanged. In Kate's mind, Thomas' sexual patronage is laced with threat, and as she becomes more convinced of his collusion with Veronica to replicate the Ellie Siddell murder with her as its victim, this newly revealed adult world is all the more shocking to Kate for her own complicity within it. Sexual knowledge and its consumption represent alluring danger, and her performance of paedophilic fantasy for Thomas is charged with affects both frightening and forbidden: '"Was this the way people really behaved?" I would ask myself in mock affront' (2002: 104).

Kate's obsession with the murder consequently takes on unsettling force. Ellie's body is the ultimate consumable form in both *Murder at Black Swan Point* and the numerous rumours and theories that flow around its central event. She is displayed and dissected via imagination, and in the pursuit of the desire 'to know' as much as she is at her murderer's hands. Kate's participation in this is made clear, generating and compounding her fear and paranoia of the Marnes as she maps out and transposes Ellie's story on her own. From Veronica's book, Kate feels as if she has 'already seen inside' the Siddell home and Ellie's room: 'Her clothes carpeted the floor', she narrates. 'It was hard to believe she'd brought her lover here, but she was still only nineteen. And I bet every time Graeme Harvey led her to the single bed, and pushed away a layer of debris, Ellie wished she'd remembered to tidy up' (2002: 70).

Veronica chronicles the police investigation as they 'bagged nearly sixty items from the house [...] over half [...] from off her bedroom floor', laboriously listing for the public reader Ellie's private life: '[A] pair of pink underpants; a sports bra; a T-shirt [...] two towels; candy wrappers' (2002: 70); '[t]he list [...] also included brown matter labelled "blood scrapings", samples of Ellie's blood, her hair, her nail and muscle tissue; scrapings from under her fingernails; and the knife found lying next to the body' (2002: 71). Such details, readily consumed by Kate, and fostering her paranoia, lead her to see her house as perfect crime-scene material: 'At a certain hour, as dark swelled, axe murderers started growing in the flower beds. Or else Margot did' (2002: 129). She imagines Veronica's blade entering her body just as Margot's supposedly had Ellie's, and as she makes love to Thomas, Kate spins with nausea, 'grainy black-and-white photos of Ellie Siddell's body' (2002: 27) sliding before her eyes. Later, 'after reading [Veronica's] book', she relates, 'I walked around my house as if visible from every angle; suddenly the walls were made of eyes. Like some primitive version of hell, every vase knew I was bad' (2002: 58).

Veronica's text treats Margot in a similar way: her life story and private spaces are opened up to public view. In the true crime book, all aspects of the event are purportedly detailed: from Margot's frenzied slashing at Ellie and the amount of blood left at the scene, to what Kate imagines is the murderer's maniacal drive to Suicide Cliffs in which she 'slipped and slid all over the road, Ellie's blood still staining her hands' (2002: 71). Public fascination with the true crime text is thus shown to signify the collusion of 'public anxiety, consumerist pleasure and pornographic scandal' (McCann 2000: 10), highlighting the paradoxes of a culture that seeks to keep violence or crime unspoken while desiring to imbibe, in textual form, what is held up as forbidden and irrational. The anxiety of the hidden coming to light and the satisfaction of its revelation are coexistent.

Yet as the distinct registers of private and public are blurred, knowledges leak and lines of reason, truth and order are breached. Understanding this, Kate questions Veronica's attempts to affect an 'ethical stance' as a true crime writer, wondering whether she could 'get inside the criminal mind, while bending backwards to then show her horror of the deed? In every chapter, she'd tried to cloak her own fascination as social responsibility. Her own perversion as research' (2002: 72). The idea of 'getting inside the criminal mind' testifies to this anatomical approach with its frisson of pleasure and horror; 'psychiatric profiling', Kingsley Kookaburra notes, 'provide[s] rich ore indeed' (2002: 30). Kate considers the true crime genre as encouraging the public to feed on the secrets of suppressed or interior spaces while also declaring its aversion to it, and she applies this layered form to an internalized reading where badlands also exist in the mind. Veronica's assertion that 'I had to acknowledge there's a struggle within all of us [...] An eye for an eye' (2002: 100) informs Kate's view, and in the classic psychoanalytic model of the 'murderous' psyche ('we are all killers in the unconscious of our desires' Mark Seltzer explains [1997: 17]) – she claims self-recognition in the murdering villainess: '[T]hese horrific crimes were not just the things other people did. These deeds were with us; they were in our nervous systems. We read true-crime books to learn about ourselves' (Hooper 2002: 105).

Tellingly, however, Kate maintains a blinkered view to history, and the crime-ridden landscape in which she is situated. While colonial crimes are continually referenced, these are, superficially at least, non-indigenous concerned crimes, specifically the history of convictism that the text describes as a kind of primal stain on the pristine colony. This is a potential blindness of the novel which seems to focus on acceptable horrors that at once fascinate, even while they might horrify – something that the prominence of convict history in Tasmania's tourist industry endorses. However, Hooper's text is not so straightforward. In between the lines of official history, Kate learns from her students, there 'must be another story, which has to be imagined, written in blood. Always true, this blood story will haunt you and keep you awake, and the grown-ups should never know of it' (2002: 237).

This other story is the founding history of colonial murder and dispossession. It is the story of a never ceded claim that haunts non-indigenous place.

And so, as with the gothic tradition of the unhomely, houses are insecure and animated in *Child's Book*, open to intrusion and their own strange plans. When she wakes to an unfamiliar view of her familiar back yard, Kate wonders if '[d]uring the night the house had taken off [...] relanding with each angle out' (2002: 142). Parents dream of infanticide, and children of murder and violence, shaped by adults' desires and the lies they weave. Thinking her pupils too young for Tasmania's 'issue of genocide' (2002: 33), Kate has the children write Dreamtime stories; the day after sending off postcards to the Tasmanian parliament urging the passing of the Aboriginal Land Act, her students appear 'crying because their parents had re-educated them. They were going to lose their backyard and therefore the new swing set and trampoline' (2002: 35) – a reference to the paranoid public discourse following the Mabo decision. Similarly evoked in McGahan's *The White Earth*, the trampoline is a banal signifier of settler-colonial anxiety that distracts from the history that Mabo exposed. At the same time as she reiterates this repression, Kate acknowledges the 'airbrushed prison' (2002: 233) of hushed tones, secreted excess and denial that these responses foster. 'The idea that [children] needed to be protected from the truth was surely a way for adults to protect themselves', she argues.

Promiscuous pasts

According to Rosalind Smith, true crime texts operate on an affective level, activating 'a level of imaginative sympathy' (2008: 24) that enables the frisson of vicarious experience that the gothic model suggests. At the same time, she argues, this sympathy is about proximity as much as it is distance. True crime affects because it 'brings readers close' (2008: 25). That Smith begins her discussion of true crime genre with a reference to Hooper's text is telling. Although Smith does not address this, it is not just non-fictional crimes that leave us 'haunted by a "blood story"' (2008: 25). The performative genre play of *Child's Book* reiterates this: it is an adult fiction about true crime, written, supposedly, for children. Neither is the text straightforward colonial gothic. Hooper's world may well be haunting but it also exceeds its own gothic overtures, working beyond a paradigmatic model of surface/depth relations, beyond those hidden things that trouble and assail us. Her narrative poetics move away from gothic limits and instead towards an inextricable entanglement that implicates the reader too, sometimes explicitly addressing them, and does not end cleanly at the covers of the text. Forms proliferate in the novel that speak of complicities, ruptured certainties and the destabilized ground in imaginative, ontological and epistemological terms.

Here, the economy of transaction between containment and consumption that sustains the gothic commodity is superseded by uncertain, non-linear effects. While the gothic does gesture to the proximity of crimes and things that unsettle, the eruptive nature of the repressed returning necessitates a foundational ground above which surface abrasions speak only cryptographically, signifying something 'below'. Environmental 'disorder' speaks of these repressed histories and a correlative alienation for non-indigenous Australians, as Chapter 4 suggested, requiring redemptive correction. Hooper's badlands refuse this however, mobilizing a topography instead where a poetic opening of the ground only illuminates deferral. Here, any attempt to go beneath the surface of an event will see the logic of revelation reflected back at it, rather than a 'truth'. Instead, her text suggests that, on the surface of things amidst an assembling world, our relations with the past are negotiated outside commodification or constraining conceptual lines.

Jacques Derrida's 'spectre' is a useful counterpoint here to the Freudian psychanalytic model, with his concept of 'hauntology' offered against ontology as a certain ground for history and being. For Derrida, haunting is not a question of belief or disbelief in ghosts: it is a conception of time – as I explore in the following chapter – that is temporal and indeed 'untimely'. '[H]aunting is historical, to be sure', Derrida writes, 'but it is never docilely given a date in the chain of presents, day after day [...]' (1994: 4). Unlike the psychoanalytic move to reveal and heal repressed histories, Derrida's haunting eludes settlement, introjection and the notion of restoration. The ghost can never be expunged; instead it continues to move on the networked surface of the world, never fully realized in knowledge (aka Derrida's concept of *différance*). Spectrality is this refusal of foundational ground in meaning and origin, and the dichotomous rendering of states. Not present or absent in ontological terms, the spectre relates to both past and present but inhabits neither. It is a recurrence even when it appears for the first time. The ghost in the network speaks of the past, but also of the future. '[E]verything [...] comes back to haunt everything', Derrida explains, 'everything is in everything else' (1994: 146).

From this perspective, Kate's experience of unhomeliness in Endpoint and her unsettling absorption in Ellie's narrative can be read as her grounding in a bumpy narrative of a 'promiscuous' (Gelder and Jacobs 1998) environment that insists on presencing its pasts. Her growing awareness that the truth of Ellie's murder can only ever be approximated realizes her distance from 'what happened' as she imaginatively moves towards it. This does not seal off the crime but rather disseminates its reach. The animal detectives are also unable to resolve Ellie's death and Margot's disappearance, as they parody the ontological desire for firm ground and evidence as truth – 'the kookaburra was not shy in peeling back the surface to uncover a protagonist's most basic emotions' (Hooper 2002: 30).

Margot's body is not recovered from below Suicide Cliffs; facts resist cohesion in the text, and narrative gaps refuse 'to restore the common light of day' (Parkin-Gounelas 1999: 137) that would settle disorder. Kate is unable to match Ellie's story with her own profiling of the Marnes' plans and recognizes that '*Murder at Black Swan Point* would offer no clues. Each chapter ended with another unanswered question [...] its author had no idea what had happened – 315 pages, but all she'd needed to scratch on each was I DON'T KNOW' (Hooper 2002: 186). Rumours cannot be reconciled, nor fragments pulled together in a straight narrative line. Despite the traces left behind in DNA samples, the abandoned car, the blood in the Harveys' bathroom – in the 'exchange theory' of criminal detection, Kate relates, 'just as a criminal leaves traces at a site, so they take them with them where they go' (2002: 152) – there is no linear correlation between these, no balance of cause and effect as 'all the possibilities branched off endlessly' (2002: 194). The association between childhood and the realization of true crime's unstable ground – which would otherwise provide an identifiable foundation for Endpoint's 'bad' side – overturns a positivist tradition in which the child's eyes are equated with untainted truth. Kate asks her class, '[w]hat if we lived in a world where everyone told the truth? [...] Can you always know the truth?', and Lucien's response is telling: '[Y]ou can change the truth. But it usually happens over years [...] Truth is a flexible substance' (2002: 52). Narratively and spatially, the text challenges a planar view of the world where relations are measured and ordered.

'[O]ur desire to "not get lost", to leave a clue, is so strong', Kate remarks, bemused by the fact that 'Margot hadn't left behind a suicide note'. She had 'left nothing' (2002: 194) as either a trail or marker, no statement of intent, no confirmation of presence. Yet to become 'lost', as the text indicates, is neither to absent oneself from the present nor to attain a reconciled place for there is no one beginning to which the story can return. Kate's privileging of childhood as the only space in which tragedy fully resounds seeks to find this line between the jaded and the pure, but turns to a point of dichotomous collapse. Her summation that '[u]ntainted by a hundred other learned horrors, [children] are haunted for the appropriate length of time. They ask a thousand unanswerable questions. The story stays with them; they dream of it' (2002: 79) is thus ironically self-reflexive. As her own enquiries and obsessions reveal, there is no measure appropriate for the effects of haunting. Evidence of the crime, unable to be gathered together, appears and disappears, wavering and shadowed, as does the past with its own transgressions. Can our obsession with the 'facts' – of knowing what happened in sequence – be an ontological buttress, another kind of protective picket fence, against an admission of the horrors of the past and, in the Australian context, the 'blood story' of colonization to which we are all connected?

Diverse forms of knowing and remembering are resonant for thinking about Hooper's text as a refusal to keep working within violent and exclusive ways of conceptualizing subject/object, past/present relations. Without denying its conceptual lineage as a non-indigenous text, *Child's Book* wants to think about inheritance differently, as something that permeates, that is enrolled with us: something atmospheric rather than final and stuck in a temporal circuit of eruption and subsidence. Her badlands are alive with remembering, heaving and sighing as they rearrange with attempts at narrative closure. 'Knowing who the murderer had been', Kate admits, 'wouldn't keep me safe' (2002: 197). The resolution of 'the crime' is continually deferred as Kate realizes that her particular experience is 'part of history' (Gibson 2002: 50). The past is not separate from the self. Papered-over walls and levelled ground cannot erase the past, for there is no 'below' or behind the surface into which they can be repressed. Kate's recollection of her father's school 'built on a graveyard' (Hooper 2002: 187) makes literal a metaphoric view of Australian non-indigenous ground, and articulates what it is to 'live with history' (2002: 186–87). 'Bones poked out of the earth', she recalls, 'and it was realized some of the coffins would need to be exhumed. When the chains of a crane accidentally broke, a coffin came crashing down into the schoolyard. One little boy was expelled for running up and trying to prod a wedding ring off a skeleton's finger' (2002: 187). The dead do not just pile up, one on top of the other, beneath the earth: they break through instead.

This kind of irreverent and performative relation to the past in the present is replayed by the children in Hooper's text who run and scream through the grounds of Port Arthur. Dressed up as pickpockets and forgers, they enact an historical stage rather than isolating it, floodlit and single-voiced. Defying prescriptions of authenticity, '[t]hey waltzed and wrestled' amongst 'diseased' (2002: 107) façades: '[wearing] their faux rags they looked like a children's theatre troupe performing the off-cuts of *Oliver!* [...] They had heard of one convict who, trying to escape overland, found a dead kangaroo and wrapped himself in the animal's fur. Lucien was allowed to be the kangaroo man, and Darren and Henry were suddenly the officers out hunting' (2002: 96). The kangaroo-cloaked figure creates a spectral moment in the text, where genocidal histories unsettle this single-storied performance of colonial pasts.

Amidst the exhibits and cases at Port Arthur, displaying the hard evidence of the past (objects found or recorded in story; the torturer's equipment alongside mock-ups of 'the crime'), the children 'reeled around, delighting in their nausea' (2002: 96). The carton of cigarettes, stuck onto the wall for demonstrative effect, and emptied of its contents by pilfering hands, signifies its own encounters with previous irreverence, ironically mimicking the past and exceeding the ordered boundaries of traditional museology. What can be read as history commodified, even vulgarized in this way, is breached by relations and the continual production of meaning that encounter initiates. The Endpoint community's whitewashing of the past is placed next to this. The same gravestones painted over now lie broken and scattered about the cemetery: '[K]ids', Kate observes, 'maybe even the dead's direct descendants […] had nothing better to do' (2002: 36), a recognition, unsettling for its own breach of social codes perhaps, that the past refuses to remain in its 'place'. Our relation to it cannot be prescribed. This kind of practice does not abstract memory from place, nor necessarily debase it as it creates different, unsettling proximities. Instead, it generates new forms through which to imaginatively bring the past close and in the process reconfigure a relation with the ground.

Kate marvels at the contrast between the alive-ness of her students and the 'dead place' (2002: 107) that is Port Arthur. Yet at the same time she notes the ground at her feet: the penitentiary's floors are carpeted with 'yellow daisies and milk-thistles' (2002: 88); the 'crude windows framing the most uncanny views: serene Opossum bay; rolling green hills; an English country garden of weeping willows […] planted by homesick officers' (2002: 88). The desire to remake and smooth over an uncomfortable landscape is evident all around, and yet, in the stone ruins, in the re-emergence of growth, and the 'long high cry and sudden note change' (2002: 88) of the whipbird, Kate feels a resonance of 'the horror that existed [here]' (2002: 88). These badlands are both alive and spectral, morphing as she moves amongst them. Kate notices rocks, 'bruised purple, bruised red – swollen with history' (2002: 31), while 'leaves whisper […] rumours' (2002: 125) above dirt that 'smelled rich with its own fertile plans' (2002: 79). 'Each giant boulder vibrated with alarm. Each tiny pebble quivered underfoot' (2002: 9), while Graeme Harvey's grief in Kate's imagination 'lurked like a mushroom cloud over the peninsula' (2002: 29).

This is an environment in which the seen and unseen move together. Curvilinear rather than rectilinear, with voices, shadows and multi-directions, the very ground on which Kate stands is unstable, throwing her continually out of balance as it records 'the traces of […] impact[s] that will not quieten down' (Carter 1996: 17). Here, past things refuse to stay at an ordered distance. In *Child's Book*, rocks 'like mouths, like tongues, like pornographic things', and 'boulders […] like the buttressed walls of a cathedral', 'curvaceous, almost bulbous' (Hooper 2002: 12), refuse the fantasy of a stable and secure ground. Kate must constantly negotiate her footing. This topography resists a smooth imperial gaze as the weathering of surfaces, the grooves in stone and incomplete tracks, bring always-composing environmental relations to the fore. 'Every molecule was now changing' (2002: 185), Kate states, taking in the disequilibrium and tremors of the ground beneath her feet.

Repeated references and allusions to spatial disorientation in the text – vertigo, nausea, agoraphobia and claustrophobia – model the characters' disequilibrium, and the reader's own unsettled relation to the novel and its performative, self-referential narrative. 'Trees planted too close to the walls scratched my bare arms', Kate tells us (2002: 212); '[a] branch scratched at my face and again I felt seasick' (2002: 215). She is immersed in her world, not saved or in harmony, but uncomfortably, unnervingly enrolled. Her world is alive, resounding with what she perceives as moral condemnation, even down to the vases in her home that watch and judge her. At a bed and breakfast with Thomas, the 'Persian rug gave a slight electric shock' (2002: 17) beneath Kate's feet; the trees lining the side of the road as they drive back to the school, lunchtime over, lean in, 'writhing, mournful' (they 'made me nervous' [2002: 32]) and birds glare down as Kate stumbles into the playground. 'I felt certain I was in trouble' (2002: 44), 'a naughty little girl, late for school' (2002: 43).

Her sudden realization that Thomas and Veronica wish her ill induces dizzying uncertainty, and her inability to discern fantasy from reality is described with the disturbing force of an oceanic swell. 'Before me the horizon line trembled', she describes. 'I'd been dumped by a wave. I stood feeling its slap, the way it belted my body' (2002: 168). The ocean, a different surface of the world, speaks here of disorientation rather than healing (Gemmell) or failed ambition (Astley). Like a 'huge animal drawing breath' (Hooper 2002: 78), its unpredictable momentum is analogous to the pitch and roll of Kate's desire and terror, which, rather than speaking of her moral 'wrongness', indicates her proximity to the Marnes and their secreted threats, and the story through which her anxiety snakes. This has implications for the reader of the text too. Since Kate's voice keeps the reader in touch with the textual ground, her constant shifts between poise and fall create the effect of nausea in the narrative itself. There is no straight narrative line for the reader to follow in this landscape of convergence and divergence, as if many worlds and truths were simultaneously opening and closing.

These oceanic entanglements recall Stacey Alaimo's new materialist elaboration of the transcorporeal, where the sea – 'dynamic, intra-active, watery' – speaks to an inter-penetration of material bodies, energies and immaterial affects that defines being in the world. Oceanic forms convey ontologies of convergence and immersion and refuse the possibility of clean separation and containment. Profound relationality is the condition of being which means that – despite efforts to the contrary – things can still 'pollute for eternity' (Alaimo 2012: 487); 'there is no solid ground, no foundation, no safe place to stand [...]' (2012: 490). Spatial disorientation is the sign of enmeshment; vertigo marks out rearranged proximities. Distances collapse and extend around the self, dispelling ontological security and confusing relations between the subject's position and its surroundings. Synonymous with the dark antithesis of human reason, vertigo toys with ontological dissolution as the ground opens up, potentially and unpredictably treacherous, and without foundation. Kate's feelings of nausea as she and Thomas drive down the main street of Endpoint, with is flower boxes and cottages 'fashionable in England two centuries ago' (Hooper 2002: 41) lining the road, suggests this agoraphobic anxiety, and gesture to the pervasive attempted erasures of colonial aesthetics.

As if intuiting the renunciation of environmental memory, and in keeping with a modality of flat surfaces suppressing unsettled ground, Kate is unnerved by the formal lines of colonial architecture: 'I wished we could lock the door and speed straight through this town', she states (Hooper 2002: 41), indicating a desire for the anonymous mobility of the colonial subject. Yet, simultaneously, she notices a slight asymmetry in these 'classicist principles', a dimensional irregularity particular to the walls of this town, an irregularity that is both historicized and localized. '[D]esigned by convict architects and built of local stone' (2002: 41), these shapes may speak of imported ideologies imposed upon the ground, but as their asymmetry suggests, they can never fully perform this imaginary. What this wavering of colonial lines also speaks to is the shadowing of Western culture's repressions as externalities that – in a network – will inevitably reappear. These are the elements of places detached by dominant national imaginings that privilege non-indigenous security and a related obsession with stable (and deep) ground. But what Hooper realizes in millennial Australia, as pasts return and illusions are broken, is that there is no immunity in a network. We are all implicated together, with uneven experiences in consequence.

Child's Book generates a world without straight lines as Kate's surroundings refuse any submission to linearity. Distances are unsettled between self and other, as proximities change, oppress or rearrange environmental positions. The connection between agoraphobia and claustrophobia is thus evident: an expression, as Paul Carter writes, of the 'oscillation between the desire for contact with the other and a fear of it, between the desire to enter into a relationship and panic at the thought of it' (2002: 32). This is not, Hooper suggests, a wholesome desire: it can be ugly and potentially toxic. Most of all it gestures to the so often repressed realization that the ground is not stable and assured. Kate's waves of nausea and spatial uncertainty suggest this oscillation between desire and fear with perverse consequences, ones that never bring her any closer to a disclosure of 'what happened'. Rather than leaving things secreted away this means instead that the narrative of the past cannot be controlled; Ellie will not be given up to contemporary consumption and the 'event' of her murder will never be finalized. Its effects continue to resonate. What would seem an abyss, a gap in reason and a frightening void for the ontologically firm, becomes, like the forms Hooper offers in her textual ecology, an interval or place of recomposition, requiring the moving figure to twist and bend into different shapes. In this light, Kate's nausea, like Carter's agoraphobe, 'bears witness to the invisible topography of relations' (Carter 2002: 71), the violence, damage, making and remaking, that is the assemblage of Australian environments.

Hooper's text creates an environment in which no one relation to, or moment of encounter with, the past is identical with another. In this environment there is nothing – neither narratives nor certain belonging – to hold the subject firm. Where ontological security is dissolved, a view of an ecology veiled by shadows, like the ephemeral quality of smoke, appears. This veiling does not hide or lock away terrible pasts but suggests their presencing that defies revelation. The cigarette that Kate, in her mind, sees Margot sucking down with post-coital glee after her frenzied attack on Ellie, performs this clouding of the event, trailing from its burning tip indecipherable but relational lines, dancing and drifting off. The interweaving of sex, death and disappearance in this scene conveys the erotics of possibility that play generatively between the revealed and the hidden. The sexual charge of Margot's 'crime' is echoed throughout the text as Thomas and Kate's liaisons (an asymmetrical mirroring of Ellie and Graeme's) teeter between violence and pleasure, invoking a doubled promiscuity: one is Margot's breach of good girl behaviour, venturing into the forbidden and the taboo, and the other is the irresolvable uncertainty surrounding her 'becoming lost': '[t]his figure, Margot Harvey, had broken out of the mould, and went blazing into the night, howling, "No! No! I will not be civilized about being replaced! I will not retire gracefully!"' (Hooper 2002: 57). As Margot vanishes into the darkness, the trail of smoke in her wake resists her erasure but also speaks to a flirtatious impermanence that evades the monogamy of reconciled meanings and settled uncertainties.

Despite its performative gestures towards 'solving' the crime of Ellie's murder, with its animal detectives on the case, *Child's Book*'s defers resolution, leading critic David Farrier to classify the text, *after* Deborah Bird Rose, as 'Anthropocene noir' (Farrier 2017). Writing outside the millennial years when 'the Anthropocene' was conceptually normalized in cross-disciplinary discourse including literary criticism, Farrier applies Rose's concept to Hooper's emphasis on entanglement and complicity from which there is no outside from where the reader can get a purchase on 'what happened'. For Rose, 'Anthropocene noir' expresses the end of externality brought about by climate change, where we are deeply immersed in the world we have created. Everyone is complicit in this ecological crime, though with varying degrees of responsibility. The power of poetics to illuminate the politics and ethics of climate change is made clear by Rose, who deploys Val Plumwood's famous concept of 'shadow places' in her elaboration of Anthropocene noir. As the world warms, the exploited places and communities of global capitalism are revealed as entirely connected to us all. Shadows relay a haunting that is like Derrida's ghost, implicitly of the present and the future. Of course, as Elspeth Probyn points out in her work on more-than-human ecologies in the Anthropocene, 'the über threat (of climate change) does not cast its shadow equitably upon all of us' (2016: 105).

For Farrier, then, read in light of a continued pervasive resistance to recognizing the reality of climate change impacts and shared, if uneven, responsibility for these, *Child's Book* evinces 'a mode of ecological consciousness alert to the incalculable nature both of non-human and human relations and of risk in "Anthropocene noir"' (Farrier 2017: 5). He reads it as 'a formal response to the (literary) problem of how to describe ecological crime' (2017: 7). The novel's refusal to offer Kate – and her reader – a safe space from where to declare her comprehension, and thus her tactical separation as analytic observer from the violence and disorientations that arise in the text, mean that everyone is implicated. However, the 'crimes' of the text are more pointed in the historical situation of the text than Farrier's retrospective reading allows. Writing out of the millennial years, Hooper captures what, ironically, Janet Deakin in Astley's *Drylands* so wanted to be: the 'voice of her times'. In Hooper's text, this voice is not prophetic; rather it is symptomatic. It speaks from the milieu of anxieties that brewed amongst non-indigenous Australians in these years, confronted and destabilized by the realization that they could no longer keep the past at bay. Their 'place' was irrevocably unsettled by the fact of colonization and dispossession, and the subsequent violence committed in its wake. Kate notes that '[p]eople, disgusted, went on and on, once again, about how Australia had forever lost its innocence' (Hooper 2002: 200–01). While it is Ellie's murder that rightly generates this disgust, the echoes of settler-colonial discourse in the millennial years reverberate, evoking the 'loss of innocence' motif that recurred in the post-Mabo period. John Howard's famous declaration of non-indigenous Australia's white-picket-fenced goodness in 2001, in the face of historical evidence to the contrary, epitomizes this.[2]

Such innocence is a product of myth, nothing more. The text's spatial forms, as well as Kate's conceptual and embodied navigation of the world around her, refuse the fantasy of externality that Rose's, and Plumwood's, political visions contest. There is no effective quarantine here. The text repeatedly infers that the opposition between 'bad' and 'good', innocence and guilt, is not so clear cut. There is no solid ground on which an 'innocent' can stand firm. Kate's feeling of dissolution, as she looks at herself in the mirror hanging on her family home's wall, gestures to this instability where becoming occurs in elastic proximity rather than a straight and commanded path. '[A]ll the comforts of my past had stood up and left', she relates, 'there was no one to tell me who I was anymore [...] I had got lost in someone else's life' (2002: 144).

Kate's 'lost' world of childhood, imbued with nostalgia, is countered by her students who already annotate their sweetened stories with darker things: 'I had seen the scribble added to their fairy tales, I'd noted where they tore the pages' (2002: 232). These children already live, write and imagine between the lines of a rectilinear world. Their seemingly awkward, stumbling steps, and the free-flowing dance movements with which they approach a wide-open space on the lawns of Port Arthur, countenance that same approach to the ground. Kate wonders at the text's end: 'Maybe the first stories we are told are the ones we find our way back to' (2002: 236). But there is no originary place to which Kate can return, the novel concludes, as things are not put right and mysteries not resolved. Like the crimes that haunt the text, any gesture of retracing, of returning to the scene, involves a different repositioning of the subject in relation to what she seeks to know.

Without the possibility of a conclusive ending, Kate's proposition that 'perhaps all perversity comes gift-wrapped in the banal' (2002: 213) takes on particular light. Without the formal separation of surface and depth, the 'banal' and the 'perverse' fold into each other, with no sharp edges to distinguish them. '[N]ot all things have to be so momentous!' (2002: 224), Thomas shouts at the knife-wielding Kate. To consider truth as the light of revelation, uncovering and laying an object bare, demands the weight of empirical terms, heavy, inviolable and unbreachable: a pinnacle of reason beneath which lurks darkness. On an unstable, disconcerting ground, however, topographic inconsistencies that can throw the self out of balance at any time admit a mode of living with the past that sidesteps the monumental, bringing the partial, the ruined and the unresolved into relation. The Port Arthur buildings that 'had seen the end of the world [...] would keep rotting until they were just piles of bricks' (2002: 107), over and around which people pass and children dance. Echoes reverberate in and out. A story rendered in the sound of 'rain drumming' and the angle of sunlight 'slanted just so' (2002: 237) will be remade with the closing in of night, or the unrolling of clouds in a dark sky above. In between the lines of an imaginary grid lies an unsettled and 'pockmarked' (2002: 237) ground. There is no single truth rooted in a deep and stable connection to place.

Hooper concludes her text on the blustery coastline of Tasmania, on the very edge of the continent where anxieties of the irrational are most clearly articulated. This reiterates the text's connection between ontology and a topography that resists the pressures of a colonial imaginary. Looking out to the stormy ocean – the space of unreason famously identified by Kant – Kate's stands on the edge of cliffs that are '[s]helves of rock, like diving boards or planks, jutted' (2002: 237) from vertical walls battered sheer by the waves, and their unpredictable rhythm. Her unstable footing on the 'windiest place in the whole world' – a wind that, blowing 'straight from Antarctica', speaks with all the spareness of this enigmatically unhomely continent – models her relation to the past. As she tips back and forward, Kate moves neither closer to nor further from a conclusion to 'the crime' but negotiates her ongoing relationship to its undisclosed dimensions that continues to destabilize the ground at her feet. Unlike Gemmell's Antarctica, these winds are not restorative. Feeling faint, as '[w]ind stung at my face', she watches and tilts with the ocean's syncopation, as waves 'now rose like walls of glass, then shattered, leaving smashed shells – or the ground-up bones of suicides – by my feet' (2002: 238).

There is nothing whole or wholesome in what the sea throws up for Kate, and *Child's Book* refuses reconciliatory poetics in its approach to Australia's badlands. Being in place, or a move towards belonging, involves a negotiation with the effects of violence and damage rather than the symbolics of restored and continuous environmental forms. While a lullaby can simultaneously speak of death and comfort in Hooper's text, the spatial spirals of vertigo express more than the subject's dislocation or ruptured belonging. In the instant between falling and hitting the ground, or tumbling from childhood into an adult realm, the ground is understood in all its promiscuity:

> From miles away all the waves rocked in with their ancient come-on, that old tease: *I-might-not-break*. If the sea is a crib endlessly rocking, don't tell me the bough won't rot, baby won't fall. How can you look down without some awareness of the end's proximity, and not be slightly seduced? Close your eyes: listen to the sea. You're so near to it – the cradle and the grave – even if you never want to die.
>
> (Hooper 2002: 238)

The 'end's proximity' is also its distance: there is no final conclusion reached. The rocking cradle suggests oscillation as it rises and falls, untethering it away from its iconic place as a stable point of beginnings. On the ground upon which Kate stands, unpredictable and unsettling, mobility does not mean moving on, or a possibility of transcendence. It is a condition of the network, a local set of relations occurring. This ground is opposed to what Robyn Dripps argues is its Western abstraction into the passive planarity of 'site'. Grounds, she argues, 'operate with great(er) nuance' than site. They 'resist hierarchy. There are no axes, centres or other obviously explicit means of providing orientation [...] (they are, instead) open networks, partial fields, radical repetition, and suggestive fragments'. Importantly, Dripps contends, within 'this textual density edges, seams, junctures, and other gaps reveal moments of fertile discontinuity where new relationships might grow' (2005: 71).

In a *Child's Book*, as in Dripps' account, topographic attunement does not secure a firm place to rest ('If everyone told the truth there'd be no surprises',

Kate's student Annaminka intuitively exclaims [Hooper 2002: 231]). This is not to say that the text rejects the possibility of meaningful relations with place. What it does suggest are the problematics of an imaginary investment in non-indigenous belonging that idealizes stable ground, a holding nation and a united society, and in which 'bad' pasts and environmental estrangement are the only things standing in its way. Place relations are negotiated with, rather than in spite of, unsettling forces, complicities and proximities. In the following chapter, I elaborate the question of time as it plays into these themes. Temporal imaginaries are imminent to spatial imaginaries in literary narratives and beyond, and in the discourses of non-indigenous belonging at the millennium, time and un/timeliness were touchstones of debate. The 'haunting' of the nation by its colonial pasts and their subjects was at play here, articulated across contexts. So was the realization that time and matter 'out of place' was not terminal or pathological, but a condition of living within the frame of the postcolonial Australian state, global modernity more widely, and in the maelstrom of history as it presents in the now.

NOTES

1. For instance, the convict Alexander Pearce who notoriously killed and ate fellow escapees.
2. See Tony Wright (2016) for context of Howard's famous metaphor for an Anglo-Celtic dominant Australia maintained through tight border control.

Chapter 7
Toxic Imaginaries: Undoing Origins and Endings

As the previous chapter discussed, Hooper depicts a world without securing limits, where effects radiate in unpredictable and generative ways. Her ambiguous ground of childhood becomings provides a challenge to non-indigenous disease focused upon national beginnings, while unsettlement is given an active force in the text: it is a mode of habitation and one that cannot know or control the totality of things. In Hooper's mobile, opaque and unresolved textual forms, possibilities for living with the risks of the present, and which bring the past close, are flagged outside a dichotomy of restitution and disabling harm. These turn our attention instead towards relationality and entanglement as the condition of being in place and in the present-with-the-past.

At the same time, her text is absent of Indigenous characters and explicit stories. It is haunted by its own spectralizing of the colonized, and we must read into the 'blood story' that the text materializes in its spatial and temporal forms. In a sense, we could say that the text's preference for *malformations* – eruption, disorientation, collapse – references its own inability to address Indigenous colonial history directly. This inability might logically be seen as a deficiency connected to caution or fear: on the one hand a perpetuation of silence, of writing Indigenous people out of the story yet again. At the same time, a counter impulse in the text is undeniably evident – like its own mobile forms, *Child's Book* pushes against a tradition of absence. 'Haunting' here means something other than teleological inevitability: the passing of something that has gone and continues to indelibly mark the future. Haunting is, instead, about mobile arrangements of place, others, and events that propel ongoing ethical provocations. As Elspeth Probyn asserts in line with this, the 'past is not there to explain the present' (1996: 113) but to generate movement, uncertainty and possibility on the assembling surface of the world.

A particular idea of time informed prevailing cultural responses to the revelations of the millennial years, and the trope of untimely, unsettled pasts that haunt the national conscience commonly characterized these. Facing 'the toxic legacy of colonialism' (McCann 2006: 54) was correspondingly positioned as the necessary path to cleaning up the nation, metaphorically and literally, in terms of environmental impacts. A well-ordered home is swept clear of untimely matter. Shame, as a manifestation of haunting, evidences an inability to keep events in their place (Schaffer 2001: 6). This chapter considers the affordances of an imaginary that works with, rather than against, this discourse and the poetic dimensions of toxicity, and returns to a discussion of McGahan's *The White Earth*, alongside Christos Tsiolkas' *Dead Europe*, in such a light.

The prevalence of haunting tropes in a narrative of national reconciliation (or its failure/refusal) accorded with correlative discourses beyond Australia, notably in other settler-colonial contexts where the still affective legacies of dispossession and colonial violence were also being appraised. In countries such as Canada, South Africa, Colombia, India and the United States, literary works were deploying ghostly thematics (for instance, Toni Morrison's *Beloved* [1988] and Arundhati Roy's *The God of Small Things* [1997]), while critical historical and postcolonial scholarship explored ideas of the spectral and upset temporalities to explore new ways of thinking about living historical legacies (the work of Avery Gordon [2011], for instance). These narratives intersected with state-initiated processes of historical reconciliation in some of these countries – such as the Canadian Royal Commission on Aboriginal People (1992) and our own *Bringing Them Home* Report – in a broader public awareness of the weight of historical wrongs driving questions of reparation and decolonization through particular tropic imaginaries: 'the ghostly, the spectral, and the uncanny' (Cameron 2008: 383).

As other critics have also pointed out (Cameron 2008; Gelder and Jacobs 1998), the ghost is problematic as a motif of traumatic legacies and historical complicity in that it reperforms an evacuation of embodied Indigenous presence. It dwells in the space of absence and erasure, even while it calls to address an historic problem. The point is that ghosts can be mobilized to suggest a past that has passed. Tim Winton's *Cloudstreet* (1991) is an example of this, where the Indigenous haunting of Cloudstreet – the 'great continent of a house' (1991: 51) – represents prior occupation, in the wake of which comes non-indigenous occupation, possession and eventually belonging once the ghost has been put to rest. This is a problem of the Western temporality that haunted imaginaries routinely subscribe to. The ghost is not just matter out of place but matter out of time. Haunting disturbs the chronological order that underscores the colonial narrative: it is a profound force of unsettlement that – even with the weight of public opinion shifting to collective acknowledgement of past, non-indigenous wrongs – in the millennial years was seen as something to ultimately overcome in a future-focused move.

A projected vision of living with the past, as part of an elaborated reconciliation process, thus articulates with classical Western ideas of artefactual history, 'speaking out' of a time that is gone. Here, touchstones of Western chronology such as origins and ruins are activated as icons of an irreducible movement forward. These, then, allow for haunting to be countenanced if it fits within a narrative of non-indigenous settlement, or of non-indigenous unsettlement that can be ultimately alleviated. So, while colonial ghost stories speak of anxious tenure on the part of the colonizer (Gelder and Jacobs 1998), they also function with the same potential as the pastoral discussed in Chapter 2: as a narrative tactic of claim. The proliferation of nineteenth-century ghosts attached to the colonial tourist trails in Australia – the mansions and iconic sites of national 'founding' such as Port Arthur – are indicative of this. Indeed, these become a further tool of erasure (as Peter Read unwittingly demonstrates in *Haunted Earth* [2003]), this time via equivalence (as Read's narratives of 'parallel' 'deep' belonging seek to acknowledge), or in many cases, via the projection of origins. The colonial ghost signals new beginnings.

The spatial stratification of the ground invested in an archaeological approach to history endorses this practice: the past is buried or layered beneath the surface of the present. Digging down uncovers and highlights descent, explaining current presence and giving an ordered genealogy to place. Lying beneath the new, the old is where it 'should' be: remembered but removed from a distinct living present. Origins are fetishized as something we have left behind and nostalgically recall, out of touch with the now. Such temporal junctures in a linear staging of history support the idea that the past is done. Calls for the nation to get over 'what happened' mobilize such discontinuity, suggesting that present social, economic, and political violence is in no way related to historical violence; that the past has no efficacy in the present; and indeed – at its extreme – that injustice no longer occurs, but is what occurred *before*.

If the present is continuously passing, then the capacity to seal oneself off from one's responsibility for harm in the world – the fantasy of immunity – is achieved. Damage will always precede the living subject's place in this temporal chain. This excludes all that is outside authorized memory, the presences that threaten to erupt through and upend dominant narratives of settlement. Kept encysted in temporal structures, the ongoing legacies of an event are, in this frame, refused outside chronology. Instead, what overspills temporal containment in the 'past' is presented as a transcendent material artefact that reasserts foundational ground rather than contesting it. Place is thus equalized and the land reduced to sameness in a continuous unfolding of the future. Sharp and heavy, these foundations speak of terminal epochs and sustain discourses of erasure, such as the 'dying race' and the climate apocalypse to come.

Cleave's depiction of a dank and empty Tasmanian landscape performs this version of time that logically moves from damage to repair, finding space for non-indigenous futures in the 'wake' of Indigenous history. The discourses of reconciliation circulating prominently in these millennial years deployed time similarly, invoking a clear future and a new nation that is beyond its past tensions and damage. John Howard's address to the 1997 Reconciliation Convention made this clear: 'We must be realistic in acknowledging some of the threats to reconciliation [...]. It will not work if it is premised solely on a sense of national guilt and shame' (1997b). In this discourse, 'haunting' is a retarding force that scrambles time and damages the possibility of non-indigenous belonging and national cohesion. Ghosts, in this sense, are far from radical eruptions; instead their invocation – the temporal and spatial form of their emergence and effects – reaffirms chronological time and its privileged imaginaries.

Temporalities of anxiety

Time is central to the pursuit of non-indigenous belonging, and to the multiple currents feeding into this in the millennial years. As I flagged in the introduction, the cultural event of the millennial period informed and was informed by a set of anxieties that accrued around its various mythical iterations: as an exceptional calendar moment; as a mystical/religious harbinger; and as a technological threat (Y2K). These can be understood in part through the long-standing investment by Western, Christian-based culture in the idea of apocalypse and the 'end of time', dating back to the twelfth century BC (Garrard 2004: 85).

Despite these theological origins, the appeal and influence of eschatological thought is strongly secular and has come to signify either the threat or supposed realization of a way of life obliterated, for instance in the discourses already attached to techno-modernity and globalization. This includes the capacity of these 'forces' to wipe away older cultural practices and values, to instil superficial and ungrounded relations between people and places, and, relatedly, to reduce existential matters and embodied community to the instrumentality of technological and market-based logic. These 'calculated asphyxiations of rampant globalization' (Dixson 1999: 6) result in what J. M. Powell termed this 'premillennial' phase, 'a global epidemic of doubt' (2000: 1–2). This, as we have seen, manifested in particular ways in an Australian context.

There is, of course, nothing 'natural' about time: concepts of temporality are structures of logic, practice and control. The prime linear model, the *chronos*, of Western temporality, as has been widely discussed in social theory, is actively universalized by systematic impositions that, as Barbara Adam writes, 'naturalize machine time' as human time. Not only has this system been 'traded globally', it has also been crucial to colonization, 'defining in and out groups, distinguishing between the developed, developing and "non-developed" world [and] designating some activities as productive while rendering others invisible' (Adam 2006: 119). In Australia, temporality is a key ontological register through which colonial power is asserted and Indigenous specificity and sovereignty denied, employing tactics such as Adam outlines.[1] More than this, though, the imposition of a colonial temporality performs its own version of historical erasure. The colonial frontier brought with it a renewed sense of time 'from the beginning', resetting an imagined local calendar to the Year Zero (Rose 1997b: 28), before which history loses consequence. This linear conception of time thus clears the ground for non-indigenous belonging and 'Australian' time. It gives shape to the nation's founding narratives.

This Year Zero, Deborah Bird Rose explains, 'cuts an ontological swathe between "timeless" land and historicized land'; 'whatever happens within that Year Zero will be disjunctive with what follows as well as what existed before. This is a moment of transcendence' (1997b: 28) – the ultimate colonial fantasy of the imperial foot striding out its claim over virgin ground. Non-indigenous presence is installed where absence is fabricated and simultaneously, Indigenous presence (read as 'pre') is placed in the land as somehow past (now disjointed from 'post'). The rhetoric of bringing light into 'dark' lands is based on this temporal structure. By forging a break between before and after, the frontier's 'progress', which leaves settlement and cultivation in its wake, positions everything else as 'behind' in a discourse of legitimacy for genocidal practices.

At the turn of the millennium, then, in a postcolonial nation such as Australia, the renewed prospect of collapsed time was potentially threatening for the non-indigenous majority who had spent the last 200 plus years constructing a new history of time in place. As Chapter 2 contended, the making of colonial place involved the actual and imagined flattening and erasure of space, opening it up for privileged forms of movement and traversal. This was a project of time-making too. It inaugurated a new epoch, a cause for both celebration (sovereign claim) and insecurity (Australia as an immature entity). The paradox at work here feeds a perpetual framing of Australia in the non-indigenous imaginary as both prehistorical (outside modern Western timescales) and belated (Carter 1994–95), as always one step (or more) behind other cultures of the West. It is this paradox that feeds negative assessments of Australian literature, pathologically consumed by 'nihilism, nothingness, the "horror of primal experience", "the terror at the basis of being"' (Carter 1994–95: 14). Such a view expresses the colonial psyche well: these 'horrors' may connect to emptiness, but this is a wilful emptiness born of repression, denial and violent complicity with what the resetting of time actually entails.

A fear of being out of time thus rubs against the cultural narrative of non-indigenous Australians as agents of temporality. Yet, even as it is unsettled (or Gelder and Jacobs would say, made uncanny), epochal thinking continues to inform narratives of non-indigenous belonging. Western epistemology generates anachronism, focusing on the spectre of 'the end' while deferring its reality. Places and times are constantly remade in an image of progress; the new is what is desired and ruins are fetishized, signalling the forward movement of time. Within this temporal structure, 'the past' is potentially facilitating or arresting. Its recollection is a performative tactic of 'moving on' (in healing discourse, for example), or a creeping force that hinders and retards requisite progress.

In this vein, the positioning of the redeemed ruin created by colonial culture, its damaging legacies, its making of wasted lives and environments as the key to national renewal and non-indigenous belonging, is a theme of millennial postcolonial narratives. It activates an imaginary of the colonizer as pollutant (Chapter 4), but also, informed by Western temporal traditions, it is shaped by a fundamental fear in the modern Western subject of 'matter out of place'. As anthropologists and cultural theorists of waste alike have argued,[2] waste confronts the boundaries of the enlightenment subject. It destabilizes categories of self/other, inside/outside and also past/future, categories that are maintained by 'waste management' practices, designed to separate the subject from its own waste, spatially and temporally. Overspill of these boundaries challenges the narrative of tactical separation based upon ontological visions, which are subsequently 'toxified' – open to pollution and challenge from outside.

McGahan's child protagonist, Will, can be read as exemplifying this toxicity in *The White Earth* as his ear literally rots, and he is consumed with nausea and fever. As he comes closer to discovering the 'secrets' of Kuran Station, his illness blossoms, the rot sets in deeper, and his world combusts in a terrifying conflagration of everything he is attached to. Similarly, Christos Tsiolkas' 2005 novel *Dead Europe*, follows a young Greek-Australian man, Isaac, in his travels around Europe as he is increasingly assailed by ghosts of the past. These ghosts are all in some way part of Isaac's inheritance, a trail between the bloody wars of Western Europe and the 'clean' untainted air of Australia. Like Will, the closer Isaac gets to his ghosts, the sicker and more deranged he and the world around him become. On his mother Reveka's return to Australia, after pursuing her son across a decaying Europe, she notes that '[t]here was no blood in the wind' here (Tsiolkas 2005: 406). The fact that both novels suggest at their conclusion that the clean Australian sky and the raised Kuran station may not be entirely free of their ghosts questions these readings, of course. Yet, the tropes of illness, toxicity and infection are instructive as the poetics of these forces – creeping and taking over different registers of bodies and spaces – indicates their resistance to chronologic fantasy.

As *The White Earth* and *Dead Europe* also indicate, ghosts represent a form of origins, and in doing so, they highlight the irony in non-indigenous Australian belonging discourse that, even as colonial culture works to rid itself of certain ghosts, others are embraced or even cultivated. This is the paradoxical result of historical erasure and the dictates of chronological time. In a landscape voided of history by the Year Zero, ghosts are valuable points of legitimacy, signalling temporal depth and genealogy, an accretion of presence in a place. As a kind of detritus of the past, they model architectural or other cultural ruins: evidence of enduring occupation with embedded narratives of 'struggle' that can feed the cause of legitimation. Yet, the isolation of the ruin as an icon of particular presence, failed or otherwise, is a narrative process. It involves the work of shutting out other presences that precede, come after, or sit alongside these stories. Time, once again, is deployed to this purpose.

The Romantic view of architectural ruins connected the enlightenment project of revelation to chronologic temporality. The ruin enabled access to past times, while also speaking of tomorrow. 'When we contemplate ruins', architectural historian Christopher Woodward insists, 'we contemplate our own future' (2001: 2). This mediating link between past and future suggests a chronology in which the ground is conceptually solid and firm. The notion of an accessible real or authentic past contained in foundations is implicated in a psychoanalytic discourse of surface and depth dichotomy, in which 'the real' resides beneath the metaphoric (or otherwise) ground. Archaeological practice was analogized by Freud in this way, wherein 'stones speak' (Freud in Woodward 2001: 55) and 'every fragment must be uncovered, studied and analysed as a piece of evidence in a larger meaning' (Woodward 2001: 55). In this perspective, the subject of history is constituted in structured, hierarchical form: its processes of 'healing' involve overcoming disconnection and, restoring fragmentary narratives to an articulate whole. The focus in psychoanalysis on the event, or 'the scene of the crime' (Ball 2000: 17), where the protective barriers of consciousness are first broken through, constructs 'an etiological reading of identity that is built around the concept of traumatic origins' (2000: 17). This suggests that 'everyone must be equally traumatized as the bedrock and result of socialization' (2000: 40) and conversely that everyone can be equally healed.

The allure of ruins in Western culture is, as critics have contended, a reactivation of apocalyptic fantasy (the breakdown of systems, structures and lives) and an aesthetized reassurance of lineage. This is the capacity of one's own 'civilization' to endure in the face of disaster, something recurrently activated according to the pressures of the time, and a fantasy wielded for Western advantage. Indigenous endurance and the 'ruins' of precolonial culture are not accorded such visibility of value. Speaking about the limit of ruins' capacity to impel responses of feeling and action in the face of climate change, Malcolm Miles suggests that 'images of ruins are seductive and lead to inaction' (2014: 73). More than this, though, the attention to ruins is inevitably selective. It extracts the material presence that is framed as 'ruin' from its entanglements in wider milieu and is blind to what the weight of its historic, aesthetized discourse obscures. In doing so, it elevates particular catastrophic events over others.

As the colonial endeavour requires that Indigenous occupation be rendered past, the visibility of the complex, historical presence of Indigenous people on the land claimed as Australia had to be actively positioned as prehistory. The non-conformity of material traces to the Romantic ruin was one way of doing so. Indigenous 'antiquity', after all, as Muecke writes, 'does not provide any "loosened building blocks" – ruins like old castles – out of which a "new order" can be constructed' (2001: 125). However, the idea that Indigenous occupation is transitory and ephemeral is a wilful mythology, as the widening scholarship on Indigenous modes of material occupation and land management practices make clear (Gunditjmara People 2010; Pascoe 2014). Indeed, the colonizer's practice of reusing Indigenous building materials for their own – exemplified in the Western Districts of Victoria, where the stones once used for Indigenous dwellings were taken for colonial fence structures, now subject to state heritage listing – indicates the narrative, as well as physical, work needed to render Indigenous presence gone without trace (Gunditjmara People 2010).

The subjective nature of 'ruins', as material traces of prior presence, only further demonstrates the problematic of an archaeological view of matter 'out of time' in which we can reach back into the past and materially encounter its reality. This is in sympathy with parallel representational discourses that accord language the power to similarly reveal meaning in the world. Both positions consider their objects of concern – language, historic traces or ruins – as conduits for positivist accounts of the world. They are extracted from the dynamic 'mesh' of a broader ecology of relations (Ingold 2011). This is the mesh that, in a different account of things, in a different imaginary, sees multiplicity and entanglement as the conditions of existence and as the dense narrative terrain of the postcolonial nation.

Rethinking ruins and origins

Despite Woodward's chronological account of the classical ruin, he also insists that 'no writer saw the same colosseum' (2001: 23); 'you can never step into the same ruin twice' (2001: 53). These concessions usefully suggest the inability of the ruin to 'speak' in any total way, or allow direct access to a particular past. They open up to the possibility of an origin that is only ever contingent and that, paradoxically, cannot be charged with a chronological weight. While the ruin can be traced to its point of construction through time and events, contact with the ruin (as the past) is situated in a present that initiates continually changing forms of relation to it. Every experience of meeting with the ruin will involve a reconfiguration, or an 'upheaval in relations of proximity', that, according to Elspeth Probyn, 'any account of the past produces' (1996: 113).

In her millennial landmark work on queer belonging (1996), Probyn offers the concept of 'suspended beginnings' (1996: 96) in place of origins and the weight of foundational narrative. This suggests the endless production of points of ontological departure. Her examination of childhood and its cultural currency as a time 'to remember' in life offers an understanding of our own beginnings, or the place from where one comes, as never directly accessible in memory. While chronology demands a solid foundation for descent, childhood for Probyn does not ground who we are in a firm and irrevocable context. It is, instead, an 'event' that in any attempt to approach its past as concrete or empirically contained will be confronted by a phantasmic reality. Childhood as an event, Probyn insists, is a 'multilevel production' and 'a tangled discursive skein' (1996: 95) that cannot be gathered together as a totalized, universal experience. The place of childhood beginnings is therefore understood as non-ordered and without hierarchy, which holds significant implications for the past in the present. If considered through this perspective, the epoch-making moment that displaces precolonial time is confronted by an unstable assemblage of singular experiences that defies a foundational account.

Indeed, official colonial history was always an elastic composition, comprising stories to and from 'home' that, as Carter points out (1999: 60), suffered serious time delays, mixed with locally generated events. As ships arrived in Australia from England, the colony constructed a local chronology based only upon the arrival of information from elsewhere, rather than the actual 'originary' time of its occurrence. From its founding, it was already out of step with its own linear narrative: not belated, but non-chronologic. While the colonial endeavour constructed its narrative of settlement, exploration and claim as a straight path to progress, empowered to cement the foundations of the 'new' world by the vested authority of the 'old', the isolation of the colony from the rest of the world meant that the formation of an historical record for Australia was, from the first, characterized by duplication, interval and disjuncture.

This revision of colonial founding refuses a view of the past, and our relations to it, that monumentalize, order, or bestow primary ground in the act of remembering. The past does not certify meaning – the *one* meaning or truth – and evades capture. Origins 'must be pried from [its] position as individualized and precious possessions' (Probyn 1996: 97). There are no solid platforms of self-evidence from which to speak. The longing for lost origins as a legible and certain ontological base is tantamount to the (colonial) need for straight, sharp lines and smooth surfaces. These material forms enact a line of descent that starts with the Year Zero, sustaining the representation of the past as over, and ideally in its place. This imaginary encysts points of crisis and locks them away, much like radioactive waste, bunkered in the earth. Such waste is imaginatively stripped of value, placed out of sight and out of mind.

As the counterpart to the commodity that operates and has value in a system of exchange, waste speaks of its residue. This is what cannot be contained in official narratives and what remains when value is extracted by those empowered to do so. 'Wasted' materials, lying about or hidden below the ground, suit an account of linearity and a discrete story of cause and effect. Yet waste constantly challenges both moral and economic values, asserting itself as material traces of what the rational principles of the market economy and traditional formulations of time exclude. It inevitably seeps through the chronologic structures of Western thought. Radioactivity, as a material force and conceptual form, offers a resistant counterpoint to the logic of temporal and spatial containment that sustains the colonial mindset.

Adam has theorized the fallout from nuclear events as a rupture to the constraints of chronology. Radiation, she asserts 'poses problems for traditional ways of knowing and relating to the world' (Adam 1998: 138). Materially present but visibly absent, thus challenging positivism's link between observable evidence and reality, radiation upsets the equation between visual apprehension and the assumption of a detached, neutral and disembodied observer. In this fantasy, which echoes the colonizers' own, the observer 'cast[s] no shadow' but instead, strides the stage as an 'externally constituted' subject. In this two-dimensional cast, 'contexts, bodies and sensualities are lost to irrelevance' (1998: 142). But the material conditions of radiation, however, insist on immersion. It flips the conditions from 'observer' to 'temporal participant' (1998: 142), which is a condition, not just of a radioactive place, but of being in the world. Radioactivity speaks metaphorically and generally, as well as specifically and materially.

The inter-implication of past/present/future, rather than their distinct separation, is evident in radioactivity that is both irreversible *and* elastic. Hidden from view and out of linear time, its effects are nonetheless present. While invisibly permeating the living world, it also materializes in ways that cannot always be predicted and that do not map onto proximal geographies. Presaging what, later, Timothy Morton would posit as the conditions of the 'hyperobject' (2013), something so significantly distributed across time and space that it exceeds any systematic attempt to map and know it, Adam describes the dispersal of radiation from a nuclear centre as inequitable, unpredictable and as 'presenting' in multiple ways.

The existence of 'radiation "hot spots"', sometimes only a matter of metres from other less contaminated areas (Adam 1998: 149), as well as the dispersal of radiation across vast distances and through various life forms (for example, traveling through waterways, or moving through the air to eventually fall as nuclear rain) indicates the untimely and indeterminate nature of radioactive fallout. Indeed, the half-life of radioactivity, and its ability to produce death 'in degrees' (1998: 144) rather than in one cataclysmic swoop, reveals diverse 'life-cycles of decay' running 'from nano-seconds to millennia' (1998: 138) that distend a linked chain of causation. The explosion itself loses its status as the point of origin back to which effects can be tracked.

Consequently, Adam argues that there can be no position outside such disaster from which to contemplate the 'event' at a remove. The permeation of the body by toxic radiation and its activation in living cells disregards a demarcation between taxonomic elements and, as it acts and impacts upon the material, radiation makes itself evident eventually and at dis-junctured times. The dispersal of radiation throughout the bodies of all life forms – entering waterways and seeping into the ground or hanging in the air to come down as nuclear rain – significantly confronts the discourse of returning the Earth to a 'pristine' state. The notion of reversibility mobilized in relation to colonial legacies becomes illusory since the interpenetration of body/environment and radiation cannot be turned back, even while its effects are not wholly known.

What Adam demonstrates in her reading of radioactivity is, in line with Probyn's account of suspended beginnings, that the impact and meaning of an event can never be wholly explained with reference to one measurable, trackable point of origin. Whenever such attempts are mobilized, be it rhetorically or physically (a delimitation of effects, for example), there will always be a remainder that falls outside. Effects continue to matter; radiation moves outward unevenly and there is no means of leaving it behind. This is what so unsettles a constituency desiring to clean up and order its past. In this alternative imaginary of colonial place, 'ruins' may take on a different meaning. This is not as talisman of origins, or the future to come, that rises directly from the past; instead, ruins cast through a radioactive imaginary signal entanglement and complicity that cannot be planned against. They reference the instability of the temporal and spatial constitution of the colonial mindset, as a condition of living in the wreckage of colonization.

Dissolving immunity

Working with rather than against this offers poetic opportunities. In what I call toxic imaginaries, an irregular ground, disconcerting proximities and infective ecologies are not an affront to progress. They are an enactment of entangled lives, and the impossibility of extracting ourselves from our shadow places/others. This makes for transcorporeal realities in which bad stuff can 'pollute for eternity' (Alaimo 2012: 487). It is fruitful to return to McGahan's *The White Earth* in light of this. Here, haunting, ghostliness and ruins are prominent tropes, and are frequently the focus of scholarly criticism of this text (Merrilees 2007; Delrez 2011). Will's narrative can be read as a story of disabling inheritance: the 'taint of "bad blood" and bad deeds reappear[ing] [...] to forecast the death of the future' (Morris 1988: 177). The protagonists' obsession with origins – John's and then, by indoctrination, Will's – expresses the colonizer's anxious need for a foundational ground that wipes away past presences. The gothic Kuran House seems an excessive performance of these origins gone bad, destabilized and ruined. As Will realizes early on, there is something hidden and horrible at the heart of this house. True to gothic convention, he defies his uncle's and the housekeeper's instructions to 'stay away from the upstairs' (McGahan 2004: 19).

In pursuit of whatever is being kept from him, Will, with stolen keys, eventually makes it into his uncle's special room and finds, in a chest, the icon of what haunts both Kuran Station and his Uncle John. It is a uniform, over eighty years old, of the Queensland Mounted Police. Vested with the authority of the uniform, John's father Daniel once rounded up, dispossessed and murdered the Indigenous people of the Kuran Downs. As Will dresses up in his great-grandfather's garments (though he is yet to discover its history), the uniform becomes a sign of inheritance, of the family's bad blood. The lock and key that hide the uniform away indicate the necessary imaginary upon which colonial culture rests, discursively containing events and their memory. Here, it seems, is an alternative origin, or causal event, of the trauma that requires repression. It is following this discovery, plagued by nausea, pain and the smell of rot, that Will determines to 'purge' himself 'of heat and dust and disease' (2004: 302), of the doubts and ghosts that trail after him on Kuran Station. 'They [...] could only be driven out by something certain and clear', he believes (2004: 293).

As Will comes to realize, however, no one version of the past or vision of the future can be trusted. Will reflects: 'Nothing was solid, not the land, and even less so its history. He had been told so many stories – but which one was he to believe? He had seen none of these events with his own eyes, walked none of the world with his own feet' (2004: 285–86). Will's justification for not knowing who to believe (a lack of accessible material evidence) is significant, not just for its rearticulation of linear logic, but also for what the reader now knows are its damaging effects. If the past is imagined to be out of touch with the subject, whether suppressed, or transcended in linear fashion, then there can be no need for acknowledgement of and redress for historical harms. Any accountability can be absolved. Despite John's instruction to Will on the importance of 'knowing where you belong and taking responsibility for that place' (2004: 109), his notion of belonging depends upon a refused recognition of the human history of the land, and a denial of complex human presences that do not fit with a linear story of settlement. The fetishization of Kuran house as a talisman of the past, for both John and Will, cannot be sustained in contemporary Australia, and the ghosts that come to Will during his hallucinatory journey through Kuran station seem to affirm this. These ghosts – the burning man, the lost explorers and the bunyip (the latter two, archetypes of the Australian colonial ghost story) – speak of a history that won't settle and disturb the colonizer's fantasy of erasure. They give voice to what Paul Carter terms 'the "hiss" of history' (1999: 15).

However, a different emphasis on spatio-temporal forms in McGahan's text opens up the question of time in the direction of networks, beyond a model of repression and eruption. The novel's opening 'event', the death of Will's father, could be considered foundational – as the traumatic moment that underscores and is the ultimate shaping force in Will's future. Yet, the poetics of this event refuse that kind of reading. They are radioactive. Will's observance of his father's death suggests a view of memory as uncontainable and untimely. No matter how much we may want the past to remain at a distance, it is still there as a force in the present, brushing against us and whispering in our ears. Recalling Astley's bacterial analogy, this is a world highly susceptible to, indeed defined by, 'mutual infection' (Bennett 2001: 168), where assemblages of matter and energy constantly shift and recombine in an endless and unpredictable flow.

Looking out one day from the back verandah, Will is surprised to see, large in the sky, 'the mushroom cloud of a nuclear explosion': 'It loomed over the house [...] great jets were arcing out from the main body, like the trails of slow meteorites. Down below, ash was beginning to fall, black flecks spiralling in the air' (McGahan 2004: 1). Later, of course, Will learns it is not a nuclear explosion that he has seen but the wake of his father's immolation. Yet, the powerful sign of the mushroom cloud remains 'loom[ing] in his memory' (2004: 2), representing disaster, loss and change, but also – in McGahan's hands – the scattering of effects, the rearranging of temporal sequence and the intangibility of memory.

Radioactivity and its miasmic residues thus confront the subject with a responsibility born from unpredictable proximity. From this initial poetic, infection and toxicity is an ongoing motif in the novel that confirms for Will his inability to escape from the weight of the past. The mystery ache and odour emanating from what he thinks is a deep rot in his brain conveys this corrosive burden. Initially, Will's contact with Uncle John and his cronies appears a catalyst for the pain, with its attendant nausea. Glimmers of other stories that his uncle does not tell him also bring it on. Standing in John's office, the administrative centre of the Australian Independence League, he notices a painting on the wall – a pastoral image of Kuran

House. As Will stares at its depiction of '[h]orses graz[ing] on long grass [...] their riders leaning easily upon their backs', from the farthest edges of the scene something else takes shape as his head begins to radiate with pain and nausea: 'Black men, looking out from the shadows [...] phantoms' (2004: 46–47). This is a past that will not go away. As Will describes, 'the ache was never acute, but it was ever present, a throb that seemed to penetrate deep within his skull' (2004: 173).

The disordered spatial relations that dizziness and nausea represent further convey a sense of uncertain memory, and a proximity to the past that profoundly unsettles. Will is unable to locate the source of the pungent smell that hangs about him, 'a scent of something rotten [...] faintly revolting but impossible to pinpoint' (2004: 250). Even though it is a part of him, emanating from his diseased ear, and even more disturbing, from his brain cavity, the site of his consciousness, 'it seemed', thinks Will, 'to come from everywhere and nowhere' (2004: 287). His belief that the scent is one of death and decay, even if he cannot trace its source, inspires his journey deep into Kuran station alone and on foot. This is a pilgrimage to what he believes is the spatial origin of all the damage and consequently the place that can redeem and heal him: the site of the Aboriginal massacre led by his great-grandfather. Yet out there, in the landscape, he becomes lost and disoriented; his ear throbs, ghosts plague him. 'Everywhere he looked there was haze and smoke, vague shifting shapes that could have been anything' (2004: 285–86). There is no clarity nor cleanliness to be found and the culmination of the journey is seemingly empty of the revelations that he desires. The secret waterhole that Uncle John has represented to Will as the sacred spring of the property is revealed to be dusty and dry.

The disease in Will's ear suggests a cohabitation of a daily and embodied attachment to origins (the fact that the infection can indeed be traced to a medically verifiable cause that disrupts his ability to perceive) and a networked refusal of foundational ground. A different kind of relation to past events is possible, McGahan recognizes. In his text, even though Will is visually confronted by evidence of the massacre and he can see and touch the bones of the traditional owners for himself, this knowledge does not prevent 'a confusing rush of violence that he could not grasp' (2004: 317). Despite all the foundational weight attributed to it, the land of Kuran Station is not solid and does not support one truth alone, of either history or identity. Will begins to recognize this as, before his eyes, the land becomes something other than certain, other than present, other than 'white'. 'Every pale tree trunk, every half-guessed clump of grass, even the chorus of cicadas – they were nothing, and yet they were something unspeakable' (2004: 315).

The bunyip-like creature that appears to Will during the height of his fever and disorientation suggests unresolved histories: 'Old things still wait', it tells him. 'In special places' (2004: 315). Ultimately, there is no one secret to uncover, no heart to penetrate in the messy narrative of Australia's colonization. Kuran House that promised so much to John and Will, eventually collapses in on itself, a burning and twisted wreck that belatedly offers the cleansing that Will has feverishly pursued (in another heightened gothic trope). However, the result is not a rebirth; there is no origin attained. Will is left damaged, physically and emotionally, and the fantasy of autochthonous claim collapses: 'All of it wasted, all of it ruined' (2004: 376). Homeless and orphaned, there seems no hope for Will except his reprieve from the violent imaginaries imposed by his Great Uncle's obsession, and the colonial cultures to which they attach. These are not the great ruins of the West, talismans of pasts that will usher in the future. They are, rather, the space of something else emerging. These are the entangled effects of a past whose origin is never firm and whose events can never be known or held in total.

Returning to Probyn's suspended beginnings, the impossibility of containing an event in a linear chain means that 'the worst thing [...] can't ever really be past' (1996: 98) since it has no fixed place in a narrative account of what happened, where and to what effect. That is, remembering involves not a direct retracing to the past, but 'a deeply disturbing experience in rearranged proximities' (1996: 114) that occur in the present. The past does not reassure us, Probyn insists. Its recollection 'is profoundly dislocating, disorientating [...] the past is bent into strange shapes so that what should be farthest away is in fact the closest' (1996: 114). This is what it means to live in history, in a toxic present, on an ever-assembling ground. The affordances of toxicity as textual form are thus profoundly discomforting. They suggest proximities and immersions that disturb as they bring things close.

Tsiolkas' *Dead Europe* asks for revisiting in these terms, too. As another non-indigenous Australian text published at the tail end of the millennial years, it is an infamously graphic, even sadistic, depiction of rapacious global capitalism and the ghosts of history that mark its shiny facades. While mostly set in Europe, the book speaks to its Australian context as it activates traditions of non-indigenous Australians 'looking back' to their generational countries of origin, in particular, the long-considered centre of Western cultural life. Critical perspectives on this text are mixed, with some scholars finding its depictions of extreme anti-Semitism disturbingly complicit to the point of reproducing and perpetuating these views. Isaac, the young photographer who heads to Europe like so many second- and third-(and more) generation Australians during the unsettled years of his early adulthood, is as horrified by the racism that seems endemic to European sociality as he is willing to give voice to these prejudices himself.

Robert Manne's critique of the text understands Isaac's anti-Semitism as a cynical co-option of a specific and overwhelming history of racist violence and murder to explore a more general 'weight of the past' (2005). Manne reads Isaac's expressions of anti-Semitism as a reaction to the oppressive, unmoveable weight of the Holocaust, and its ongoing demand for shame and repentance by non-Jews. This is evidenced by the 'exterminatory desires' that Isaac expresses on walking through the Venetian Jewish ghettos and reading in an old Jewish man's face the mark of 'eternal exhausting vengeance': 'For one deranged, terrified moment – I promise only a moment, it passed, I willed it away immediately – I wished that not one Jew had ever walked on the face of the earth' (Tsiolkas 2005: 158). Thus, Manne argues, 'if [Isaac] is to flourish, it is from this burden that he must be freed' (2005). In Manne's interpretation, 'the Jews' bear responsibility for Isaac's entrapment in history. Isaac describes Jewish characters as vampires, cursed and vengeful – the same elderly man bites Isaac's hand, spits in his face, and hisses "a continuous low sound that cautioned and threatened like a snake". The decrepitude of the water-eaten city is echoed in the man's "decaying dying face"' (Tsiolkas 2005: 154). When Isaac returns to his hotel he notices that the teeth 'marks on my wrist were burning' (2005: 158).

Catherine Padmore agrees that the depiction of Jews in *Dead Europe* is stereotypical and alienating, and certainly, as we are distanced from Jewish characters by Isaac's focalization, we are potentially refused from counter engagements with, or understandings of, Jewish experience. However, Padmore's take on the novel's performance of anti-Semitism is different to Manne's. She sees the novel not as participating uncritically in racist sentiment, but as exposing what she calls the 'viral' capacities of anti-Semitism and racial hatred, how it infects and moves through times, families, communities and populations (Padmore 2008). This offers another way to understand the vampiric figures that stalk Tsiolkas' text: the trope of infection – of being bitten and thus tainted with the capacity to hate. This, the novel suggests, can also be understood through this history, as it presents a modern Europe laced through with a premodern world of superstition and the claims of inheritance that bind more and more tightly to Isaac. His family, we are told, is cursed, tainted with legacies of sexual violence, murder and anti-Semitism, and the ambiguity of Isaac's genealogy plays with the notion of 'bad' blood carried through the generations.

For it is not just others who manifest vampiric tendencies: Isaac himself metaphorically, and eventually literally, feasts on the vulnerable. His modes of exploitation grow, from photographing unwitting subjects, to wielding uneven sexual power, and finally, literally drawing on the blood of others. Isaac does not simply document the degeneracy and collapse of contemporary Europe, however, he is an active participant in a world full of damage, filth, horror and alienation. This is 'discrepant cosmopolitanism' (McCann 2010) exposed: the parasitic nature of global capital at work in the fantastic cities of the West, animated, paradoxically, by the deadening effects of consumerist excess and the abjection of others. The illegal migrants that Isaac encounters in Gerry's warehouse recall Agamben's 'bare life' subjects (1995), reduced to base material conditions without the protection of the law. In the red-light district of Amsterdam, Isaac narrates, in a monotone voice evocative of the undead:

> I will walk among schizophrenic homeless men and women and their snarls for money will appal me and I will understand the urge to wipe them off the face of the earth. I will enter a porn cinema and have sex with three men [...] I wish to have my fill of bodies, to consume and devour. I will be the first to come and as I spray my scent on the face of the pale-skinned German, he will reach out for my hand and I will slap it away.
>
> (Tsiolkas 2005: 302)

As McCann points out, the vampire is the emblem of capitalist culture, identified by Marx. The 'death' of Marxism under the ascendency of fragmented capital and individualistic culture leaves unchecked stark divides between the elite and the abject. Older and more recent histories of violence and destruction – the brutality of premodern Europe, World War II, the Greek civil war – hang heavy over Europe, refusing to rest. Tsiolkas literalizes this haunting through the spectres that populate the text, most prominently the ghoul-boy, Elias, who shadows Isaac closely all the way back to Australia. *Dead Europe* offers a kind of inverted bildungsroman, in which Isaac's journey is one of violent undoing as the past begins to overwhelm him. The reader is positioned inside this experience, via his first-person narration, profoundly visceral and transcorporeal, and spatial forms of crossing, contamination and entanglement:

> There are prostitutes outside the closed gates of the Earls Court tube station. I sniff. Rats and sewage, shit and piss and blood, it is all coursing beneath my feet [...] I can see the blinking lights of an off-licence. I can hear the thump-thump of music. I walk past each of the women. I am smelling them, testing their odour. I am not interested in their appearance. The first woman smells of heroin [...]. The second woman smells of decaying flesh. I know at once that she is dying. The third woman's odour is soft and appealing.
>
> (Tsiolkas 2005: 375)

The text is intensely sensorial, centralizing bodily responses and encounters – sex, desire, pleasure, drug use: bodies are vital, as well as abused and debased, and are a primary means of negotiating and knowing the world. Moreover, the text moves restlessly between times and places (back and forth between pre-civil war time and contemporary Europe, and in and out of Isaac's life growing up in Australia;

and through Greece, to Venice, Vienna, Prague, Paris and London – a perverted grand tour); there are no firm edges. Everything bleeds, shifts and transmits. Elias seems to dissolve into Isaac, and we are left at the text's conclusion with a vision of the spectre wrapping himself around Reveka, the protagonist's mother, who has made a deal with the Devil to 'save' her still-vampiric son (feeding on his family's blood on the journey back to Australia) and take on his burden.

This is a toxic imaginary at work, where we cannot disentangle from the things that haunt us. The text suggests specific historical traumas that continue to have effects: the trauma of war and violence, of incest and rape; trauma of migration, forced or otherwise; exile, alienation and the ambiguity of home. In this maelstrom, Isaac recognizes his alienation as a second-generation Australian migrant. Europe, the touchstone for his parents, and for the Australian non-indigenous consciousness more generally, is no longer the answer: decayed, depraved, chaotic and fragmented, broken by the rise of neo-Nazism, disenfranchised populations, poverty, and inequities: 'Greece is dying [...] this is Europe now' (2005: 135). Australia's relationship with this 'centre' ('imagine that, he kept repeating, two thousand years. What does this country have to offer that is that old? Nothing. Fucking Nothing. We are going back to real history' [2005: 6]) seems radically reoriented. Australia's Indigenous past, is of course, written out of Isaac's appraisal.

Isaac expresses the paradoxical self-consciousness of the modern non-indigenous Australian, craving escape from the anxiety of youth yet desirous for new futures, clear of the past. This Australia is innocent and, as a result, anachronistic: '[T]he Greece I knew in Australia was indeed largely irrelevant to these modern Europeans' (2005: 35). Reveka's sense that there is no 'blood on the wind' when she lands in Melbourne with her son at the end of Isaac's journey speaks to the complex positioning of Australia in relation to Europe, which allows for fantasies of strategic separation and denial. And yet Australia, as a colonial artefact and ongoing colonizing culture, is absolutely a product of global modernity and far from innocent. We must read the complicities of parasitic capitalism in the colonial endeavour itself. Its legacies are global ones, locally rendered. As Padmore writes of the text's insistence on viral complicities, the racist is *not* other, it is us (2008: 443). Here, we are returned to Val Plumwood's vision of a world dense with shadow places that connect into the shiny centres of urban modernity. *Dead Europe* moves amongst the underside of the West, which reaches all the way to sunny Australia. The book's eruptions of bodily fluid, violence, racist vitriol and chaos contest the modern capitalist dream of unhindered mobility, freedom and choice: it also materializes our entanglements in the violence done to distant (or near) and invisible others.

The text undercuts its representation of an untainted Australia. Here, old and new violence belies a 'vigorous, juvenile sky' (Tsiolkas 2005: 375): asylum seeker children are kept prisoner 'out in the desert' (a reference to the Howard government's policy of 'illegal' asylum seeker detention at the time) (2005: 342); racism, colonial brutality and violence produce abject, disenfranchised bodies, subjected to the 'bare life' denial of rights (as the 2007 Northern Territory 'Intervention' into remote Indigenous communities would soon show). Is Australia really so different to elsewhere, Tsiolkas asks? Does it have the same destiny of 'the end of time' awaiting it? The crisis at the heart of this book is diffuse, but it is also ongoing, as Isaac relates: 'I was conscious of a gnawing in my stomach. It stirred, it was a living organism within me, and I knew, even as I begged it not to be so, that it was stirring, that it would seep through the lining of my stomach and into my blood'. 'It was an appetite' (2005: 353), we might imagine, for more and more consumption – the bloated excesses of material acquisition, the exploitation of others in visible and invisible networks across the world and a continued resistance to the contours of the ground. In this way, the book is not about what was but what will be. 'Isaac had not photographed the past, he had captured the future' (2005: 405), where fantasies of tactical separation between individuals, between times and places, cannot endure.

This is the toxicity of the past, active in the present and the enfolded, but not conclusive or predictable, relationships between places, times and bodies, human and non-human, that constitute our world. The temporal-spatial unsettlements of the radioactive event open up space and time to porous exchange, with resultantly reoriented proximities and therefore responsibilities. In line with Derrida's hauntology, 'haunting' in toxic imaginaries does not model repression and return. Repression is not possible in such a network of actors and energies. Radioactivity as haunting emphasizes ever-presence in a network of rearranging bodies and effects. Ghosts are with us because we lack immunity to the past overspilling its boundaries. In both McGahan's *White Earth* and Tsiolkas' *Dead Europe* this is clear. Will and Isaac, in their very different narratives, are disoriented talismans of the future, centralizing uncertainty for non-indigenous Australians as the only way of being here, into the next millennium. Just what form this uncertainty takes is a matter of imaginaries, as we realize we're all tangled up with each other. This is where hope lies, in rethinking relations with place from here.

NOTES

1. Emma Kowal makes the point that time is still used by progressives to pathologize and paternalize Indigenous others, excluding them from the time of modernity (2011).
2. For instance, Mary Douglas (*Purity and Danger* [1966]) and Gay Hawkins (*The Ethics of Waste* [2006]).

Afterword: Postcolonial Atmospheres

This book began in a particular place and time: the sun-drenched tents of Adelaide Writers' Week, as a group gathered to hear Drusilla Modjeska call on millennial Australian literature to do the particular work of shoring up the ground. It ends somewhere else, with another gathering place – Federation Square in the centre of Melbourne – six years later, and in a moment that signalled an apparently different political time. Here, on 13 February 2008 former prime minister Kevin Rudd was beamed in from Canberra as he issued a formal state apology to the victims of the Stolen Generations, acknowledging the ongoing intergenerational effects of removing Indigenous children from their families, communities and country. His clear statement of 'Sorry' as an official position of the Australian Government countered the prolonged stance of his predecessor John Howard, who he had beaten in a resounding victory the previous November. The Apology was prioritized as one of the first acts of the new parliament.

Eight thousand people came together at Federation Square to watch the Prime Minister's apology speech, connected via television cameras to the tens of thousands gathering elsewhere across the country. Rudd called on non-indigenous Australians to bring their imaginations to bear on the experience of Indigenous Australians subjected to these practices – to empathically engage and to inhabit the injustices they had suffered. Many people at Federation Square cried, Indigenous and non-indigenous, as they did elsewhere across Australia. There were cheers and a feeling of transformative shifts in a previously intractable polity, refusing to let go of erroneous non-indigenous fantasies of colonial nobility, benevolence and civilizing authority. More than a decade on from this, however, these same fantasies hold strong.

Political leaders continue to pitch a vision of the national project in Australia as ultimately well-intentioned, without the need for shame: '[W]e should be proud of our history', the then prime minister Malcolm Turnbull declared in 2017 (Murphy 2017). Not long after this, Turnbull's predecessor, Tony Abbott, claimed that 'it's hard to imagine a better Australia in the absence of the Western civilization that began here' (Abbott 2018). A series of defacements of public statues memorializing Captain Cook, as the explorer who 'discovered Australia', with protest statements such as 'no pride in genocide' and 'a racist endeavour' (referencing the name of Cook's ship, the first colonizing vessel to reach Australian shores) have been decried as 'totalitarian' acts, 'trashing our national heritage' (Knaus 2017; Hinchliffe 2018; Hocking 2019). Scott Morrison, who was to become Prime Minister in 2018, tweeted in response to a defaced statue in Sydney's Hyde Park, that such protest '[d]oes not keep one Indigenous child safe, in school, or end up in a job' (AAP 2017).

These indignant voices from the apex of political and cultural power in the country demonstrate that what in the early millennial years seemed an extreme reaction against Indigenous recognition has become normalized amongst non-indigenous political leaders. Pauline Hanson, back for a second political career, is 'now indistinguishable from mainstream politicians' (Quiggin 2019). Other racisms have only intensified, too. 'Islamophobia', as Hage calls it, manifests in a fear of 'homegrown terrorists': the ultimate 'ungovernable waste' that threatens to overwhelm (Hage 2017: 48). Interlaced with this is the continuing abjection of asylum seekers, still detained off-shore or precariously located on-shore on temporary visas for the rhetorical purpose of 'border protection' (Australian Border Force 2019). These communities, displaced from their homes and un-homed in the country from which they sought asylum, experience the reality of not/belonging as a profoundly structural position. For some there are inviolate borders that forbid their belonging. For others, borders are permeable. A 'largely white upper class [...] [is] made to feel truly at home in the world', in contrast to billions of others (Hage 2017: 39).

Indigenous activism and scholarship in the intervening years since the millennium has intensified its criticism of the 'recognition' paradigm that informed the post-Mabo years (and the Mabo decision itself), pointing to the structural harms that persist despite gestures of acknowledgement and apology in settler-colonial contexts (Liddle and Mason 2016; Araluen Corr 2018; Coleman 2019). These writers point out that recognition does not necessarily demand the remaking of the system. As Glen Coulthard expresses in the Canadian First Nations context, 'colonial powers will only recognize the collective rights and identities of Indigenous peoples insofar as this recognition does not throw into question the background legal, political and economic framework of the colonial relationship itself' (2014: 451). In Australia, this is exemplified by the fact that the landmarks of historical reckoning in the millennial years have not resulted in improved socio-economic circumstances for Indigenous people. The statistics of serious Indigenous disadvantage remain – lower life expectancy, poor health outcomes, lower levels of literacy and qualifications. There are now double the number of Indigenous children in out of home care than at the time of the Apology (Wahlquist 2018).

In May 2017, 'The Uluru Statement from the Heart', a call for constitutional reform issued by a group of 250 Indigenous delegates at the First Nations National Constitutional Convention held at Uluru, set out a proposal for full Indigenous participation in constitutional processes in an effort to counter systemic disadvantage. The delegates mapped out three key steps for participation, including a voice in the parliament, at the centre of government power. Despite then Prime Minister Turnbull's tacit support for the convention and the project of constitutional change, he quickly dismissed the Uluru Statement and its vision for reform, stating that the 'government does not believe such an addition to our national representative institutions is either desirable or capable of winning acceptance in a referendum' (Grattan 2017). Conservative columnists rejoiced, evoking the dichotomous language of the Howard years: '[T]he Uluru Statement will divide us as a nation', wrote non-indigenous commentator Andrew Bolt. 'Say no to racism. Say no to this latest plan by Aboriginal activists to change our constitution to divide us by race' (Bolt 2017).

I recount these developments at the end of this book to indicate how the millennial years – 'the era when the anxieties of settler colonial belonging were laid bare' (Slater 2018: 35) – continue to stretch, discursively, and practically, into the contemporary moment. That history, like all others, does not end when we stop telling a particular story of a particular time. Indigenous dispossession is ongoing in Australia, sustained by capitalist-colonial socio-political, economic and imaginary structures that continue to deny Indigenous sovereignty and maintain colonial visions of a land 'open' to development and resource extraction: a land on which settler-colonial subjects can find firm ground. This fantastic vison is stretching thin as the world warms, Australian rivers runs dry and species disappear. At the same time, new generations of Indigenous activists and thinkers, building on the legacies of their forebears, are mobilizing unprecedented resistance to the prevailing settler-colonial paradigm still so informed by Howard's Australia, and behind this, myopic colonial visions of an empty land, passively open to exploitation. The 'Invasion Day' protests, held around the country on 26 January, Australia Day, are now large-scale events drawing tens of thousands of Indigenous and non-indigenous people, walking together in opposition to the continuing situation of Indigenous disempowerment and disadvantage by the state that still fails to acknowledge Indigenous sovereignty. Refusing the terms of the settler-colonial state (Simpson 2014), voices of Indigenous people are claiming sovereignty through a range of practices and tactics, and rejecting 'the will of Western Enlightenment desire to violently translate Indigenous knowledge through its own taxonomy' (Hokowhitu 2016: 163).

What role has non-indigenous literature to play in these happenings, particularly when the non-indigenous voice has claimed so much already? How this book has attempted to answer this question is through the matter of imaginaries, which provide both limitations and possibilities to political futures. Imaginaries give shape to our making of, and acting in, the world, and the poetic forms and discourses that generate and sustain these are far from benign. Indeed, they can enable and legitimize violence and exclusion. The pre-eminence of certain imaginaries in the making of Australia found renewed expression in the millennial years, as the non-indigenous majority experienced a destabilization of the narratives through which they made sense of and formed attachments to place. Literary works, and the cultural expectations surrounding them, took a focus in the debates amongst non-indigenous Australians over how their belonging might be forged (or otherwise), in light of the domestic and global pressures that spotlighted the insecurity of dominant ways of being in place and the ontological implications of this. The legal and moral ramifications of the Mabo decision and the other landmark challenges to the national conscience, the unfolding reality of climate change, and the increasing alienations of capitalist modernity intersected in these expressions of disconcertion that more often than not folded back into a logic all too familiar to the colonial mind: of an individual claiming the stage alone and seeking to quell disquiet by a refusal to engage with the literal and metaphoric ground beneath their feet.

New imaginaries are needed that break from a hermetic, colonial vision for non-indigenous narratives, imaginaries informed by a reorientation of thought around time, place and the question of origins. This is an ethical imperative beyond the service of non-indigenous storytelling. It is a task that responds to the correlate place-making of this in which everyone is enrolled, and more broadly to the endemic violence of the colonial project itself: its power to install absence and control presence via exclusive temporalities and spatial practices. Other non-indigenous imaginaries were active in these years, however, as I hope I have demonstrated, brushing against the impulse to secure and smooth out.

Despite the continued investment in the idea that stories can instruct and perhaps even save us, they cannot. Stories will not secure new conditions. However, this is a source of possibility: stories are themselves active in the unfolding of things. Because of this they offer no straight map to the future. Instead, they participate in the world as it is happening. This is why the stories that we tell, from novels, to public declarations, to the poetics that literally shape our places, matter so greatly. To return to the ground at Federation Square, as the crowd listened to Kevin Rudd's words they also moved across an uneven surface that rippled with text and spatial forms. The ground here is an artwork, by Paul Carter, titled *Nearamnew*. Made of pink Kimberley sandstone from Western Australia, the work moves in swirls and flows that trace out the shape of Lake Tyrrell, a large salt-lake almost 400 kilometres away in the Mallee country north-west of Melbourne. Frequently dry, and far from the European model of a lake that it was (like so many others) hoped to be, Lake Tyrrell's salt crystals often radiate a similar, luminous pink.

Nearamnew along with the Square itself was commissioned to commemorate the one-hundred-year anniversary of Federation in Australia. In keeping with Carter's practice, it incorporates the traces of many place stories associated with the history of the site, evoking the federal constellation of the local, the regional and the global in its forms. Nine large irregularly shaped text boxes connect across the plaza, constituting the medium scale, and recalling the system of creeks and waterholes that, before colonial intervention, once fed into what is now the Yarra River flowing alongside Federation Square. Within these boxes are local stories in poetic compositions by Carter, drawn from historical records. These appear in carved stone words that are frequently incomplete and only partially decipherable. They include stories of the Kulin nation, who gathered on the banks of the Yarra for generations prior to colonization; of encounters between Kulin members and the colonizers; of the post-war arrival of migrants to Melbourne; of the particular experience of women and children; of labourers – of the many lives that have constellated in the imaginary and physical space of the nation. The global register is the lake form itself. It was derived by Carter from a Wergaia bark etching taken in the Lake Tyrrell area during the late nineteenth century, and now housed in the National Gallery of Victoria. The etching depicts the lake in flood, an event that seems near impossible now given the droughts to which the Mallee is increasingly prone. Climate change is predicted to see an intensification of water shortages, temperature rises and the region's infamous dust storms in an agricultural area long vulnerable to the unsuitability of its environment to intensive farming. In 2009, some Victorian Mallee communities were counted as Australia's first climate change refugees (Ker 2009).

The presence of Lake Tyrrell in the centre of Melbourne reminds us that places and histories are mobile, and in frequently disarming ways. The pink sandstone whorls may be striking in their aesthetics and highlight a local past dense with life and cross-cultural engagements, but they also recall places elsewhere, shadow places, that are depleted and damaged by the networks in which they are enrolled, and that they help sustain. This includes the Kimberley quarry from which the stone was taken and transported 4,500 kilometres away, and the Mallee, of course, whose agricultural colonization was a narrative, as much as a practical, process, identified as a region awaiting utilization, 'one of the most barren environments in the world' (Pierce 1987: 234) that, through endeavour and labour, could be conquered. As the dust storms, drought and mice plagues hit, this narrative proved steely, although declining and economically stressed populations across the region might also tell a different story.

The Melbourne air has long played host to the Mallee too, with topsoil from parched farms to the north (including the adjacent Wimmera country) periodically blowing down with such force that it passes through the city and across the Bass Strait to Tasmania. We might bring other aerial minglings into this picture, too, such as the radioactive cloud that floated across Melbourne in October 1956, having already moved through the air of Adelaide on its way from Maralinga, the site of the secret British atomic testing program, one of many ways in which these cities come together. Maralinga, a place that remains highly toxic and uninhabitable to its people dispossessed by the British tests (although with insufficient warnings of what the contaminating legacies would be) is another shadow place that entangles in the making of contemporary Australia. We need stories that acknowledge and work with these constitutive forms rather than deny them. These forms gesture towards what might be called a postcolonial atmosphere, an illumination of an inherently 'shared climate' (Sloterdijk 2005: 946) mobilized by entangled lives, energies and affects across times and spaces. In this atmosphere, non-indigenous centricity, spatio-temporal command and binary thinking have no stable ground. Instead, the dynamics of being-together come to the fore, the surprising, risky and disorienting 'co-produced reality' (Weir 2015: 17) that is coexistence, 'the difficult, never settled issues of our being together' (Larsen and Johnson 2017: 10). A poetics that accounts for this opens its politics to decolonization.

To return to Federation Square, on the day of the Apology, we can see the potential for a different imaginary that begins on the ground, in the folds of mobile feet, pink Kimberley sandstone, and the assembling stories that, with varying degrees of visibility, track through the space. Some are composed as fragments in rock, some spoken on screens, others in the process of writing as thousands of people, physically and virtually came together. These remain active, despite the regressions of the Australian state since, and the persistence of non-indigenous narratives that sustain its current power. The ground, in its many dimensions, is where we must look, for here dynamics become perceptible, and instability is a condition that is shared, though with vastly differing consequences. While postcolonial Australia continues to cling onto stories that support its founding logic, efforts to expose these patterns of thought and the complicity of poetics initiates new conversations much more responsive to the contemporary moment, as climate change manifests as an imminent, and for some, already arrived, dispossessing force. The Uluru statement from Indigenous leaders issued an invitation to non-indigenous Australians to 'walk with us in a movement of the Australian people for a better future' (Referendum Council 2017). This, of course, is impossible if that cohort – of which I am one – remain imaginatively tethered to the spot, afraid of moving with an unpredictable ground. Letting go means narrating ourselves differently, across a field of texts and their recomposing forms. For this we need stories that admit to a world in which our shadows are with us rather than erased.

References

AAP (2017), 'Captain Cook statue vandalized in Melbourne before Australia Day', *The Guardian*, 25 January, https://www.theguardian.com/australia-news/2018/jan/25/captain-cook-statue-vandalised-in-melbourne-before-australia-day. Accessed 28 January 2019.

Abbott, Sally (2017), *Closing Down*, Sydney: Hachette Australia.

Abbott, Tony (2018), 'Australia Day debate: There are 364 other days to wear a black armband', *The Honorable Tony Abbott MP*, 22 January, http://tonyabbott.com.au/2018/01/australia-day-debate-364-days-wear-black-armband. Accessed 16 February 2018.

Adam, Barbara (1998), 'Radiated identities: In pursuit of the temporal complexity of conceptual cultural practices', in M. Featherstone and S. Lash (eds), *Spaces of Culture: City-Nation-World*, London and Thousand Oaks, CA: Sage, pp. 138–58.

—— (2006), 'Time', *Theory, Culture and Society*, 23:2&3, pp. 119–26.

Adams, Phillip (2000), 'The boy from the bush', *The Weekend Australian*, 30–31 March, p. 24.

—— (2001), 'A vote for division', *The Weekend Australian*, 17–18 November, p. 32.

Agamben, Giorgio (1995), *Homo Sacer: Sovereign Power and Bare Life*, Stanford, CA: Stanford University Press.

—— (2005), *State of Exception* (trans. Kevin Attell), Chicago, IL and London: University of Chicago Press.

Alaimo, Stacey (2012), 'States of suspension: Trans-corporeality at sea', *ISLE: Interdisciplinary Studies in Literature and Environment*, 19:3, pp. 476–93.

Amsterdam, Stephen (2009), *Things We Didn't See Coming*, Collingwood, Vic.: Sleepers Publishing.

Anderson, Ben and McFarlane, Colin (2011), 'Assemblage and geography', *Area*, 43:2, pp. 124–27.

Anderson, Jon (2014), *Page and Place: Ongoing Compositions of Plot*, Amsterdam and New York: Rodopi.

Araluen Corr, Evelyn (2018), 'Silence and resistance: Aboriginal women working within and against the archive', *Continuum*, 32:4, pp. 487–502.

Armstrong, Gillian (1979), *My Brilliant Career*, Australia: New South Wales Film Corporation and Margaret Fink Productions.

Arthur, Paul Longley (1999), 'Imaginary conquests of Australia', *Journal of Australian Studies*, 61, pp. 136–42.

Astley, Thea (1999), *Drylands*, Camberwell, Vic.: Penguin.

Atwood, Bain (ed.) (1996), *In the Age of Mabo: History, Aborigines and Australia,* St Leonards, NSW: Allen and Unwin.

Australian Border Force (2019), 'Australian Border Force – home page', Commonwealth of Australia, https://www.abf.gov.au/. Accessed 28 January 2019.

Ball, Karyn (2000), 'Trauma and its institutional destinies', *Cultural Critique*, 46:Autumn, pp. 1–44.

Barad, Karen (2003), 'Posthumanist performativity: Toward an understanding of how matter comes to matter', *Signs*, 28:3, pp. 801–31.

Baudrillard, Jean (1983), *Simulations* (trans. Paul Foss, Paul Patton and Philip Beitchman), New York: Semiotext(e).

Bennett, Jane (2001), *The Enchantment of Modern Life: Attachments, Crossings, and Ethics*, Princeton, NJ: Princeton University Press.

—— (2012), 'Systems and things: A response to Graham Harman and Timothy Morton', *New Literary History*, 43.2, pp. 225–33.

Birch, Tony (1996), '"A land so inviting and still without any inhabitants": Erasing Koori culture from (post-)colonial landscapes', in K. Darian-Smith, L. Gunner and S. Nuttall (eds), *Text, Theory, Space: Land, Literature and History in South Africa and Australia*, London and New York: Routledge, pp. 173–88.

Birns, Nicholas (2015), *Contemporary Australian Literature: A World Not Yet Dead*, Sydney: Sydney University Press.

Blainey, Geoffrey (2001), *This Land is All Horizons: Australian Fears and Visions*, Boyer Lectures, Sydney: ABC.

Bolt, Andrew (2017), 'Uluru Statement will divide us as a nation', *Herald Sun*, 31 May, http://www.heraldsun.com.au/news/opinion/andrew-bolt/andrew-bolt-this-new-racism-is-just-apartheid/news-story/764994b3c51665da3080b38aac2901a0?memtype=anonymous. Accessed 5 March 2018.

Bradford, Clare (2008), 'The homely imaginary: Fantasies of nationhood in Australian and Canadian texts', in M. Reimer (ed.), *Home Words: Discourses of Children's Literature in Canada*, Waterloo, Ont.: Wilfrid Laurier University Press, pp. 177–93.

Brattland, Camilla, Kramvig, Britt and Verran, Helen (2018), 'Doing Indigenous methodologies: Toward a practice of the "careful partial participant"', *ab-Original: Journal of Indigenous Studies and First Nations and First Peoples' Cultures*, 2:1, pp. 74–96.

Brennan, Frank (1995), *One Land, One Nation: Mabo Towards 2001*, St Lucia, Qld.: University of Queensland Press.

Brett, Judith (1997), 'John Howard, Pauline Hanson and the politics of grievance', in G. Gray and C. Winter (eds), *The Resurgence of Racism: Howard, Hanson and the Race Debate*, Clayton, Vic.: Monash Publications in History, pp. 7–28.

Buell, Frederick (2003), *From Apocalypse to Way of Life: Environmental Crisis in the American Century*, New York: Routledge.

Bull, Malcolm (2007), 'Vectors of the biopolitical', *New Left Review*, 45:May–June, http://www.newleftreview.org/?page=article&view=2667. Accessed 13 May 2017.

Burke, Anthony (2001), *In Fear of Security: Australia's Invasion Anxiety*, Annandale, NSW: Pluto Press.

Cameron, Emilie (2008), 'Indigenous spectrality and the politics of postcolonial ghost stories', *Cultural Geographies*, 15, pp. 383–93.

Cappiello, Rosa (1984), *Oh Lucky Country* (trans. Gaetano Rando), St Lucia, Qld.: University of Queensland Press.

Carroll, John (2001), *The Western Dreaming: The Western World is Dying for Want of a Story*, Sydney: HarperCollins.

Carson, Rachel (1962), *Silent Spring*, Boston, MA: Houghton Mifflin.

Carter, David (1994–95), 'Modernity and belatedness in Australian cultural discourse', *Southerly*, 54:4, pp. 6–18.

Carter, Paul (1988), *The Road to Botany Bay: An Exploration of Landscape and History*, New York: Knopf.

—— (1996), *The Lie of the Land*, London: Faber and Faber.

—— (1999), *Lost Subjects*, Lyndhurst, NSW: Historic Houses Trust of NSW.

—— (2002), *Repressed Spaces: The Poetics of Agoraphobia*, London: Reaktion.

—— (2009), *Dark Writing: Geography, Performance, Design*, Honolulu: University of Hawai'i Press.

Case, Jo (2011), 'Aborigines, sharks and Australian accents: On Australian writing', *Kill Your Darlings*, 6:July, pp. 40–51.

Cathcart, Michael (2009), *Water Dreamers: The Remarkable Dry History of Our Continent*, Melbourne: Text Publishing Company.

Clarke, Marcus (1880), 'Preface', in A. L. Gordon, *Poems of the Late Adam Lindsay Gordon*, Melbourne: A. H. Massina.

Coleman, Claire (2017), *Terra Nullius*, Sydney: Hachette Australia.

—— (2018), 'The credibility gap', *The Saturday Paper*, 17 February, https://www.thesaturdaypaper.com.au/edition/2018/02/17. Accessed 18 February 2018.

—— (2019), 'This is not about grog, it's about depression, hopelessness, and failed government', *The Guardian*, 20 January, https://www.theguardian.com/australia-news/2019/jan/20/this-is-not-about-grog-its-about-depression-hopelessness-and-failed-government. Accessed 27 January 2019.

Collingwood-Whittick, Sheila (ed.) (2007), *The Pain of Unbelonging: Alienation and Identity in Australasian Literature*, Amsterdam and New York: Rodopi.

Collins, Felicity and Davis, Therese (2004), *Australian Cinema after Mabo*, Cambridge: Cambridge University Press.

Collins, Paul (2002), 'A journey through hell's gate', *The Age*, 29 October, p. 13.

Collis, Christy (1999), 'Mawson's hut: Emptying post-colonial Antarctica', *Journal of Australian Studies*, 23, pp. 22–29.

Coombes, Brad, Johnson, Jay T. and Howitt, Richard (2012), 'Indigenous geographies II: The aspirational spaces in postcolonial politics – Reconciliation, belonging and social provision', *Progress in Human Geography*, 37:5, pp. 691–700.

Coulthard, Glen (2014), *Red Skin, White Masks: Rejecting the Colonial Politics of Recognition*, Minneapolis, MN: University of Minnesota Press.

Crane, Kylie (2014), 'Visions, vellum and pastoral transpositions', *Journal of Ecocriticism*, 6:1, p. 12.

Crouch, David (2007), 'National hauntings: The architecture of Australian ghost stories', *JASAL: Journal of the Association for the Study of Australian Literature*, special issue, *Spectres, Screens, Shadows, Mirrors*, pp. 95–105, https://openjournals.library.sydney.edu.au/index.php/JASAL/article/view/9642. Accessed 22 April 2019.

Crowe, Shaun (2014), '"Team Australia": A nationalism framed in terms of external threats', *The Conversation*, 18 September, https://theconversation.com/team-australia-a-nationalism-framed-in-terms-of-external-threats-31630. Accessed 13 May 2017.

Curthoys, Ann (1999), 'Expulsion, exodus and exile in white Australian historical mythology', *Journal of Australian Studies*, 23:61, pp. 1–18.

Darwin, Charles and Beer, Gillian (1998), *The Origin of Species*, Oxford: Oxford University Press.

Davidov, Veronica (2015), 'Beyond formal environmentalism: Eco-nationalism and the "ringing cedars" of Russia', *Culture, Agriculture, Food and Environment: The Journal of Culture and Agriculture*, 37:1, pp. 2–13.

Davidson, Robyn (1980), *Tracks*, London: J. Cape.

Davis, Mark (1997), *Gangland: Cultural Elites and the New Generationalism*, St Leonards, NSW: Allen and Unwin.

Deitering, Cynthia (1996), 'The postnatural novel: Toxic consciousness in fiction of the 1980s', in C. Glotfelty and H. Fromm (eds), *The Ecocriticism Reader: Landmarks in Literary Ecology*, Athens and London: University of Georgia Press, pp. 196–203.

Delrez, Marc (2011), '"Twisted ghosts": Settler envy and historical resolution in Andrew McGahan's *The White Earth*', *Cross/Cultures*, 136, pp. 191–204.

Department of Climate Change and Energy Efficiency (2010), 'Risks From Climate Change to Indigenous Communities in the Tropical North of Australia Report', 5 May, http://www.climatechange.gov.au/en/publications/adaptation/risks-from-climate-change-to-indigenous-communities.aspx. Accessed 13 May 2017.

Derrida, Jacques (1994), *Specters of Marx: The State of the Debt, the Work of Mourning, and the New International* (trans. Peggy Kamuf), New York and London: Routledge.

Dessaix, Robert (1998), *(And So Forth)*, Sydney: Pan Macmillan.

Dixon, Robert (2007), 'Australian literature – International contexts', *Southerly*, 67:1&2, pp. 15–27.

Dixson, Miriam (1999), *The Imaginary Australian: Anglo-Celts and Identity – 1788 to the Present*, Sydney: UNSW Press.

Douglas, Mary (1966), *Purity and Danger: An Analysis of Concepts of Taboo and Pollution*, London: Routledge.

Dripps, Robyn (2005), 'Groundwork', in C. Burns and A. Kahn (eds), *Site Matters: Design Concepts, Histories, and Strategies*, New York and London: Routledge, pp. 59–92.

Duffy, Michael (1997), 'How to bypass the reconciliation roadblock', *The Australian*, 14 July, p. 11.

Ellemor, Heidi (2003), 'White skin, black heart? The politics of belonging and native title in Australia', *Social & Cultural Geography*, 4:2, pp. 233–52.

Farrier, David (2017), 'Animal detectives and "Anthropocene Noir" in Chloe Hooper's *A Child's Book of True Crime*', *Textual Practice*, 23:January, pp. 1–19, https://doi.org/10.1080/0950236X.2016.1275756. Accessed 13 May 2017.

Felski, Rita (2011), '"Context stinks!"', *New Literary History*, 42:4, pp. 573–91.

Flanagan, Martin (2002), *In Sunshine or in Shadow*, Sydney: Pan Macmillan.

Flannery, Tim (1994), *The Future Eaters: An Ecological History of the Australasian Lands and People*, Port Melbourne, Vic.: Reed Books.

—— (2002), 'The day, the land, the people: Australia Day address', *Australia Day*, 23 January, https://www.australiaday.com.au/events/australia-day-address/dr-tim-flannery. Accessed 29 October 2016.

—— (2005), *The Weather Makers: The History and Future Impact of Climate Change*, Melbourne: Text Publishing.

—— (2008), *Now or Never: A Sustainable Future for Australia?*, Quarterly Essay, 31, Melbourne: Black Inc.

Franzen, Jonathan (2001), *The Corrections*, New York: Farrar, Straus and Giroux.

Gaita, Raimond (2001), 'Why the impatience? Genocide, "ideology" and practical reconciliation', *Australian Book Review*, July, pp. 25–31.

Gammage, Bill (2011), *The Biggest Estate on Earth: How Aborigines Made Australia*, Sydney: Allen and Unwin.

Garrard, Greg (2004), *Ecocriticism*, London and New York: Routledge.

Gelder, Ken and Jacobs, Jane M. (1995), 'Uncanny Australia', *UTS Review*, 1:2, pp. 150–69.

—— (1996), 'The postcolonial ghost story', Current Tensions: Proceedings of the 18th Annual Conference, *JASAL Journal of the Association for the Study of Australian Literature*, July, pp. 110–20.

—— (1998), *Uncanny Australia: Sacredness and Identity in a Postcolonial Nation*, Melbourne: Melbourne University Press.

Gelder, Ken and Salzman, Paul (2009), *After the Celebration: Australian Fiction 1989–2007*, Carlton: Melbourne University Publishing.

Gemmell, Nikki (1997), *Shiver*, Milsons Point, Sydney: Vintage.

—— (1998), *Cleave*, Milsons Point, Sydney: Vintage.

Gibson, Ross (2002), *Seven Versions of an Australian Badland*, St Lucia, Qld.: University of Queensland Press.

—— (2014), 'Narrative hunger: GIS mapping, Google street view and the colonial prospectus', *Cultural Studies Review*, 20:2, http://epress.lib.uts.edu.au/journals/index.php/csrj/article/view/4052/4338. Accessed 13 May 2017.

Glascott, Katherine (1997), 'PM pushed racial split in 96: Pearson', *The Australian*, 15 December, p. 2.

Goldsworthy, Kerryn (1999), 'Undimmed outrage', *Australian Book Review*, September, pp. 30–31.

Gordon, Avery (2011), 'Some thoughts on haunting and futurity', *borderlands e-journal*, 10:2, http://www.borderlands.net.au/vol10no2_2011/gordon_thoughts.htm. Accessed 13 May 2017.

Gorman-Murray, Andrew (2010), 'An Australian feeling for snow: Towards understanding cultural and emotional dimensions of climate change', *Cultural Studies Review*, 16:1, pp. 60–81.

Government of New South Wales (2019), 'Australia Day address', https://www.australiaday.com.au/events/australia-day-address/. Accessed 20 January 2019.

Grattan, Michelle (2017), 'Turnbull government says no to Indigenous "voice to parliament"', *The Conversation*, 26 October, https://theconversation.com/turnbull-government-says-no-to-indigenous-voice-to-parliament-86421. Accessed 15 November 2017.

Graver, Elizabeth (1999), 'Walkabout', *The New York Times*, 15 August, http://www.nytimes.com/books/99/08/15/reviews/990815.15gravert.html. Accessed 13 May 2017.

Greenop, Kelly (2006), 'Uncanny Brisbane: New ways of looking at urban Indigenous place', *Proceedings of the 25th International Conference of the Society of Architectural Historians, Australia and New Zealand*, Geelong, Australia, http://kellygreenop.weebly.com/uploads/1/2/8/9/1289180/greenop_uncanny_brisbane.pdf. Accessed 23 April 2014.

Greer, Germaine (2003), *Whitefella Jump Up: The Shortest Way to Nationhood*, Quarterly Essay, 11, Melbourne: Black Inc.

Griffiths, Tom (2000), 'Travelling in deep time: *La Longue Durée* in Australian history', *Australian Humanities Review*, 18:June, http://australianhumanitiesreview.org/2000/06/01/travelling-in-deep-timela-longue-dureein-australian-history. Accessed 13 May 2017.

Gunditjmara People with Wettenhall, Gib (2010), *The People of Budj Bim: Engineers of Aquaculture, Builders of Stone House Settlements and Warriors Defending Country*, Heywood, Vic.: em Press.

Hage, Ghassan (1998), *White Nation: Fantasies of White Supremacy in a Multicultural Society*, Annandale, NSW: Pluto Press.

—— (2017), *Is Racism an Environmental Threat?*, Cambridge: Polity.

Halligan, Marion (2001), 'Introduction', in M. Halligan (ed.), *Storykeepers*, Sydney: Duffy and Snellgrove, pp. 1–13.

Hanson, Pauline (1996), 'Maiden speech to parliament', *Parliament of Australia*, http://parlinfo.aph.gov.au/parlInfo/search/display/display.w3p;query=Id%3A%22chamber%2Fhansards%2F16daad94-5c74-4641-a730-7f6d74312148%2F0139%22. Accessed 13 May 2017.

Hawkins, Gay (2001), 'Plastic bags: Living with rubbish', *International Journal of Cultural Studies*, 4:1, pp. 5–23.

—— (2006), *The Ethics of Waste: How We Relate to Rubbish*, Sydney: UNSW Press.

Haynes, Roslyn (1998), *Seeking the Centre: The Australian Desert in Literature, Art and Film*, Cambridge and Melbourne: Cambridge University Press.

Hinchliffe, Joe (2018), 'Pink paint poured on Captain Cook's statue on eve of Australia Day', *The Age*, 25 January, https://www.theage.com.au/national/victoria/pink-paint-poured-on-captain-cook-s-statue-on-eve-of-australia-day-20180125-p4yyvg.html. Accessed 28 January 2019.

Hocking, Rachel (2019), 'A racist endeavour: Captain Cook statue in Melbourne gets a makeover', *NITV*, 24 January, https://www.sbs.com.au/nitv/article/2019/01/24/racist-endeavour-captain-cook-statue-melbourne-gets-makeover1. Accessed 28 January 2019.

Hodge, Bob and Mishra, Vijay (1991), *Dark Side of the Dream: Australian Literature and the Postcolonial Mind*, North Sydney: Allen and Unwin.

Hokowhitu, Brendan (2016), 'Review of Mohawk Interruptus: Political life across the borders of settler states', *Native American and Indigenous Studies*, 3:1, pp. 162–64.

Hones, Sheila (2008), 'Text as it happens: Literary geography', *Geography Compass*, 2:5, pp. 1301–17.

Hooper, Chloe (2002), *A Child's Book of True Crime*, Milsons Point, Sydney: Random House.

Hospital, Janette Turner (2003), *Due Preparations for the Plague*, Sydney: HarperCollins.

Houston, Donna (2015), 'Crisis is where we live: Environmental justice for the Anthropocene', *Globalizations*, 10:3, pp. 439–50.

Howard, John (1997a), 'Address by the Prime Minister the Hon. John Howard MP address to Australian Day Council's Australia Day luncheon – Darling Harbour, Sydney', *PM Transcripts: Transcripts from the Prime Ministers of Australia*, 24 January, http://pmtranscripts.pmc.gov.au/release/transcript-10217. Accessed 13 May 2017.

—— (1997b), 'Transcript of the Prime Minister the Hon. John Howard MP opening address to the Australian Reconciliation Convention – Melbourne', *PM Transcripts: Transcripts from the Prime Ministers of Australia*, 26 May, https://pmtranscripts.pmc.gov.au/release/transcript-10361. Accessed 13 May 2017.

—— (2003), 'Australians at war address: Australia House, London', *PM Transcripts: Transcripts from the Prime Ministers of Australia*, November, https://pmtranscripts.pmc.gov.au/release/transcript-20994. Accessed 13 May 2017.

Howitt, Ritchie (2001), 'Frontiers, borders, edges: Liminal challenges to the hegemony of exclusion', *Australian Geographical Studies*, 39:2, pp. 233–45.

—— (2006), 'Scales of coexistence: Tackling the tension between legal and cultural landscapes in post-Mabo Australia', *Macquarie Law Journal*, 6, pp. 49–64.

Huggan, Graham and Tiffin, Helen (2010), *Postcolonial Ecocriticism: Literature, Animals, Environment*, Abingdon, Oxford and New York: Routledge.

Hulme, Mike (2010), 'Cosmopolitan climates: Hybridity, foresight and meaning', *Theory, Culture and Society*, 27:2–3, pp. 267–76.

Human Rights and Equal Opportunity Commission (1997), 'Bringing Them Home: Report of the National Inquiry into the Separation of Aboriginal and Torres Strait Islander Children from Their Families', https://www.humanrights.gov.au/publications/bringing-them-home-report-1997. Accessed 13 May 2017.

Ingold, Tim (2004), 'Culture on the ground: The world perceived through the feet', *Journal of Material Culture*, 3:9, pp. 315–40.

—— (2011), *Being Alive: Essays on Movement, Knowledge and Description*, London and New York: Routledge.

Iovino, Serenella (2015), 'The living diffractions of matter and text: Narrative agency, strategic anthropomorphism, and how interpretation works', *Anglia*, 133:1, pp. 69–86.

Jacobs, Jane M. and Anderson, Kay (1997) 'From urban aborigines to aboriginality and the city: One path through the history of Australian cultural geography', *Australian Geographical Studies,* 35:1, pp. 12–22.

Jensen, Lars (2011), 'The whiteness of climate change', *Journal of the European Association for Studies on Australia*, 2:2, pp. 84–97.

Keating, Paul (1992a), 'Speech by the Prime Minister, the Hon PJ Keating official banquet given by President Suharto Istana Negara, Jakarta', *PM Transcripts: Transcripts from the Prime Ministers of Australia*, 21 April, https://pmtranscripts.pmc.gov.au/release/transcript-8487. Accessed 13 May 2017.

—— (1992b), 'Redfern speech (year for the world's Indigenous people)', 10 December, https://antar.org.au/sites/default/files/paul_keating_speech_transcript.pdf. Accessed 13 May 2017.

Ker, Peter (2009), 'Exodus fears for Murray Towns', *The Age*, 18 March, http://alturl.com/mcrma. Accessed 13 May 2017.

Kerridge, Richard (2012), 'Ecocriticism and the mission of "English"', in G. Garrard (ed.), *Teaching Ecocriticism and Green Cultural Studies*, London: Palgrave Macmillan, pp. 11–23.

Knaus, Christopher (2017), '"No pride in genocide": Vandals deface Captain Cook statue in Sydney's Hyde Park', *The Guardian*, 26 August, https://www.theguardian.com/australia-news/2017/aug/26/captain-cook-statue-and-two-others-in-sydneys-hyde-park-attacked-by-vandals. Accessed 28 January 2019.

Kossew, Sue (2000), '"The voice of the times": *Fin-de-siècle* and the voice of doom in Thea Astley's *Drylands*', *CRNLE (Critical Review of New Literatures in English)*, pp. 177–83.

Kowal, Emma (2011), 'The stigma of white privilege: Australian anti-racists and Indigenous improvement', *Cultural Studies*, 25:3, pp. 313–33.

—— (2015), 'Welcome to country: Acknowledgement, belonging and white anti-racism', *Cultural Studies Review*, 21:2, pp. 173–204.

Kramer, Leonie (ed.), with Mitchell, Adrian (1981), *The Oxford History of Australian Literature*, Melbourne: Oxford University Press.

Lamond, Julieanne (2007), 'The ghost of dad Rudd, on the stump', *JASAL: Journal of the Association for the Study of Australian Literature*, 6:1, pp. 19–32.

Langton, Marcia (2013), *The Quiet Revolution: Indigenous People and the Resources Boom,* Boyer Lectures, Sydney: ABC Books.

Larsen, Soren C. and Johnson, Jay T. (2017), 'Indigenous coexistence in a more than human world', in S. C. Larsen and J. T. Johnson (eds), *Being Together in Place*, Minneapolis, MN: University of Minnesota Press, pp. 184–202.

Lea, Tess, Young, Martin, Markham, Francis, Holmes, Catherine and Doran, Bruce (2012), 'Being moved (on): The biopolitics of walking in Australia's frontier towns', *Radical History Review*, 114, pp. 139–63.

Levine, Caroline (2013), 'From nation to network', *Victorian Studies*, 55:4, pp. 647–66.

—— (2015), *Form: Whole, Rhythm, Hierarchy, Network*, Princeton, NJ: Princeton University Press.

Liddle, Celeste and Mason, Terry (2016), 'Fighting for sovereignty and treaties over recognition', *Advocate: Journal of the National Tertiary Education Union*, 14, http://ezproxy.deakin.edu.au/login?url=http://search.ebscohost.com/login.aspx?direct=true&db=edsibc&AN=edsibc.165925053279868&site=eds-live&scope=site. Accessed 12 November 2017.

Lindsay, Joan (1967), *Picnic at Hanging Rock*, London: Penguin.

Mabo vs Queensland (No.2), https://jade.io/j/?a=outline&id=67683. Accessed 13 May 2013.

MacCallum, Mungo (2002), *Girt by Sea: Australia, the Refugees and the Politics of Fear*, Quarterly Essay, 5, Melbourne: Black Inc.

Maddison, Sarah (2011), *Beyond White Guilt: The Real Challenge for Black-White Relations in Australia*, Crows Nest, NSW: Allen and Unwin.

Malouf, David (1978), *An Imaginary Life*, New York: G. Brazillier.

Manne, Robert (1996), *The Culture of Forgetting*, Melbourne: Text.

—— (2000), '"Unthinkable brutality? Who cares..."', *The Age*, 29 April, p. 13.

—— (2001a), *In Denial: The Stolen Generations and the Right*, Quarterly Essay, 1, Melbourne: Black Inc.

—— (2001b), *The Barren Years: John Howard and Australian Political Culture*, Melbourne: Text.

—— (2005), 'Dead disturbing: A bloodthirsty tale that plays with the fire of anti-semitism', *The Monthly*, June, pp. 50–53.

Marr, David (2003), 'The role of the writer in John Howard's Australia', Colin Simpson Lecture, Redfern Town Hall, Sydney.

Marr, David and Wilkinson, Marian (2004), *Dark Victory*, Crows Nest, NSW: Allen and Unwin.

Marsden, John and Tan, Shaun (1998), *The Rabbits*, Port Melbourne: Lothian Books.

McCann, Andrew (2000), 'Colonial gothic: Morbid anatomy, commodification and critique in Marcus Clarke's "The Mystery of Major Molineux"', *Australian Literary Studies*, 19:4, https://www.australianliterarystudies.com.au/articles/colonial-gothic-morbid-anatomy-commodification-and-critique-in-marcus-clarkes-the-mystery-of-major-molineux. Accessed 13 May 2017.

—— (2006), 'The literature of extinction', *Meanjin*, 65:1, pp. 48–54.

—— (2010), 'Discrepant cosmopolitanism and the contemporary novel: Reading the inhuman in Christos Tsiolkas's *Dead Europe* and Roberto Bolaño's *2666*', *Antipodes*, 24:2, pp. 135–41.

McCredden, Lyn (2007), 'Haunted identities and the possible futures of "Aust. Lit."', *JASAL: Journal of the Association for the Study of Australian Literature*, special issue, *Spectres, Screens, Shadows, Mirrors*, pp. 12–24, https://openjournals.library.sydney.edu.au/index.php/JASAL/article/view/9636. Accessed 22 April 2019.

McGahan, Andrew (2004), *The White Earth*, Crows Nest, NSW: Allen and Unwin.

McGurl, Mark (2010), 'Ordinary doom: Literary studies in the waste land of the present', *New Literary History*, 41:2, pp. 329–49.

McKibben, Bill (1989), *The End of Nature*, New York: Random House.

McMurchy, Megan, Nash, Margot, Oliver, Margot and Thornley, Jeni (1983), *For Love or Money*, Australia: Flashback Films.

Memmott, Paul and Long, Stephen (2002), 'Place theory and place maintenance in Indigenous Australia', *Urban Policy and Research*, 20:1, pp. 39–56.

Merrilees, Margaret (2007), 'Circling with ghosts: The search for redemption', *JASAL: Journal of the Association for the Study of Australian Literature*, special issue, *Spectres, Screens, Shadows, Mirrors*, pp. 65–76, https://openjournals.library.sydney.edu.au/index.php/JASAL/article/view/9640. Accessed 22 April 2019.

Miles, Malcolm (2014), *Eco-Aesthetics: Art, Literature and Architecture in a Period of Climate Change*, New York: Bloomsbury.

Miller, George and Amenta, Pino (1983), *All the Rivers Run*, Australia: Alan Hardy and Seven Network.

Miller, Linn (2003), 'Belonging to country – A philosophical anthropology', *Journal of Australian Studies*, 27:76, pp. 215–23.

Mills, Catherine (2008), *The Philosophy of Agamben*, Montreal and Kingston: McGill-Queen's University Press.

Modjeska, Drusilla (2002), 'Why I am not reading fiction', Adelaide Writers Week, 4 March, Adelaide.

Moran, Anthony (1998), 'Aboriginal reconciliation: Transformations in settler nationalism', *Melbourne Journal of Politics*, the Reconciliation Issue, 25, pp. 101–31.

Moreton-Robinson, Aileen (2003), 'I still call Australia home: Indigenous belonging and place in a white postcolonising society', in S. Ahmed (ed.), *Uprootings/Regroundings: Questions of Home and Migration*, Oxford: Berg, pp. 23–40.

—— (2013), 'Towards an Australian Indigenous women's standpoint theory: A methodological tool', *Australian Feminist Studies*, 28:78, pp. 331–47.

—— (2015), *The White Possessive: Property, Power and Indigenous Sovereignty*, Minneapolis, MN: Minnesota University Press.

Morgan, Ruth (2014), 'Imagining a greenhouse future: Scientific and literary depictions of climate change in 1980s Australia', *Australian Humanities Review*, 57:November, pp. 43–60, http://australianhumanitiesreview.org/2014/11/01/issue-57-november-2014. Accessed 13 May 2017.

Morris, Meaghan (1988), 'Panorama: The live, the dead and the living', in P. Foss (ed.), *Island in the Stream: Myths of Place in Australian Culture*, Leichhardt, NSW: Pluto Press, pp. 160–87.

Morrison, Toni (1988), *Beloved*, New York: Random.

Morton, Timothy (2012), 'An object-oriented defense of poetry', *New Literary History*, 43, pp. 205–24.

—— (2013), *Hyperobjects: Philosophy and Ecology after the End of the World*, Minneapolis, MN: University of Minnesota Press.

Muecke, Stephen (1997), *No Road (Bitumen all the Way)*, Fremantle, WA: Fremantle Arts Centre.

—— (2001), 'Devastation', *UTS Review*, 7:2, pp. 123–29.

—— (2010), 'Public thinking, public feeling: Research tools for creative writing', *TEXT*, 14:1, http://www.textjournal.com.au/april10/muecke.htm. Accessed 13 May 2017.

Mulligan, Martin (2000), 'Towards a "whitefella dreaming"', *Overland*, 161, pp. 58–61.

Murphy, Katherine (2017), 'Changing colonial statues is Stalinist, says Malcolm Turnbull', *The Guardian*, 25 August, https://www.theguardian.com/australia-news/2017/aug/25/changing-colonial-statues-is-stalinist-says-malcolm-turnbull?CMP=Share_iOSApp_Other. Accessed 2 February 2018.

Murray, Timothy (2000), 'Wounds of repetition in the age of the digital: Chris Marker's cinematic ghosts', *Cultural Critique*, 46, pp. 102–23.

Native Title Act (1993), 'Commonwealth Consolidated Acts – Native Title Act 1993', http://www9.austlii.edu.au/cgi-bin/viewdb/au/legis/cth/consol_act/nta1993147. Accessed 13 May 2017.

Nettelbeck, Amanda (2007), 'Contact history, social memory and the construction of white belonging', *Australian Cultural History: The Journal of the History of Culture in Australia*, 26, pp. 195–209.

Padmore, Catherine (2008), 'Future tense: *Dead Europe* and viral anti-Semitism', *Australian Literary Studies*, 23:4, pp. 434–45.

Palmer, Vance (2012), 'What is significant in us will survive', in R. Manne and C. Feik (eds), *The Words That Made Australia: How a Nation Came to Know Itself*, Collingwood, Vic.: Black Inc., pp. 69–71.

Parkin-Gounelas, Ruth (1999), 'Anachrony and anatopia: Specters of Marx, Derrida and gothic fiction', in P. Buse and A. Stott (eds), *Ghosts: Deconstruction, Psychoanalysis, History*, London: Macmillan, pp. 127–43.

Pascoe, Bruce (2014), *Dark Emu: Black Seeds – Agriculture or Accident?*, Broome, WA: Magabala Books.

Pearson, Noel (2012), 'Keating and the speech we had to have', *The Australian*, 10 December, http://www.theaustralian.com.au/opinion/columnists/keating-and-the-speech-we-had-to-have/news-story/24e0622a03662ccafebd207adc66c61d?sv=ed7cacb3701157684fc35f-8d8870e94d. Accessed 4 September 2015.

Pierce, Peter (ed.) (1987), *The Oxford Literary Guide to Australia*, Melbourne: Oxford University Press.

—— (1999), *The Country of Lost Children: An Australian Anxiety*, Cambridge: Cambridge University Press.

Plumwood, Val (2008), 'Shadow places and the politics of dwelling', *Australian Humanities Review*, 44:March, pp. 139–50, http://australianhumanitiesreview.org/2008/03/01/issue-44-march-2008. Accessed 13 May 2017.

Pollak, Michael and McNabb, Margaret (2000), *Hearts and Minds: Creative Australians and the Environment*, Alexandria, NSW: Hale and Iremonger.

Porter, Libby (2010), *Unlearning the Colonial Cultures of Planning*, Farnam and Burlington, UK: Ashgate.

Potter, Emily (2012), 'Climate change and non-indigenous belonging in postcolonial Australia', *Continuum*, 27:1, pp. 30–40.

—— (2014), 'Programme: Dreaming, timekeeping, becoming', in J. McGaw and A. Pieris, *Assembling the Centre: Architecture for Indigenous Cultures*, London and New York: Routledge, pp. 100–20.

Potter, Emily and Oster, Candice (2008), 'Communicating climate change: Public responsiveness and matters of concern', *Media International Australia*, 127:1, pp. 116–26.

Powell, J. M. (2000), 'Revisiting the Australian experience: Transmillennial conjurings', *The Geographical Review*, 90:1, pp. 1–17.

Probyn, Elspeth (1996), *Outside Belongings*, New York: Routledge.

—— (2016), *Eating the Ocean*, Durham, NC: Duke University Press.

Probyn, Fiona (2002), 'How does the settler belong?', *Westerly Magazine*, 47, pp. 74–94.

Quiggin, John (2019), 'Socialist Utopia 2050: What could Australia be like after the failure of capitalism?', *The Guardian*, 17 January, https://www.theguardian.com/politics/2019/jan/17/socialist-utopia-2050-what-could-life-in-australia-be-like-after-the-failure-of-capitalism. Accessed 24 January 2019.

Read, Peter (1996), *Returning to Nothing*, Melbourne and Cambridge: Cambridge University Press.

—— (2000), *Belonging: Australians, Place and Aboriginal Ownership*, Melbourne and Cambridge: Cambridge University Press.

—— (2003), *Haunted Earth*, Sydney: UNSW Press.

Referendum Council (2017), 'Uluru Statement from the Heart', 26 May, https://www.referendumcouncil.org.au/event/uluru-statement-from-the-heart. Accessed 17 April 2018.

Rifkin, Mark (2014), *Settler Common Sense: Queerness and Everyday Colonialism in the American Renaissance*, Minneapolis, MN: University of Minnesota Press.

Riggs, Damien (2004), '"We don't talk about race anymore": Power, privilege and critical whiteness studies', *Borderlands e-journal*, 3:2, http://www.borderlands.net.au/vol3no2_2004/riggs_intro.htm. Accessed 13 May 2017.

Robbins, Paul and Moore, Sarah A. (2013), 'Ecological anxiety disorder: Diagnosing the politics of the Anthropocene', *Cultural Geographies*, 20:1, pp. 3–19.

Robinson, Alice and Tout, Dan (2012), 'Only planet: Unsettling travel, culture and climate change in settler Australia', *Australian Humanities Review: Ecological Humanities*, 52:May, http://australianhumanitiesreview.org/2012/05/01/only-planet-unsettling-travel-culture-and-climate-change-in-settler-australia. Accessed 13 May 2017.

Rose, Deborah Bird (1997a), 'Dark times and excluded bodies in the colonization of Australia', in G. Gray and C. Winter (eds), *The Resurgence of Racism: Howard, Hanson and the Race Debate*, Clayton, Vic.: Monash Publications in History, pp. 97–116.

—— (1997b), 'The year zero and the North Australian frontier', in D. B. Rose and A. Clarke (eds), *Tracking Knowledge in North Australian Landscapes: Studies in Indigenous and Settler Ecological Knowledge Systems*, Northern Territory: Australian National University North Australia Research Unit, pp. 19–39.

—— (2004), *Reports from a Wild Country: Ethics for Decolonization*, Sydney: UNSW Press.

Roy, Arundhati (1997), *The God of Small Things*, New York: Random House.

Royal Commission into Aboriginal Deaths in Custody (1991), National Reports, http://www.austlii.edu.au/au/other/IndigLRes/rciadic/. Accessed 13 May 2017.

Rundle, Guy (2001), *The Opportunist: John Howard and the Triumph of Reaction*, Quarterly Essay, 3, Melbourne: Black Inc.

Rutherford, Jennifer (2000), *The Gauche Intruder: Freud, Lacan, and the White Australia Policy*, Carlton, Vic.: Melbourne University Press.

Schaffer, Kay (1989), *Women and the Bush: Australian National Identity and Representations of the Feminine*, Adelaide: South Australian College of Advanced Education.

—— (2001), 'Manne's generation: White nation responses to the Stolen Generation Report', *Australian Humanities Review*, 22:June, http://australianhumanitiesreview.org/2001/06/01/mannes-generation-white-nation-responses-to-the-stolen-generation-report. Accessed 13 May 2017.

Seltzer, Mark (1997), 'Wound culture: Trauma in the pathological public sphere', *October*, 80, pp. 3–26.

Sharp, Nonie (2005), 'The artistic and literary imagination in Australia and beyond: Finding places of the heart amongst the gum trees', *Organization and Management*, 18:3, pp. 354–68.

Shaw, Wendy S. and Bonnett, Alastair (2016), 'Environmental crisis, narcissism and the work of grief', *Cultural Geographies*, 23:4, pp. 565–79.

Shellam, Tiffany (2015), '"On my ground": Indigenous farmers at New Norcia 1860s–1900s', in Z. Laidlaw and A. Lester (eds), *Indigenous Communities and Settler Colonialism: Land Holding, Loss and Survival in an Interconnected World*, Basingstoke, England: Palgrave Macmillan, pp. 62–85.

Simpson, Audra (2014), *Mohawk Interruptus: Political Life Across the Borders of Settler States*, London: Duke University Press.

Slater, Lisa (2018), *Anxieties of Belonging in Settler Colonialism*, New York: Routledge.

Sloterdijk, Peter (2005), 'Atmospheric politics', in B. Latour and P. Weibel (eds), *Making Things Public: Atmospheres of Democracy*, Cambridge, MA: MIT Press, pp. 944–51.

Smith, Rosalind (2008), 'Dark places: True crime writing in Australia', *JASAL: Journal of the Association for the Study of Australian Literature*, 8, pp. 17–30.

Stanner, W. E. H. (2011), *The Dreaming and Other Essays*, Melbourne: Black Inc.

Starford, Rebecca (2016), 'The White Earth', Copyright Agency (Reading Australia), https://readingaustralia.com.au/essays/the-white-earth. Accessed 13 May 2017.

Tacey, David (1995), *Edge of the Sacred: Transformation in Australia*, East Melbourne: HarperCollins.

Terrill, Ross (2000), *The Australians: The Way We Live Now*, Sydney and Auckland: Doubleday.

Thomas, Martin (1998), 'Morphic echoes, stony silences: Reading an Australian landscape', *UTS Review*, 4:1, pp. 42–66.

Timms, Peter (2001), *Making Nature: Six Walks in the Bush*, Crows Nest, NSW: Allen and Unwin.

Treddinick, Mark (2003), *A Place on Earth*, Kensington: UNSW Press.

Trigger, David (2008), 'Place, belonging and nativeness in Australia', in F. Vanclay, M. Higgins and A. Blackshaw (eds), *Making Sense of Place: Exploring Concepts and Expressions of Place through Different Senses and Lenses*, Canberra: National Museum of Australia Press, pp. 301–09.

Tsiolkas, Christos (2005), *Dead Europe*, Milsons Point, Sydney: Vintage.

Tumarkin, Maria (2001), '"Wishing you weren't here…": Thinking about trauma, place and the Port Arthur massacre', *Journal of Australian Studies*, 67, pp. 197–205.

Turner, Graeme (1986), *National Fictions: Literature, Film, and the Construction of Australian Narrative*, Sydney: Allen and Unwin.

Turner, Stephen (1999), 'Settlement as forgetting', in K. Neumann, N. Thomas and H. Ericksen (eds), *Quicksands: Foundational Histories in Australia and Aotearoa New Zealand*, Sydney: UNSW Press, pp. 20–38.

Veracini, Lorenzo (2007), 'Settler colonialism and decolonization', *Borderlands e-journal*, 6:2, http://www.borderlands.net.au/vol6no2_2007/veracini_settler.htm. Accessed 13 May 2017.

—— (2011), 'Introducing settler colonial studies', *Settler Colonial Studies*, 1:1, pp. 1–12.

Verran, Helen (1998), 'Re-imagining land ownership in Australia', *Postcolonial Studies*, 1:2, pp. 237–54.

Vidler, Anthony (1992), *The Architectural Uncanny: Essays in the Modern Unhomely*, Cambridge, MA and London: MIT Press.

Wahlquist, Calla (2016), 'It took one massacre: How Australia embraced gun control after Port Arthur', *The Guardian*, 15 March, https://www.theguardian.com/world/2016/mar/15/

it-took-one-massacre-how-australia-made-gun-control-happen-after-port-arthur. Accessed 13 May 2017.

—— (2018), 'Indigenous children in care doubled since Stolen Generations Apology', *The Guardian*, 25 January, https://www.theguardian.com/australia-news/2018/jan/25/indigenous-children-in-care-doubled-since-stolen-generations-apology. Accessed 8 April 2018.

Watson, Irene (2001), 'Keynote', *In Conversation,* Postgraduate Conference English Department, 15 November, University of Adelaide.

—— (2002), 'Buried alive', *Law and Critique,* 13, pp. 253–69.

Weaver-Hightower, Rebecca (2010), 'The Sorry novels: Peter Carey's *Oscar and Lucinda*, Greg Matthews' *The Wisdom of Stones* and Kate Grenville's *The Secret River*', in N. O'Reilly (ed.), *Postcolonial Issues in Australian Literature*, Amherst, NY: Cambria Press, pp. 129–56.

Weir, Jessica (2015), 'Lives in connection', in K. Gibson, D. B. Rose and R. Fincher (eds), *Manifesto for Living in the Anthropocene*, Brooklyn, NY: Punctum Books, pp. 17–21.

Weir, Peter (1975), *Picnic at Hanging Rock*, Australia: Australian Film Commission.

Westling, Louise (2012), 'Literature and ecology', in G. Garrard (ed.), *Teaching Ecocriticism and Green Cultural Studies*, London: Palgrave Macmillan, pp. 75–89.

Williams, Raymond (1973), *The Country and the City*, Oxford: Oxford University Press.

Windschuttle, Keith (2000), 'The break-up of Australia', *Quadrant*, September, pp. 8–16.

Winton, Tim (1991), *Cloudstreet*, Melbourne: Penguin.

—— (2001), *Dirt Music*, Sydney: PanMacmillan.

Wolfe, Patrick (1999), *Settler Colonialism and the Transformation of Anthropology*, London: Cassell.

Woodward, Christopher (2001), *In Ruins*, London: Chatto and Windus.

Wright, Alexis (2013), *The Swan Book*, Artarmon, NSW: Giramondo.

Wright, Tony (2016), 'In wanting what he'd been denied, John Howard picked two words and a fence to save career', *Sydney Morning Herald*, 28 February, https://www.smh.com.au/politics/federal/in-wanting-what-hed-been-denied-john-howard-picked-two-words-and-a-fence-to-save-his-career-20160228-gn5k5r.html. Accessed 6 May 2018.

Index

N

O